DEER WARS

DEER WARS

Science, Tradition, and the Battle Over Managing Whitetails in Pennsylvania

2006

BOB FRYE

PHOTOGRAPHS BY GREGORY D. SOFRANKO

The Pennsylvania State University Press
University Park, Pennsylvania

A KEYSTONE BOOK

A Keystone Book is so designated to distinguish it from the
typical scholarly monograph that a university press publishes.
It is a book intended to serve the citizens of Pennsylvania by
educating them and others, in an entertaining way, about
aspects of the history, culture, society, and environment of the
state as part of the Middle Atlantic region.

LIBRARY OF CONGRESS
CATALOGING-IN-PUBLICATION DATA

Frye, Bob, 1967–
    Deer wars : science, tradition, and the battle over manag-
    ing whitetails in Pennsylvania / by Bob Frye.
        p.   cm.
"A Keystone book."
ISBN 0-271-02885-8 (pbk. : alk. paper)
1. White-tailed deer hunting—Pennsylvania.
2. Wildlife management—Pennsylvania.
I. Title.

SK301.F79 2006
799.2'765209748—dc22
2006002084

TO *Mandy, Derek, and Tyler,* WHOSE SACRIFICES MADE THIS POSSIBLE

CONTENTS

FOREWORD BY GARY ALT

Deer management influences all of us—whether you hunt or not, whether you're trying to grow shrubs in the suburbs or in a country garden, whether you're a farmer, a forester, or just trying to drive across our state. Restoring white-tailed deer to their previous range in the early 1900s, after being exterminated from many areas during a century or more of overexploitation, has often been touted as one of wildlife management's greatest success stories. Ironically, after decades of overprotection, one of the greatest challenges of wildlife management today is to balance this important game species with its forested habitat and with the increasing conflicts of our human society. Attempting to raise more deer than the land can sustain is one of the greatest mistakes in the history of wildlife management and one that threatens the health and sustainability of our forest ecosystems, the viability of our farms, the health and safety of our people, and, if not corrected, the future of sport hunting as well. The management of no other wild animal has been so controversial, so contentious, nor has carried such grave consequences.

Knowing the troubled history of deer management and the irresistible challenge of attempting to correct one of the greatest mistakes in my profession was what attracted me to accept a newly created position as supervisor of the Pennsylvania Game Commission's deer management section in September 1999. To increase our credibility, my team and I planned to launch some of the largest research programs ever done on whitetails in the wild. We also knew that taking deer management from where it was to where it needed to go would require some of the largest policy changes that have ever occurred in the history of deer management in Pennsylvania. I was looking for someone I could trust to document our successes and failures in an impartial way. It was at a press conference in Harrisburg, a few days into my new job, that I first met Bob Frye and recommended that he write this book.

Over the past six years since then, Bob and I have been in constant touch. We've had scores of phone conversations, most lasting more than an hour, where I would pour my heart out about what we were doing and why. He kept our confidentiality and documented every detail. He never told me what he thought. He just relentlessly asked questions and quietly listened and wrote. When I testified at Game Commission public meetings, Bob was always there. When I testified before the Game and Fisheries Committee at the capital, Bob was there. Whenever we had important field research projects going on, key lectures, or other major events, Bob was usually there.

Bob has interviewed an amazing array of characters on all sides of the deer management issue—in fact, I can't think of any major player he hasn't interviewed. In his unbiased, reporter-style coverage, he almost never takes a position; he just reports what other people say, often providing quotations from others with conflicting views.

This book certainly represents the most comprehensive documentation of the history of deer management in Pennsylvania and how it has influenced various aspects of our society and the economy of our commonwealth. You will read, time and time again, how respected scientists and visionaries like Richard Gerstel, Ross Leffler, and Roger Latham have pled with their government to implement responsible wildlife management and balance deer with their habitat and human society, and how they were struck down by the political pressures from those who wanted more deer—at any price—which ironically ruined the habitat and the deer herd they were trying to protect. It seems unfathomable that this recurring management nightmare could persist for more than seven decades and that it still continues today. It's an environmental version of one of those old westerns in which the villain strikes repeatedly and we keep waiting, with great anticipation, for the "good guy" to come along and right the wrong. But time is running out—and so are seed sources—for our forests.

How did this happen? Why hasn't this problem been solved? This can best be explained by looking at the history of the problem. Precolonial white-tailed deer populations were probably maintained at relatively low densities in the old-growth forests of eastern North America. This was thought to have been the case, in part, because of the limited browse and other foods available for deer in old-growth forests, but also because of natural predators such as wolves, cougars, and Native Americans. Before colonization, more than 90 percent of Pennsylvania was forested, but by 1890 70 percent of our state had been cleared for agriculture. The eighteenth and nineteenth centuries were also an era of severe overexploitation of deer, as suitable forest habitat disappeared and unregulated killing, including year-round market hunting, led to declines and even extirpation from many portions of their former range.

The loss of deer and many other wildlife species and their habitats spawned a conservation movement at the end of the nineteenth century. That is when wildlife departments like the Pennsylvania Game Commission were created to restore and protect wildlife and their habitats. During the late 1800s and early 1900s nearly all of Pennsylvania's remaining forests were clear-cut, and deer were stocked in a variety of areas to reestablish deer populations. These recently clear-cut forests regenerated profusely, providing deer with the perfect food and cover in which to thrive. Also, the deer's natural predators had been removed, and new laws were enacted to provide even further protection, which set the stage for a dramatic recovery but unfortunately also for an era of overprotection and habitat destruction.

Perhaps the greatest mistake that launched nearly a century of overprotection for deer was the regulation enacted in 1907 prohibiting the hunting of does. In 1917 the executive secretary of the Pennsylvania Game Commission, Dr. Joseph Kalbfus, was frustrated in his efforts to start a doe season. Realizing that doe would have to become fair game at some point in the near future to keep deer from becoming overabundant, and knowing how unpopular this would be with hunters, Kalbfus told future director Seth Gordon, "Thank God I won't be in charge of this work 10 years from now, because someone is going to have hell to pay." No truer words have ever been spoken or better reflect what happened in the twentieth century and what's still happening today.

The "Golden Rule" of responsible deer management is that you must balance the deer herd with its habitat. The same is true of range management with cattle or sheep. If you try to raise more livestock than the range can support, they will overgraze the range and destroy it. If you try to raise more deer than the forest can support, the deer will overbrowse their forest habitat and destroy it. Once overbrowsed, the forest cannot sustain nearly as many deer as before, and it may take a long time to repair the damage. If the overbrowsing continues, it threatens the health and sustainability of the entire forest ecosystem—not just for deer but for most of the plants and animals that live there. As simple and crucial as this basic concept is, it has been blatantly disregarded, leading to immeasurable environmental and ecological damage.

Why has this happened? To understand why responsible deer management has almost never been practiced in Pennsylvania, one must understand the management system in place. It is the responsibility of the Pennsylvania Game Commission to properly manage our commonwealth's birds and mammals, and their habitats, for current and future generations. They decide what seasons and bag limits will be put in place to control deer populations. The Game Commission is funded almost totally by hunters, more than 90 percent of whom are deer hunters. Surveys have repeatedly shown that deer hunter satisfaction is closely tied to the number of deer hunters see while hunting. Deer hunters demand to see larger numbers of deer than their forest habitat can possibly sustain. They have very effectively pressured legislators, administrators, and policymakers to ensure that doe harvests are insufficient to balance deer populations with their habitat. The net result has been a disaster.

Deer populations have not been controlled properly for more than seven decades in our "big woods" areas, which has resulted in devastated forests. So little food remains that the reproduction and survival of deer is low, resulting in very low deer densities, but the habitat is so poor that even these low densities continue to overbrowse the damaged habitat. Ironically, by allowing more deer than the land could sustain, there are now fewer deer than before, and the habitat is so thoroughly destroyed that some ecologists fear that it may be impossible to restore it in our lifetime, if ever. Even more pathetic, political pressure continues to prevent enough does from being taken to allow this area to recover. It is unlikely that this problem will be solved until there is broader-based funding to ensure a wider representation of constituencies, which would allow a more ecosystem-friendly form of deer management to be put in place.

The inability to balance deer populations with forest ecosystems is not just a hunting issue. It is a serious environmental and ecological issue that may well have negative implications for the future of sport hunting. If hunters continue to prevent managers from harvesting enough does to balance deer with forest ecosystems and the other needs of human society, then we will be forced to find alternative, nontraditional solutions to this problem. The return of market hunting, for example, may be one of those alternatives.

It is my hope that through education we can get hunters to balance deer with their habitat and with the rest of society. I am a hunter, and hunting is very important to me. Some of my greatest memories of my grandfather, my father, and my son involve deer hunting. But if recreational hunting is to continue, we must ensure that it is done responsibly and we must demonstrate that we can, and will, balance deer with their habitat, thus providing a free environmental and ecological service for everyone. If we can do that, hunting is likely to be better in the future than it has ever been in the past.

ACKNOWLEDGMENTS

To my way of thinking, the white-tailed deer, more than any other animal, speaks to wilderness, at least here in Pennsylvania. I know they flourish today amid our housing plans and city parks, and they often end up dead along our roads. But it's easy to see with the mind's eye a Native American or an early pioneer stalking a white-tailed deer or carrying one home for the table, its meat and bone and hide the difference between hunger and health, comfort and suffering.

I've always felt a connection to those early hunters whenever I've gone into Penn's Woods with a gun or a bow. That's why deer and deer hunting have always been nostalgic, even romantic, for me.

My affection for deer also made writing this book a labor of love. This was not something I accomplished alone, however. I owe a debt of gratitude to many people—more than I can name here—who helped bring this book to life.

The people who make up the staff of the Pennsylvania Game Commission proved to be, almost without exception, dedicated, patient, and helpful. Gary Alt, Marrett Grund, Bret Wallingford, George Kelly, and Chris Rosenberry, biologists one and all, indulged me in countless phone interviews and in-person get-togethers, and allowed me to tag along in the field on all of their various research projects. Duane Diefenbach, Eric Long, and the students who did the legwork on those studies deserve a round of applause as well. This book would not have been possible without their experience and knowledge.

Game commissioners, particularly Roxane Palone, Russ Schleiden, John Riley, and Bob Gilford, were free with their time and thoughts. Bob Boyd was a wealth of information on chronic wasting disease. John Dzemyan not only came out in the sprinkling rain to show Greg and me around Pennsylvania's big woods, he also supplied me with a copy of Roger Latham's September 1950 issue of *Game News* and helped me track down Richard Gerstell. Joe Kusack's wonderful book, *The Pennsylvania Game Commission, 1895–1995: 100 Years of Wildlife Conservation,* was a historical goldmine. Jerry Feaser was great about directing me to the right people to talk to within the agency and helping to set up interviews.

Charlie May, the best woodsman I ever knew, provided the perfect opening for this book. Emil Nelson's diaries, supplied by his grandson and my good friend Jeff Nelson, were a one-in-a-million find. How better to understand the rebirth of a species than to learn from one of the men who brought it about?

Merlin Benner deserves kudos for always being available to talk about deer and their relationship to state forests. Mike Pechart and Jeff Grove were invaluable in putting me in touch with farmers around Pennsylvania.

What can I say about Lou Calandrella? Who would have thought that tagging along with a guy who picks up road-killed deer for a living could be so much fun? He's one of the funniest people I've ever met, period.

Roger Cowburn, Richard Gerstell, Jim Seitz, Jim Morrison, Blaine Puller, Cindy Adams Dunn, Bryon Shissler, Doug Gilbert, Michele Clarke, Ray Martin, David Laux, Don Morris, and others all invited Greg and me into their homes or workplaces, or met us in restaurants or in the field. The time they gave us made all the difference.

Tony DeNicola showed his persistence by talking to me for several hours over multiple days, whenever we could get cell phone reception. Shug Davis and Bridgette Irons, leery about meeting with a couple of hunters, still managed to squeeze Greg and me in between protests one weekend. I appreciate their giving us the benefit of the doubt.

A diehard if only moderately skillful hunter, I thoroughly enjoyed talking to fellow sportsmen for their perspectives on managing deer. I was fortunate, too, that so many on both sides of the debate agreed to share their thoughts. Walter Poole, Ed Grasavage, Ron Freed, Greg Levengood, Schuyler Frey, Lowell Graybill, and the others, I thank you all.

Special thanks go out to the family and friends of Gary Alt. There's no way you can write about Pennsylvania and deer in the twenty-first century without talking to Alt, who continues to be at the eye of the storm. Fortunately, not only was Gary himself open and honest with me, but those closest to him were, too. His children Lindsay and Garrick, father, Buck, and friends Larry Schweiger, Tim Carr, Bob McDowell, and the rest all made priceless contributions to this book.

Jim Loree and David Creegan invited us to visit their deer farms at a time when those in their industry are sensitive about being painted in a bad light. I appreciate their giving us a chance to listen to their side of the story.

As for all of the others among the more than two hundred people who are either quoted in this book or who supplied reports, documents, and other information, please know that I appreciate your contributions. As a writer, I know that getting the right word or right fact from just the right person often makes all the difference. I am grateful to have had your help.

I have to thank Greg Sofranko for being such a big part of this book, too. Spike, we put in a lot of hours and covered a lot of miles getting this done. It was great having you along as a friend, partner, and driver.

My wife, Mandy, and sons, Derek and Tyler, deserve my thanks, too. Doing the research for this book and then writing it meant time away from home and hours squirreled away in the office, pounding away at the keyboard. Thanks, guys, for picking up the slack.

Finally, I want to thank Tony Sanfilippo and the Keystone Committee for giving Greg and me the go-ahead to do this book, and also to our copyeditor at Penn State Press, Suzanne Wolk, for her expertise in shepherding us through this process.

Bob Frye
North Huntingdon, Pennsylvania
January 1, 2006

1

HOW MUCH IS ENOUGH?

The door of the one-room schoolhouse burst open with a bang, quieting in an instant the normal before-class chatter. Goosebumps rose on the flesh of the students, in part because of the icy blade of cold air that knifed through the room.

More than that, though, it was the look on the face of their classmate. Eyes wide, hair askew from ripping off his cap, out of breath from running through the snow, he was stammering, the words running together like water droplets over a falls.

Charlie May was one of the students who turned to see what the stir was about. Only minutes before, he had settled into his seat after hanging his coat on a peg by the door. It was just before Christmas 1931 and there were several inches of snow on the ground.

That hadn't kept May from walking to school, of course. It was only a few miles from home, and he was all but a man anyway. Fifteen and in eighth grade, his last year of school, he'd soon be leaving books behind to join the rest of the men in Gowan City, Schuylkill County, in working for the Reading Coal Company. His relative maturity left him immune to some of the crises that occasionally sent his younger classmates into a frenzy. This was to be something different, though.

"Hey! Hey everybody! You'll never guess what I just saw!" yelled the excited youngster at the door behind him. "I saw a deer track!"

It took a second for this to sink in, and then the room was on fire with excitement. Just imagine, a white-tailed deer track, and in the snow on the same road the children walked to school every day! It was almost unthinkable. Even the teacher—whose first instinct must have been to put down the sudden disturbance before it led to general mayhem—got caught up in the pandemonium.

"Get your coats on, everyone," the teacher said. "We're going to go see it."

"It seems funny now, but my dad said the whole class walked about a mile in the snow just to see that track—it wasn't even a deer, just a track—because it was unheard of," said Charlie May, the same-named son of that Schuylkill County teenager. "I remember my dad telling me that was one of the few times he ever saw a deer track as a kid, and he was in the woods a lot, more than most. There just weren't many deer back in those days."

I was thinking of that story as I pulled the minivan over to the edge of the road. It was an August evening, seven decades removed from Charlie May's last year of school, and the air was just beginning to cool. My wife, Mandy, and I had weathered the afternoon heat by swimming with our sons, Derek and Tyler, in the lake at Laurel Hill State Park, in southwestern Pennsylvania's Laurel Mountains. When we left, an hour or so before dark, we decided that rather than head straight home, we would detour on some side roads to look for deer.

Now we were parked on the edge of the two-lane blacktop, the driver's-side tires in the gravel, watching a six-point buck. It was the sixth or seventh deer we'd seen so far, but the first with antlers. It had crossed the road in front of us from right to left, inexplicably leaving the security of Forbes State Forest for a forty-yard strip of greenery that stood between us and the Pennsylvania Turnpike, a cross-state, four-lane superhighway. It was just inside the tree line, peering back at us over its shoulder. Derek, then age nine, and Tyler, then age six, craned their necks to get a better look.

"Can we unbuckle?" Tyler asked, frustrated by his inability to get closer to the window on the deer's side because of the restrictions of his seat belt.

We saw a truck coming toward us and tried to catch the driver's eye, hoping to alert him to the buck's presence. I'm not sure he knew what we were trying to tell him—he slowed only a little—but fortunately the buck never moved.

We stayed another minute, then left when it seemed we might be the reason he was staying so still, so close to the road. If that deer was going to get hit by a vehicle, we didn't want to cause it, and we certainly didn't want to see it.

We continued through that state forest area, swung by some game lands managed for wildlife by the Pennsylvania Game Commission, then drove along a few roads at the base of the Laurel Ridge, where houses are sandwiched between the road and the woods. Having chosen the air conditioning of our minivan over the extra ground clearance of our Wrangler earlier in the day, we stayed on the pavement now.

Still, in that final hour of daylight we saw thirty-nine deer, not an unusual number by any means. Only that one was a buck—a telling fact at the time—but we saw several spotted fawns, including one set of triplets and two sets of twins. We saw some fat, healthy-looking deer. We saw a doe or two that seemed gaunt. We saw so many deer of so many kinds that before our trip was over Derek and Tyler had tired of watching them. "Uh-huh," they'd say without lifting their heads when Mandy or I would say, "there's one!" or "there's a bunch!"

"Would we have been home already if we went straight there?" I heard Tyler ask.

"Yeah, we've been driving for an hour, and it takes an hour to get home from the park, so we'd have been there by now. But mom and dad want to look for deer," Derek said, before going back to looking at the dog encyclopedia that he carried with him everywhere we went that summer.

Both kids love animals, both love to go for hikes, both look forward to tagging along with Dad in hunting season. If they're the first to spot a deer, they brag about how good their eyes are. But deer are everywhere, and they see them all the time. Coop them up in the van for more than an hour, and the novelty of spotting whitetails loses its appeal.

If that might have shocked Charlie May in 1931, it doesn't shock his son today. The younger May spent about thirty years working as a wildlife conservation officer with the Game Commission, serving in Fayette County, in the state's deer-rich southwestern corner. During that time he was in the woods more than most, as his wiry frame and tanned skin attest. The difference is that the younger May enjoyed, each day, the potential to see more deer in a single afternoon than his dad could ever have imagined.

"Seeing deer today for a lot of people is like seeing cows," May said. "They're everywhere. Unless someone sees a really, really big buck, they don't even mention it to me anymore."

While Derek and Tyler and May's neighbors might take all of those deer for granted today, their counterparts just a few generations ago couldn't do the same. Pennsylvania is a big state by eastern standards, comprising forty-five thousand square miles divided into sixty-seven counties. Yet in 1916, about the time the elder May was born, hunters killed only 1,722 deer, all bucks. In 1931 the statewide harvest was still less than a hundred thousand.

Today, drivers kill that many or more on the roads each year. Hunters take another four hundred thousand annually, and still the deer population was thought to be something like 1.6 million animals heading into the fall of 2003.

At first glance, it's hard to consider this population explosion anything but a wonderful development, especially in Pennsylvania, which has considered the white-tailed deer its state animal since 1955. Whitetails are unquestionably beautiful. Watching one bound across a field in great leaps, its signature white tail held high, or dodge and weave through an oak forest, you can't help but wonder at their combination of form and function. Does have the deep brown eyes and long lashes of a movie starlet. Bucks, especially those in the rut, have a primeval masculinity about them that bespeaks raw power. They're lithe, fleet, and have the grace of a Baryshnikov. Just about everyone, hunter or nonhunter, likes to see them. What both sexes share, though—and this is what makes them so potentially devastating—is the ability to destroy the very habitat they rely on to survive.

"Deer are second only to humans in their impact on a forest ecosystem," says Dr. Gary Alt, former head of the Game Commission's deer management section, where he was responsible for recommending when and how to control deer numbers. "They can, and will, dictate what other animals will survive there." The trick for Alt and biologists like him all around the country is not figuring out how to manage deer. That's relatively simple. The trick is figuring out how to manage the people who love deer. That's much harder.

Ask how many deer are enough and the answer you get may vary widely, depending on whether it's a hunter or a farmer or a forester or a homeowner doing the talking. When people as often as not want to manage deer populations based on values and desires instead of the amount of available habitat, the right answer is not always the popular one.

Dr. Joseph Kalbfus, a dentist by day who served as the Game Commission's first executive director, knew as much nearly a century ago. Speaking in 1917, he said that the biologist or executive who tried to manage deer based more on science than on social pressures was in for a fight.

"Thank God I won't be in charge of this work 10 years from now, because someone is going to have hell to pay," Kalbfus wrote. How right he was. Almost ninety years later the job of managing deer on the basis of their impact on habitat, and not on how many animals people want to see, remains a challenge.

"I've been on the [Game Commission] board for years, and I see no organization standing in line to take on deer management in Pennsylvania," says Steve Mohr, until recently a commissioner from Lancaster County. "It's no small task."

It is, though, perhaps the most important task facing the agency at the beginning of the twenty-first century. In Kalbfus's day, few people, other than the hunters who went to the woods in search of them, interacted with deer. Today, each and every one of the state's 13 million residents is likely to see or be affected by deer somewhere along the line. That's raised the stakes considerably.

Vern Ross, executive director of the Game Commission, knew as much when he persuaded Alt to dive into the deer debate. Ross said then that deer management was "the issue that would decide the future of the Pennsylvania Game Commission and the future of hunting in Pennsylvania." Bruce Smith, the York County Republican who chairs the Game and Fisheries Committee in the state House of Representatives, agreed when he said that "deer hunters and deer management can make or break the Pennsylvania Game Commission."

These are pretty dramatic statements, but they're also probably close to the mark. After all, it was the decimation of the state's deer herd that in large part sparked the formation of the Game Commission. And it's the debate over deer that may very well determine what happens to the agency in the future.

To understand what could happen in the future, though, it's necessary to first take a look at the past. History shows that there was no shortage of deer in Pennsylvania when the first European settlers arrived. The Keystone State was home to wildlife of all kinds—deer, elk, turkeys, even caribou and bison—in great abundance.

"The food the woods yield is your elks, deer, raccoons, beaver, rabbits, turkey, pheasants, heath-birds, pigeons and partredge innumerably; we need no setting dogs to ketch, they run by droves into the house in cold weather," wrote William Penn, founder of the state, upon his arrival in Pennsylvania on October 29, 1682. Penn was equally enthusiastic about the state's rich wildlife resources in other letters, like the one he wrote to the Earl of Sutherland on July 28, 1683. "I have had better venison, bigger, more tender and as fatt as in England," he wrote.

Settlers were quick to take advantage of that bounty, by whatever means necessary. Deer were taken in such quantity that the state enacted its first hunting regulations on August 26, 1771. That's when Provincial Governor Sir William Keith outlined a law that protected "buck, doe, fawn, or any other sort of deer whatsoever" from January 1 to July 1. Violators paid a fine of twenty shillings, though Indians were exempt.

This restriction did little, though, to slow the market hunters who could make money by selling venison to the residents of America's growing cities. They continued to kill deer by any means possible, including many that are now illegal. They shot deer over salt licks. They chased them with dogs. They even perfected the art of jacklighting, or shooting deer at night, often from a boat, with the aid of a pitch-pine torch. The light from the torch transfixed the deer momentarily, giving the shooter time to score a killing hit.

Hunters of the era, who wrote of taking as many as a hundred deer each fall, decimated the herd. Things got so bad that Potter County residents circulated a petition seeking "passage of a law to prevent all persons, except actual residents or the holders of lands, houses or tenements, in the county of Potter, from killing or destroying any deer therein, at any period of the year whatsoever." That request failed to become law, and the devastation continued unchecked. Other laws were adopted later, but to no effect. In 1869 the state legislature limited deer season to September 1 to December 31; in 1876 it was shortened again, from October 1 to December 31. In 1895 it was scaled back one more time, from October 15 to December 15.

All of this was too little too late. Constant hunting pressure, combined with widespread clear-cut logging that, in the practice of the day, left entire mountainsides without a single tree standing, had destroyed the deer population. With 70 percent of what had been "Penn's Woods" converted to agricultural fields by the 1890s, there were few deer and little food or cover for those that remained.

John M. Phillips, a prominent businessman who went on to become one of the state's leading conservationists, summed up the situation in a story he told at the fourteenth American game conference in New York City. He and a friend were hunting in what is now the Allegheny National Forest region, between Ridgway and Brockway. They jumped a buck in the morning.

"About six inches of snow had fallen, so we tracked it all day, camped on the trail that night, followed it the next day, then rested overnight at the town of Brockwayville. In the morning we took up the trail again and succeeded in jumping and killing the buck," Phillips said. "During all that long chase we didn't cross another deer track. I said to my friend, 'I am done—I think I have killed the last deer in Pennsylvania.'"

He hadn't, but he probably wasn't far off the mark. The harvest in 1906 was estimated at only eight hundred deer, 350 of which were bucks. The following year, when Pennsylvania had its first-ever bucks-only season, the kill dropped even lower, to two hundred bucks and thirty illegal does.

Things began to change only when sportsmen began to lobby aggressively for changes in deer management. First, in 1895, hunters led the way in creating the Pennsylvania Game Commission, the state's first agency mandated with protecting wildlife. In 1913, with the help of a letter from former president and conservationist Theodore Roosevelt, sportsmen prompted the inauguration of a $1 hunting license to fund the Commission.

In the years between those two events, the Commission, again with the backing of hunters, established refuges known as game preserves. The first was formed in Clinton County in 1905, and several others followed. They had several things in common. They averaged about thirty-two hundred acres. All hunting was prohibited. And they were located on state ground in the hope that game populations would take root there, then spread onto other property.

To speed things up, the Game Commission stocked white-tailed deer on those preserves beginning in 1906. The first shipment of fifty deer was purchased from a wildlife propagator in Michigan. Over the next nineteen years twelve hundred more deer were purchased from commercial deer farms in Pennsylvania, Kentucky, Maine, Michigan, New Hampshire, New Jersey, North Carolina, and Ohio, and were stocked throughout Pennsylvania.

A friend and fellow deer hunter, Jeff Nelson, provided me with a fascinating firsthand account of how those refuges and stocking efforts worked. Over lunch one day, he showed me some documents belonging to his grandfather, Emil L. Nelson, who was a game warden for the Game Commission in the early 1920s. One of the mementos Emil passed down to his grandson was a blueprint-like map of game preserve 29, located in his district in Warren County. Dated April 18, 1922, and signed by chief of lands W. Gord Conklin, the map shows a parcel bounded by Warren Boro to the north, the Allegheny River to the west, Minister Creek to the south, and Clarendon Boro to the east.

There's no way to tell what the many lines and numbers on the map mean. The map does, however, provide a wonderful reference when you're looking through some of Emil's old notes. Jeff gave me two shirt-pocket-sized notebooks that Emil carried when he was on duty. Bound in leather and still in excellent shape, they smell slightly musty, like old library books that haven't been cracked open in quite a while. They're veritable treasure chests of information, though.

Emil, using his own form of shorthand, penciled inside each notebook a record of his activities on a daily basis. His notes speak of a hardworking man from a long-ago era. In 1923 he wrote, "working about buildings," "had horse shod," "working on telephone lines," "fighting fire along east line," and "with two men planted 2,350 seedlings." He recorded how many miles he traveled each day and how he did it—for example, "12 car, 6 foot, 6 trolley." There are details about his expenses, too: eighteen cents for the trolley, ten cents for the phone, and $1 for stamps.

There are camp names and rosters, arrests—"Arrested Arthur Woodland. $25 fine paid. Rained all day"—and all sorts of scribbles, figures, and odds and ends. What's most interesting, though, are the notes Emil Nelson kept about releasing deer into game preserve 29. The notebooks cover various months between December 1921 and March 1923. There are many, many references to Emil's trips to Clarendon—perhaps there was a train station there?—to pick up deer and return empty crates that might be used to bring more whitetails in. He also recorded details about what happened to the deer after they were released.

A sampling of his notes looks like this:

Dec. 19, 1921: Unload deer. 4 bucks, 2 does
Dec. 20, 1921: Paid express on deer $80
Dec. 29, 1921: To Clarendon and return for deer. 4 fawns, 2-point buck
Jan. 5, 1922: 4 does. One died 1/6/22
Jan. 6, 1922: Clarendon and return for deer. 11-point buck and buck fawn
Jan. 9, 1922: Paid express on two does. Crates $16.35. Deer $27.80. Dinner
    40 cents. Telegram 53 cents.
Jan. 15, 1922: Brought out alfalfa for deer
Jan. 31, 1922: Found doe one mile from Clarendon
Feb. 12, 1922: Found one doe, hind quarter part eaten
Feb. 23, 1922: Found fawn, no marks
March 13, 1922: Found 10 point buck
March 11, 1923: Clarendon SGL, two trips looking for shipment of deer
March 12, 1923: Brought out three bucks, two does

Flipping gently through Emil's notebooks, I'm amazed. Emil stocked a deer here, two there, a half dozen somewhere else. He took some pictures of the animals. Jeff showed me a few dim black-and-white prints, one of them capturing a child staring eyeball to eyeball with a seemingly travel-weary and dazed buck. And now we've got more than a million and a half deer? It seems incredible.

What undoubtedly helped bring the deer back was that, at the same time the refuges were being established and the stocking effort was under way, sportsmen were lobbying to have deer hunting restricted to bucks only. The idea—a good one in the circumstances of the day—was to boost the herd by saving as many antlerless deer, or does, as possible. The Game Commission listened, and doe seasons were closed from 1907 through 1922 and periodically thereafter.

All of these factors—game preserves, transplanted deer, less hunting pressure—were in play at the same time that the state's forests were beginning to grow back. Most of deer's natural predators had been eliminated, too, courtesy of a culture that saw everything from hawks to wolves as evil. The result was a boom in the size of the deer herd.

"It was what I call a perfect storm," said State Representative Dan Surra, an Elk County Democrat who counts many hunters and anglers among his constituents. "You look at the old pictures. There wasn't a tree left standing in Pennsylvania. I mean every hillside was clear-cut down to the dirt. I knew a storeowner who told me that in the 1920s, if you found a deer track, you scooped it up and made soup out of it.

"But as soon as the forests started to grow again, all at the same time across the whole state, the deer herd just went crazy. There was so much browse and feed that the deer couldn't help but explode."

Roger Cowburn of Galeton, Potter County, described those days to me as we sat in his home amid the antique railroad equipment he collected. Perched on a stool by his bar, surrounded by several deer mounts and the rack from a moose he had collected in a lifetime of hunting, the seventy-three-year-old Cowburn talked about living in what was the heart of Pennsylvania's deer country in the mid-twentieth century.

Cowburn grew up in the woods, the son of a hunting father. In time he put his woodsman's skills to use guiding "flatlanders"—people from outside the state's mountainous north-central area—on deer hunts, informally in the 1950s and, beginning in 1966, from a lodge he ran for five years. The lodge employed eight other guides and hosted as many as fifty-six hunters each week of deer season.

"Back in 1952 and 1953, there was one farm where I could take you and you could see five hundred deer in one field every night," said Cowburn. "One time in doe season, in 1966, we guided twenty-three hunters, and we had twenty-three deer by lunchtime." Roger passed away in 2006.

No one should have been surprised by that kind of success. Pennsylvania's deer herd, by the Game Commission's estimates, doubled between 1913 and 1915, doubled again by 1919, again by 1921, again by 1924, and again by 1927. That trend continued for decades, with the size of the herd spiraling upward unabated.

The problem with that unchecked growth is the same one that has plagued the Game Commission and its biologists ever since. Namely, the hunters and

policymakers who set the direction of deer management in the decades that followed the population explosion couldn't or wouldn't change, even though Pennsylvania's deer herd and the woods it called home certainly did. While the deer herd
went from being too small to being too large for the available habitat, and the ratio
of bucks to does got out of balance, hunting seasons generally stayed the same.

Pennsylvania could get away with mismanaging deer fifty years ago, says Gary
Alt, because the state had fewer people, fewer roads, fewer cars, fewer suburban
housing developments. Today, deer affect people everywhere. That means it's past
time to undo the mismanagement that Alt calls "the greatest skeleton in the closet
of the Pennsylvania Game Commission" and develop strategies that balance deer
populations with the available habitat.

"Hunter expectations were developed in an era with extremely high deer densities," Alt says. "That caused a love affair with seeing lots of deer. They loved it so
much they got hooked on it. That fueled their desires. The result, though, was that
those desires prevented proper deer management, and caused billions of dollars in
ecological damage. We have to realign those expectations with reality.

"We have never done that, at least not over the long term. If you want to look at
where we've failed in the past as game managers, it's been our inability to educate
the general public and communicate among ourselves about what the problems
caused by deer are and how to fix them."

Certainly, biologists have tried. Richard Gerstell was a young go-getter with the
Game Commission in 1935, a Yale graduate and one of the agency's first full-time
wildlife managers who went on to a distinguished career as a biologist and author.
Despite his talents, though, he couldn't make hunters or the general public understand the relationship between deer and their habitat.

We talked about that one warm summer evening in 2000. I had been reading
some of Gerstell's work, and when I learned that he was living in Lancaster
County, I gave him a call. He was ninety years old then and still a gentleman, but
his memory had, in his own words, started to slip. He wasn't sure how much help
he would be, but he agreed to a meeting.

Photographer Greg Sofranko and I were scheduling interviews all over the state
then, taking people as we could get them. On this occasion we left my home, east
of Pittsburgh, at about 4:00 A.M. for an interview in the woods of McKean County,
then several hours later set out for Lancaster. Arriving while dinner was still being
served, we found Richard, his wife, and the other residents dressed in blouses and
skirts and jackets and ties. They were being served by waiters and waitresses outfitted

Richard Gerstell warned hunters as early as the 1930s about the need to balance deer with their habitat.

in black pants and crisp white shirts and bow ties. Still in our boots and jeans, wearing camouflage ball caps, we waited on a bench in the hallway, trying not to get mud on the carpet and feeling like a couple of wayward gardeners.

Richard, though, put us at ease. Still thin and dapper, he led us out to a garden where we sat on a bench and talked for more than an hour. We talked a lot about the dead deer that he and others used to routinely discover each winter. The deer were generally young ones, those least equipped to survive the harsh conditions found in forests that had too many deer and not enough food to sustain them.

"They went down the worst whenever the weather hit them, like a bad snow. There were a lot of them that starved," Gerstell said. "Some places you never saw that, but in other places you did."

Gerstell tried to educate sportsmen about the need to balance deer with their habitat in an article he wrote for the *Pennsylvania Game News* magazine entitled "Pennsylvania Deer Problem in 1935." Gerstell warned of the need to balance the deer herd with the forest ecosystem. "Steps must be taken to remedy present conditions or both the deer herd and the deer range will suffer unprecedented and irreparable losses," he wrote.

What concerned Gerstell was that deer were dying in winter because of malnutrition. Field officers for the Game Commission did a survey from December 16, 1934, to May 1, 1935, in which they collected 964 deer that had died from "pathological causes"—that is, something other than old age, gunshot wounds, accidents, or the like. Of those deer, fewer than 1 percent died from poisoning. Fewer than 1 percent died from parasites. Another 7 percent died of unknown causes. The majority—881 of the deer, or more than 91 percent—died from malnutrition. Gerstell theorized that the number was even greater, though, because at least some of the deer that died from unknown causes were probably victims of malnutrition, too.

"This state of malnutrition was, of course, due to the fact that the density of the deer population throughout a large part of the deer range exceeded the carrying capacity of that particular portion of the range," Gerstell wrote. "As a result, many deer actually 'starved' to death with full stomachs. Such a state of affairs seems impossible, but such, unfortunately, was indeed the case and the facts are easily explicable.

"The demand for food exceeded the available supply and all suitable and attainable food was consequently devoured without fulfilling the demand. The deer, therefore, consumed various greens, twigs and other materials in an attempt to satisfy their craving for food and in doing so filled their stomachs, but the material contained therein was so low in actual food value that although the stomach was full, the animals perished from lack of nourishment."

Such a situation should not be allowed to continue, Gerstell argued. Overpopulation and inadequate food made the deer herd especially susceptible to disease. Worse, the drain the deer were placing on the state's forestland would "permanently reduce its food producing capabilities."

The answer to the problem was not artificial feeding, a tactic that some sportsmen advocated then as well as now. For starters, such a project would be prohibitively expensive. Emergency feeding was tried on a large scale during the winter of 1935–36, Gerstell noted, at a cost of $28,000 in feed and labor, and had minimal effect. Thousands of deer were still found dead of starvation the following spring.

What's more, Gerstell estimated that a deer herd comprising half a million animals would eat about a million pounds of food per winter day, based on a rate of two pounds of food per hundred pounds of deer. To feed ear corn to even one-fourth of the deer herd would cost about $25,000 per week, and the effort would probably have to be sustained for eight to ten weeks. That put the effort of feeding just a portion of the deer herd at $250,000 in 1938 dollars.

Worst of all, Gerstell warned, was that even if you could save deer one winter using artificial feeding, what then? The resulting overabundant deer herd might yet starve after the weather changed, when even the bounty of summer would not be enough to feed them all. And any deer that made it to the following winter would arrive in poorer shape than the ones saved a year before.

Gerstell concluded that the only real solution was for hunters to shoot more does, thereby decreasing the deer population enough to let the forest repair itself. He knew that this advice went against tradition. In the previous twenty years hunters had killed 216,826 bucks in Pennsylvania, but only 83,969 does. But he was convinced that an expanded doe harvest was best not only for Pennsylvania's forests but for its deer.

"Since a carefully regulated open season on antlerless deer would result in the removal of many of the 1935 fawns which will be during the winter most susceptible to the inroads of malnutrition and since such a season would also tend to balance the sex ratio of the deer herd by the removal of does, does not such a season appear to be the most logical solution to the Pennsylvania deer problem?" Gerstell asked.

Logical, yes. Popular, no. Following Gerstell's advice, the Pennsylvania Game Commission held a doe season in 1935, its first since 1931. A total of 46,668 does were harvested, but there was such a backlash from hunters that the season was closed for the following two years.

When 1938 rolled around, the Game Commission had decided that simply adding a doe season wasn't enough. Instead, the agency closed buck season and forced hunters to shoot does exclusively. It was a plan the Commission had tried once before. From 1915 to 1927 Pennsylvania held only four doe seasons, with harvests ranging from a low of eight to a high of 1,295. That didn't solve the problem, so biologists closed the buck season in 1928. Hunters killed 25,097 does, but they didn't like it, and doe season was closed in 1929.

If biologists thought things would be different in 1938, if they thought Gerstell's work had convinced hunters of the need to shoot does, they were wrong. The deer herd had grown so much that hunters killed more does in 1938 than anyone probably imagined possible. The harvest was 171,662, almost double 1931's state-record deer kill, when bucks and does were both legal. But hunters reacted angrily again, and doe hunting was shut down by 1941.

Still, biologists continued to warn that the deer herd was too large for the available habitat. In an August 1940 *Game News* article, the same John M. Phillips who once worried that he had shot the last deer in Pennsylvania wrote about the devastation—both to the environment and the deer herd itself—brought about by the overabundance of whitetails.

He noted that the Game Commission, by its own count, lost 75 to 90 percent of the thousands of trees, shrubs, and food plots it planted as wildlife habitat each year to ravenous deer. Despite those plantings, and despite the supplemental feeding of wildlife carried out by various sportsmen's groups, the state lost more than nine thousand deer to starvation in 1939. "Many were found in and along the streams and the April trout fishermen say the stench from the decaying carcasses was nauseating and the water not fit to drink," Phillips wrote.

Robert McDowell, chief of the Game Commission's Wildlife Research Division, wrote about the same kind of thing in a letter to the Commission's executive director, Thomas D. Frye, on March 30, 1950. He described the ugliness found during a winter survey that year on state game preserve 59 in Pleasant Valley Township, Potter County.

"We checked two miles of stream in Fish Hollow. In these two miles, on March 27 and 28, we found 26 dead and dying deer—22 were fawns; 4 were mature does, 3 yearlings and one older. All deer were suffering from malnutrition as proven by examining the marrow of the femur. No animals were suffering from pathological conditions and there were no heavy manifestations of nasal botflies," McDowell wrote.

An examination of the deer's stomach contents found corn (put out by the Game Commission), poor browse, spruce (from roadside plantings), and grasses. Artificial feeding in the form of timber cuts meant to provide additional browse was not the answer. "It is evident that cuttings made in January and February will not maintain a large number of deer," McDowell concluded.

Phillips also wrote about the impact of too many deer on other wildlife species. "It is variously estimated that there are from five hundred thousand to a million deer in the state. They have not only destroyed their own food so that many thousands die during the winter, but have destroyed the ground food and cover for small game, which gives sport to the great majority of our hunters," he wrote. "Our cottontails and snowshoe rabbits, grouse and wild turkeys are disappearing in many sections where deer are too plentiful."

If Phillips's words had any effect, it was apparently minimal, because a few years later Ross L. Leffler, president of the Game Commission, felt compelled to write about the same subject. In an article in the September 1944 issue of the *Game News*, Leffler blamed the Commission for failing to educate hunters about game management. He promised to correct this shortcoming, but then urged hunters to look beyond their own immediate wishes and do what was right for the future of hunting and wildlife—namely, get the deer herd under control. "Furthermore," he concluded, "the 640,000 licensed hunters of this state must remember that there are over 9,000,0000 additional residents of Pennsylvania who have a stake in its wildlife and in the natural resources with which the Keystone State is so richly endowed."

Leffler, in looking at the state's landscape, did not place all of the blame for the lack of forest regeneration on the overabundant deer herd. As trees grow old, they

An average adult doe will have twin fawns in areas of good deer habitat, so populations can outgrow the habitat quickly.

naturally shade out competition from below, he noted. But allowing deer to become so numerous that they were eating almost every shoot that sprang from the ground had exacerbated the problem. And because the kind of reckless, hell-bent timbering that had created the conditions so favorable to deer early in the twentieth century were never likely to be duplicated again, it was up to hunters to control deer numbers.

"Unless we have strict management of deer herds, there will be little or no deer hunting in this state 25 years from now," Leffler wrote. "You will probably want to blame the Game Commission for that. In one of our counties where there do not seem to be a great many deer now, some of the people will say, 'Well, it's because we killed off the does.' But it is actually because we did not kill them off early enough in the game."

Until Gary Alt arrived on the scene, however, no one carried the message about the need to balance deer and their habitat to the public as passionately as Roger Latham. Latham should have been, and was for a time, one of the bright lights of the Game Commission. A graduate of its first class of trainees at what is now the

Ross Leffler School of Conservation for wildlife conservation officers in 1936, he served for about five years as a game protector, until the outbreak of World War II.

After spending time as the leader of a Pittman-Robertson project and at Cornell University for the War Department, Latham returned to the Commission full-time in 1946. He stayed a little more than year, until he was granted a two-year paid leave to complete his degree at Penn State University. There he studied on a scholarship awarded by the Wildlife Management Institute in Washington, D.C.

He came back as a senior research technician, then advanced to chief of the Commission's Wildlife Research Division. He was a star on the rise, and he looked the part. A picture of him examining a dead deer in the 1950s shows a dark-haired, athletic-looking young man in his prime.

Ultimately, though, Latham was fired, his sin having been to argue for trimming Pennsylvania's deer herd. He wanted hunters to shoot more deer overall, and to shoot more does in particular, to bring the herd into line with their available habitat, to prevent the possible outbreak of disease, to make the state's forests a better home to a greater variety of plants and animals, and to make the deer themselves healthier, bigger, and less susceptible to starvation.

His most valiant effort to broadcast this message came in September 1950, when the Game Commission issued a special edition of the *Pennsylvania Game News* devoted entirely to deer management. Latham, who wrote the entire issue, laid out everything from the life history of white-tailed deer and the management problems they presented to possible solutions.

"In this issue the well-qualified author presents a clear and unbiased account of the recreational value of the Pennsylvania deer herd, as well as its devastating effects if not properly controlled," read the foreword. Latham said the goal of the Game Commission's deer management effort was to provide the "best possible deer hunting on a sustained basis—that is, maximum production for next year, 10 years later, and for generations to come." He also said, though, that well-meaning hunters who didn't understand how to reach that goal had hampered the effort for thirty years.

The problem was that hunters had not kept pace with changes in the state's forests. At the beginning of the century Pennsylvania's forests had been young and brushy, sprouting from the hillsides that had been clear-cut only a decade or so earlier. They offered lots of browse and could support one deer on every eight to ten acres. Two decades later, it took twenty-five acres of forest to support a single deer, Latham said, because the state's forests had entered the "pole timber" stage,

When deer herds are allowed to grow too large, browse lines—areas of forest where nothing grows below six feet except plants deer don't eat—become common.

when trees are too small to produce large amounts of mast but too large to provide browse.

Sportsmen and game managers who failed to notice that change, and who called for ever-higher deer populations, were being irresponsible, Latham argued. He suggested that whereas the state had had too few deer in 1905, it was beginning to have too many in some places as early as 1925.

Latham compared raising deer in the state's forests to raising cattle on a farm. Every farmer knows he can support only so many cattle on a finite piece of ground. If the number of cattle is kept in line with the ability of the range to grow good grass, the herd grows fat and healthy. Try to run too many cattle, and they grow thin and give less milk. The herd destroys its own range and the land is unable to support as many cattle as before, perhaps forever. The same is true with deer: the forest can only support so many. "Unfortunately," Latham wrote, "the herd has been maintained above the level of the true carrying capacity since the early 1920s."

This problem was not unique to Pennsylvania. The famous conservationist and author Aldo Leopold, professor of wildlife management at the University of Wisconsin, estimated in the 1930s that thirty of the forty-eight states were experiencing problems with overbrowsing by too many deer. Reducing deer herds was the only sure way to prevent a "tragic shrinkage" of both a deer herd and its range, he wrote.

Pennsylvania was already beginning to see that shrinkage, as Leopold had warned years before Latham arrived on the scene. He estimated that half of the total deer range in Pennsylvania had already been depleted. "In 1931 the Pennsylvania herd was estimated at 800,000 and the carrying capacity of the range at 250,000. The several doe seasons prevented a serious die-off, but not before thousands and thousands of acres of good range was spoiled," Leopold wrote.

Anyone who looked at Pennsylvania and saw mile upon mile of forest needed to realize that deer are not spread uniformly across that land, Latham argued, especially at certain times of year. In winter, deer move from the tops and sides of mountains to the valleys that offer the most shelter, especially when the snow is deep. The result is that the majority of deer concentrate on just a portion of the forest—3 to 4 million of the 10 to 15 million acres that are occupied during warmer weather—at a time when food is scarcest. At such times, deer "eat themselves out of house and home" and suffer the dire consequences, he said.

"During the 1935–36 winter it was possible to count from 50 to 100 dead deer while walking for a mile or less along some of the state's mountain streams," Latham wrote. "Today, nine out of 10 of these valleys are 'eaten out,' and they have become death traps for the deer which remain. To permit animals to suffer in this manner and to permit this waste of a natural resource is surely not judicious management!"

The impact of too many deer was visible not only on the forest but on the deer themselves. Experiments at the Game Commission's wildlife experiment station revealed that deer body weights had dropped over a period of twenty to thirty years, when deer populations were climbing, Latham noted. Whereas bucks weighing 200 pounds field dressed—meaning with their insides removed—were once common, and weights of 150 pounds or more were average, by 1941 the average buck weighed 105 pounds. Some were as small as 80 to 90 pounds.

Average antler sizes had also decreased. The number of ten- and twelve-point bucks had dropped as spikes became increasingly common. That was a bad sign, Latham said. "Any spike buck is an abnormality, reflecting the over-browsed condition of the range, and spikes are common only when the animals are improperly nourished. That is, bucks should normally have from four to 10 points the first time they produce antlers at 18 months of age."

Malnutrition among does was obvious when examining fawning patterns, Latham continued. A healthy adult doe should give birth to twins or triplets and, in good range, as many as 30 percent of yearling does—those six to seven months of age—might produce fawns. Pennsylvania was seeing little or none of that. Most does were not having fawns their first year, and few gave birth to more than one fawn their second year. "The important consideration here from a management standpoint is that 50 well-fed does will produce as many, and perhaps even more, fawns as 100 poorly-fed does," Latham wrote.

The good news for hunters, he continued, was that if deer were kept in line with the available habitat, sportsmen could have healthier forests, a healthier deer herd composed of larger animals, and good populations of other game and nongame animals, all at the same time. The question was how to bring that about.

Latham suggested two means of balancing deer and their habitat. The first alternative was to prevent the forest, or at least a large portion of it, from ever maturing. Some advocated just such tactics, calling for the Game Commission to regularly bulldoze, cut, burn, or otherwise harvest large tracts of timber. Such talk was impractical, Latham said, because the state did not own enough forest to indefinitely support large numbers of deer. What's more, the state's residents— hunter and nonhunter alike—could ill afford to waste the timber and other natural resources provided by the forest "just because a few selfish individuals want to maintain deer in such numbers that they constitute an ecological menace."

The only option, Latham said, was to reduce the size of the deer herd, primarily through increased doe hunting. He was decades ahead of his time in advocating all-age, all-sex hunting seasons. Expecting some to oppose that idea—and boy, did they ever—Latham tried to temper fears about what reducing the herd meant.

"Many hunters . . . will immediately oppose any such suggestion because they feel that the proposed herd reduction will ruin their sport. Many sportsmen visualize a wholesale slaughter followed by years and years of poor hunting," Latham wrote. "Fortunately, the wildlife manager's meaning of herd reduction is far different from this. He wants to reduce the number of animals held over the winter when browse is at a minimum and when deer may die by the thousands. There would actually be little or no reduction in the numbers of deer available for the hunting season. Instead of ruining the deer hunting as many sportsmen believe, the wildlife manager is confident that the hunting can and will be improved by herd reduction."

Latham laid the responsibility for managing deer at the feet of hunters, and said they had to decide whether they wanted to do it the right way—relying on "scientific study and management by well-trained wildlife men"—or the wrong way, based on "the whims, fancies, and selfish desires" of well-meaning but misguided sportsmen.

Like the man in the fairy tale who was presented with a pile of gold coins for his good deeds, hunters had been given a treasure in the state's deer herd, Latham said. The question was whether they would make the same mistake as the man with the coins. Overcome by greed and oblivious to the fairy's warnings, he tried to stuff his sack too full, putting more and more coins in until the seams parted, and his fairy and all of the gold disappeared.

The Game Commission had spent decades warning hunters they were trying to stuff their sack too full, Latham said. As a result, the state's forests and fields were already bursting at the seams with deer. "Has not the Game Commission warned repeatedly for the past 20 years that the bag contained more than it could safely hold?" Latham asked. "Have not the seams begun to break and the gold pieces started to trickle through (winter mortality)? And is there no imminent danger that the whole bottom may fall out if some of the pieces are not removed and the strain relieved?"

Hunters did not get the message, or did not care to listen if they did. When the 1950 deer season rolled around, counties still had the option of overruling the Game Commission and closing doe seasons. Fourteen did just that, and the statewide doe kill decreased from 84,121 in 1949 to 31,515 in 1950, just when Latham said it should be increasing.

By 1951 the Commission had persuaded the state legislature to give it complete control over doe seasons, but it did not prove a much better steward than the hunters had, at least initially. The kill still did not rise appreciably in either of the next two years. Hunters took 37,952 does in 1951 and 37,829 in 1952.

This prompted Latham to write another article in February 1953 that dripped with the frustration and bitterness he was obviously beginning to feel. It appeared in the *Pennsylvania Game News* and was entitled "Too Many, Too Long!" He told hunters to sit down before reading the article, because the predictions it contained "will probably hit you right between the eyes."

"Remember the good old days when there was a whitetail behind every bush, and it was not unusual to start 50 or 100 deer on one drive? Remember how every member of some upstate families would kill a deer—including Mom and Grandpop? Remember how a car with five hunters would have four or five deer tied on the outside? And remember how hunters scoffed at doe hunting because it was just like shooting cows?

"Those lush days are about gone except for a small area in the north-central counties, and within five years this pocket will probably go as have the other great concentration areas of the state," Latham wrote. "Closing the season entirely would only hasten the process. Shooting deer down to rock bottom would help but little because now it is too late. There would be no recovery because there is no food for recovery. Much of it is a desert—a forest desert with rotting bones of starved deer."

Still hunters and game managers did not listen. Instead of shooting more does and allowing the habitat to recover, they shot even fewer, and doe hunting became a yo-yo. The 1953 doe harvest was just 16,252; in 1954 the season was closed. Doe hunting returned in 1955—hunters shot 41,111—but closed again in 1956, ending Latham's career with the Commission in the process. When he continued to argue for more aggressive doe hunting, he was fired on August 21, 1957.

It was a sad end to a sorry chapter, but it hardly signaled the end of efforts to control deer numbers. Biologists managed to get a doe season back in 1957, and they never lost it again. Those who followed Latham, including fellow Game Commission biologist and contemporary Glenn L. Bowers, also continued to carry his message.

"There is little doubt that had more deer been harvested in earlier years, our forests would be more productive of deer food today, and also would provide better living conditions for small game species such as snowshoe hares, cottontails and grouse," Bowers wrote. "We could have maintained a large deer herd in better condition—heavier animals with better racks and an increased rate of reproduction—if closely regulated harvests of antlerless deer had been accepted by sportsmen."

Deer management took a bit of a scientific turn in the 1960s, when the Game Commission developed its first comprehensive deer management policy, which set deer density limits for different types of habitat. In 1964 the agency began to try to calculate the size of its deer herd and allocate antlerless licenses accordingly, based on a "minimum deer population index." That same year it created a special regulations area in parts of counties bordering Philadelphia to check the booming urban deer population there.

But this was too little too late. It was obvious even then that what Gerstell, Phillips, Leffler, and Latham had predicted had come to pass—the first areas in the state to recover from turn-of-the-century logging practices, the first places where the forest had come back, the places considered "the deer woods" for so long, were showing the effects of overbrowsing. Areas outside the traditional deer range, which were behind the curve in terms of regeneration, had become the better places for deer.

"A most apparent fact is that the best deer, from the standpoint of size and health, are found in places not necessarily considered deer country," reported Game Commission biologist Lincoln Lang in 1965. "On the other hand, many of the poorer quality deer are found in our Big Woods country where deer populations are usually high."

That situation persists today, nearly four decades later. The population of Pennsylvania has grown by 3 million people since Leffler wrote his article about the need to control deer for the good of all in 1944. The deer herd is also larger, numbering somewhere around 1.5 million animals. And the counties that routinely produce the most deer, and the biggest bucks in terms of both body size and antlers, are located outside the traditional deer range. The state's northern tier may have most of the deer camps and most of the public land and most of the deer hunting tradition, but it's the southwestern corner of the state, home to the city of Pittsburgh and innumerable suburban housing developments, that has given up more big bucks and more deer overall every year for a decade.

"When you read the history of deer management in this state, it reads like a horror novel," Alt says. "Every time anyone tried to change things by talking about deer in relationship to their habitat, they just got killed. They either quit, got transferred, or got fired. Even now, when you look at the problems facing us and when you talk about the solutions, it's kind of eerie. It sounds just like it did all of those years ago when Aldo Leopold and Roger Latham and Richard Gerstell were talking about deer management."

The question, then, is what the sportsmen, policymakers, deer managers, and others who care so deeply about deer will do this time around. In Emil Nelson's day, when their fathers and grandfathers were hunting, the answer to the question of how best to save deer was to not shoot very many of them. Today, ironically enough, the answer to saving Pennsylvania's deer—and their habitat—seems to be to shoot a lot of them, at least in the short term. Will the policymakers who set deer seasons give them the chance to do it, and will sportsmen respond?

It's probably too early to say. Like his predecessors, Alt ran into his share of opposition for advocating higher doe harvests. He came to the deer section's top job with a lot of credibility, earned over two decades as a pioneering black bear researcher. But he did not survive either, quitting in frustration after five years on the job. Steve Mohr had warned everyone early on that this might be Alt's fate. "Sportsmen are not going to put blinders on. As long as progress is being made, they're going to be willing to give him time. But they want him to produce. There's a lot of that attitude out there."

George Venesky, a former Commission board member who was removed from his post by then–Pennsylvania governor Tom Ridge—largely, he believes, for not going step for step with Alt and the deer team—was even more blunt. "If sportsmen don't see progress, it will be 'Gary who?'" Venesky said. "He's a great guy and people have a lot of respect for him, but this is a different ballgame."

The members of the Game Commission board have endured some criticism, too, not only from the people who don't want to shoot too many deer, but also from those who think they didn't listen enough to Alt and his staff. In Pennsylvania, biologists recommend seasons and bag limits. The commissioners, though, have the final say about whether to adopt them or not. Sometimes, board members have said, those decisions have to be based as much on social and political concerns as on biological ones.

Roxane Palone, a commissioner from Greene County, agrees with those who believe commissioners, sportsmen, and others must do the right thing, no matter how it affects their recreation in the short term. Hunter satisfaction is important, Palone says. She's a deer hunter, too. But the hunters of the early twentieth century were the state's first conservationists, and they put aside their own wants for the long-term good of the deer. The hunters of the early twenty-first century must be equally selfless in doing what's right for whitetails and their habitat, she adds. "Wildlife is not a commodity, manufactured on assembly lines. We cannot increase or decrease production based on a good or a bad quarter. The programs that we institute today will affect most greatly those generations after ours, as those management decisions of the past affect us now," says Palone.

"The Game Commission should not focus solely on the wishes of current hunters. There is very little it can provide in using short-term deer management, other than giving political victories to those who demand short-term solutions. Short-term and shortsighted solutions will only result in long-term failures," she says. "Our goal should be a sustainable deer herd for the generations that follow. It is morally unjust to borrow from the trust fund of our forests to give one or two generations unsustainable numbers of deer. It is unjust to leave the future forests and the next generations of hunters with a habitat devoid of regeneration, unable to provide all the benefits we're enjoyed in the past."

Bob Gilford, a former game commissioner from Clarion County, agrees, though he also stresses that deer need hunters as much as hunters need deer. "You just cannot please everyone and still do what's best for the resource," Gilford says. "I think we're going to have to withstand some public pressure. If sportsmen will stick with the program and let the habitat come back, they're going to see more deer. But they're going to have to weather a few years where they might not see as many.

"By the same token, we have to respect the hunters. Without them we have no effective way to control the deer herd. We just can't do it. If we lose our hunters, we'll have real problems."

Indeed, no one should look at Pennsylvania's hunters as the bad guys in the state's deer story, says Jim Seitz, former president of the Pennsylvania Deer Association. It was hunters who helped bring the state's whitetails back from the brink a hundred years ago, and who funded the acquisition of game lands to benefit deer and other wildlife in the decades since. Hunters will do the right thing from here on out, too, he believes, once they learn the nature of the deer problem and what needs to be done about it. Educating hunters is the key.

"We've got hunters who want to just be able to drive to a state game lands, jump out of the car, walk fifty yards into the woods and shoot a deer. That's their idea of hunting. But you can't have that. You can't continue to manage for that many deer," Seitz says. "We want to see a deer herd that's in line with the available habitat."

"It's going to be a long, slow educational process. I think we just have to keep chipping away at it," agrees George Kelly, a retired deer biologist from the Game Commission. "It took us at least 70 years to get here, so things aren't going to change overnight.

The lure of deer hunting has always been the chance to get close to nature. This won't change, though hunters in the future will have to work harder to explain who they are and why they do what they do.

"We just have to set a goal and get the train moving in that direction. And I don't think that with an ever-growing deer population the train was moving in the right direction."

For his part, and despite some setbacks, Alt also remains optimistic that Pennsylvania is on the right rack. He traveled thousands of miles around the state over the winters of 2000, 2001, and 2002, talking about the need to manage deer properly, filling school auditoriums, sportsmen's clubs, and civic centers at each stop along the way. He's come away thinking that the majority of sportsmen are willing to try new management approaches if they can be explained. "When sportsmen hear the truth and they see how deer management works, they will sign on," he says.

Alt credits game commissioners for having the courage to implement changes like antler restrictions, concurrent buck and doe seasons, and October doe seasons, too. Those things radically broke with decades of tradition and were all controversial in their time. Some remain that way today. But commissioners have stayed the course on those fronts, he says.

If there's one problem on the horizon, Alt says, it's that the Game Commission is funded almost exclusively by one constituency, namely, the hunters who buy licenses. That puts the agency in a tough spot. Biologists can determine that an area has too many deer. But if hunters—the agency's only paying customers—demand more deer than the habitat can support, what are commissioners to do? Prior to 2000 they always caved in and backed away from doe seasons, higher doe license allocations, and new opportunities to kill antlerless deer. Even in 2005, after several years of high deer kills, and just as anecdotal evidence suggested that forests around the state were starting to show evidence of tree regeneration, commissioners lowered the doe license allocation. The biggest cuts came in the wildlife management units with the most complaints from hunters.

Given that, Alt worries that no board of commissioners, no matter how committed they are to doing the right thing by deer, wildlife, and even hunters, can ultimately withstand the political pressure that comes from being answerable to only one group.

"I don't hold any animosity toward the Game Commissioners, or anyone in the agency's executive office, or on the staff. I think they're all genuinely dedicated to the resource," Alt said. "But they can't win. The system won't allow them to. You're never going to be able to move far enough and fast enough to solve this problem so long as hunters who want more deer at all costs, even when they're in the minority, can hold you hostage.

"If and when the Game Commission has a broader funding base and a broader constituency, you'll see real change, I think. But not before. The system is broken. It needs to be fixed."

Commissioners bristle at those kinds of comments. They've "stayed the course" in terms of trying to bring deer numbers into balance with their habitat, Palone says. It's true, deer numbers will have to be kept down for a while. None of the young trees that have sprouted up in forests across the state in the past few years have outgrown deer yet, and the only way to make sure they will — even on Commission-owned state game lands — is to fence deer out. But the agency is moving in the right direction, she says.

Alt, who says some of his best memories are of hunting with his father and his son, is less convinced. He remains, hopeful, though, that some day hunters and biologists, working together, can manage Pennsylvania's deer for the benefit of everyone. The job will never be easy, he says. The people with a stake in the deer issue are diverse, and they all have their own hopes and goals. But it can be done.

"Running this deer program is like piloting a plane, and the plane is going down. You're yelling 'mayday, mayday,' while someone behind you is saying, 'there's gum on my headrest,' or 'the toilet's not working,' or whatever. We must save the plane first, then we can go in and address those other issues.

"Once we do, though, Pennsylvania is going to be a model for the rest of the nation," Alt says. "Everything we do here will make it easier for biologists and hunters and deer managers elsewhere to set things right in the places where they are."

2

THE NATURE OF OVERABUNDANCE

Arthur Stewart sounded like a happy man when we talked in the fall of 2004. Superintendent of Valley Forge National Historical Park, he was less than three months away from retirement and was looking forward to getting away. He wasn't sure where he and his wife might end up. They were debating whether to stay close to the park, move to an area of Maryland he'd been eyeing, or perhaps go to North Carolina, where they have a small summer home. One thing was certain: Stewart wasn't planning to take a lot with him, wherever he went.

"I'm not packing one more box," Stewart said. "We've made eight moves over my career and I don't want to lug one more thing around. When it's time to move, we're going to decide what we really want and need and then sell the rest or give it away. Or maybe we'll eBay it."

If only he could do that with Valley Forge's white-tailed deer.

Located in southeastern Pennsylvania and famous as the place where George Washington and his bedraggled army spent the winter of 1777–78, Valley Forge is just the kind of place most people probably think of when the subject turns to having "too many" deer. The park, which contains about two square miles of forested land, had an estimated 116 deer in 1987. With no predators, hunting, sharpshooting, or anything save the more-than-occasional vehicle collision to check their numbers, though, the population skyrocketed. It grew by an estimated 15 percent or more per year over the next decade.

White-tailed deer, especially those sporting collars and tags, are a common site amid the greenery of Valley Forge National Historical Park.

The result was that, by 2000, the first time Stewart and I talked, the park's deer population stood at 1,122 animals, or 561 per forested square mile. Penn State University researchers, who came up with that estimate, called the park's deer density "among the highest of any reported area with free roaming deer in North America."

And that was just a beginning, as things turned out. When Stewart and I talked again in 2004, Valley Forge's deer population had climbed to a mind-boggling 1,460 animals, or 730 deer per forested square mile.

"There's no question there are a lot of deer here and they're impacting the park. We have to make some decisions about what to do and how to do it so we can carry out the mission of the park as outlined by Congress, to show the history of George Washington and the soldiers who were here, and also keep the park's natural resources from being destroyed," Stewart said. "But the big question is not are we going to control deer. The big question is how many are you going to kill? When do you stop? That's the hard part."

There are plenty of people living around Valley Forge who are just glad the park is finally asking those questions. Jim Morrison is one of them. I met Morrison—

president of Valley Forge Citizens for Deer Control—at a Game Commission meeting he had attended to ask for help in controlling deer. Intrigued by his situation, photographer Greg Sofranko and I traveled to his home one Sunday afternoon to talk about deer.

Morrison is a scholarly-looking sort in his glasses, button-down shirt, and casual slacks, with a nice home in this affluent section of the state. His house sits within shouting distance of the park, in an area that's surprisingly green—not rustic, or even rural, but green—given the concrete and pavement that's so common in heavily populated southeastern Pennsylvania. Just getting there required driving across the state on the Pennsylvania Turnpike, buffeted by trailer trucks speeding along faster than the sixty-five-mile-per-hour speed limit the whole way, then driving past the sprawling entrance to the park, only to arrive at what seemed like an oasis.

And it is that, for white-tailed deer as much as for people. Morrison explained this while we sat in his home looking at pictures of houses surrounded by chewed-up shrubs and flowers. His own property has been a favorite target of deer.

"I remember wondering why our bushes were looking a little ragged. Why should they be getting sick all of the sudden?" Morrison said. "Then, when I went out and started looking around, I started seeing it was deer damage."

The culprits aren't hard to find. Driving through the park, Morrison points out the window of his Taurus wagon at the deer. There are dozens of them in plain view, standing on the manicured fields of the park, staring at us from behind split-rail fences and wandering among the Revolutionary War cannons. They roam the park with impunity, feeding and bedding just yards from vehicles, joggers on an asphalt walking track, and sightseers here to get a glimpse of America's past.

Morrison pointed to mountain laurel that's stripped of all its leaves to heights of six feet. That, he said, is the work of deer, many of whom look emaciated. One doe we spotted under a tree looked to be all ears and ribs, the collar put around her neck as part of the Penn State study seemingly much too large, even considering that they're purposely left loose so as not to choke the animal.

We spied a buck bedded down just off the park's main road. It had a nice rack, but what struck me was the nonchalant way the buck stared at us, even when we slowed down. It never flinched, twitched an ear, or gave any indication of being wild. It reminded me of the buck I'd seen in a pen at the zoo in Washington, D.C., a few years earlier, standing listlessly on bare, hard-packed dirt behind a fence.

Morrison, who had a distant relative with George Washington's army at Valley Forge, wonders what those soldiers, who suffered mightily from starvation and other privations, might think, could they see the park and its countless deer—all that venison and hide on the hoof—today. He wonders, too, if the park's visitors realize how these deer have changed Valley Forge, and with it their chance to really understand what it was like for those patriots who suffered and died here more than two hundred years ago.

"Two thousand out of eleven thousand marched in here without shoes. Half didn't have a full set of clothes," Morrison said. "They had things like scabies. Man, that went through this camp like wildfire. They died from things like typhoid and typhus. They had dysentery, pneumonia. For a whole week they had no meat. The whole army. It was flour and water."

The deer wandering around the park these days would have been a welcome addition around the campfires when Washington was trying to create a new nation. Now, though, the deer, for many, are a nuisance at best and a threat to the park and those who use it at worst.

Warning motorists to be on the lookout for deer is a regular part of the job for park employees. Those rangers have to watch for deer—and the parasites they carry—themselves, too. By mid-2000 ten or so park rangers—"it may be that, it may be more," said Stewart—had contracted Lyme Disease. A tick-borne ailment that starts as a "bull's eye" rash, Lyme Disease can eventually cause arthritis, aseptic meningitis, facial palsy, motor and sensory nerve inflammation, inflammation of the brain, and occasionally cardiac problems.

Outside the park, homeowners have had to go to extreme lengths to live with deer. Driving the neighborhoods around the park, Morrison takes us past house after house that look like they're covered in giant spider webs. These are big houses, one after another. Almost all of them, nestled among the trees and green lawns and fancy shrubbery, are surrounded by nylon mesh netting or steel fencing or plastic tubing meant to keep the deer from eating their landscaping.

Rob Arnold lives just one house removed from the park boundary. He has had to fence the shrubbery and mountain laurel that grows on his property to keep the deer out and allow the plants to grow. It's obvious that the deer doing all the damage are the ones who hide out in the park by day, venturing out after dark only long enough to nibble his plants into oblivion. "All you have to do is see one of the deer with a collar around its neck from the Penn State study walking through your neighborhood to know it's their deer," Arnold said.

David Hudder, another park neighbor, has also seen what damage deer can do. He estimated that in one year he spent about $20,000 replanting shrubbery that the deer kept eating before he spent another $2,000 fencing in his bushes and shrubs. "They just come in here and graze it flat every year," Hudder said. "It's a problem because of the federal park." Things are so bad that one resident has made a business of helping his neighbors deal with deer. Drive past Jim Bizokas's house and a large sign in the front yard catches your attention. It reads, "Deer Control Services . . . we can help!"

If most people don't consider white-tailed deer "aggressive" animals, Bizokas disagrees. Bambi-like deer might not attack humans directly, but they can certainly move in on their property with a vengeance. Allow too many of them to live in an urban or suburban area and eventually they'll eat everything they can find in that area's parks, he said. After that, they'll venture farther from the woods to gobble up every flower and ornamental shrub that the neighborhood's residents have gone to great trouble and expense to plant.

"When there aren't that many food sources available, they will become aggressive. They will tear right through a polypropylene barrier," Bizokas says. Forget about using taste and color deterrents on shrubbery. They don't work now, if they ever did, according to Bizokas. "If you're using a deterrent, you will slow them down. But if you have fruit trees or major plantings, that's not going to be enough."

And there's no use trying to plant vegetation you think deer won't eat either. "There used to be a lot of things deer wouldn't eat. But as you get into urban settings, a lot of the native species are being decimated by deer. The result is that the things they wouldn't eat before they're eating now," Bizokas says. "Very few things are deer proof. And by the time you get to that point, you're probably planting things you don't want anyway."

That's where Bizokas comes in. He helps individual and corporate clients deal with overabundant deer. Business had been good, courtesy of the human sprawl that's put more people in contact with more deer. The only real way to keep deer from decimating shrubbery—short of killing a few—is to fence or screen it. What's most effective and least obtrusive is welded steel mesh fences covered in black polypropylene.

"They're fences for people who don't want fences, but also don't want deer," says Bizokas. He wouldn't tell me what those fences cost—the individual characteristics of every property "preclude off-the-cuff numbers"—but it's less expensive to install fence than "to replace irreplaceable shrubs." Some of his neighbors must agree. A drive through his neighborhood revealed house after house surrounded by black steel fence. It almost looks like the scene outside a government building,

Jim Morrison, president of the Valley Forge Citizens for Deer Control, looks at a map of properties around the Valley Forge National Historical Park that have sustained significant deer damage.

where concrete barriers have been installed to keep terrorist-driven trucks full of explosives from crashing into buildings.

I wonder what people must think, I told Morrison, if they're visiting the area for the first time, looking to buy one of these expensive stone houses. Do they know what all of those fences, starting in the grass of the front lawn, curving up and over the flowers outside the picture window, then connecting to the house on the outside wall, are for? If they don't, he replied, they learn quickly enough.

"I know one man who is one property removed from the park, who decided one fence wasn't enough. He had a regular fence, then he put up a second high fence, then he ran electricity through it," Morrison said. "And the deer still got in. They did an end run and went in through his drive.

"No one is saying they don't want any deer. Somewhere between forty and eighty would be okay. But they should be unusual," Morrison said. "That's precisely the way it was when we moved here in 1976. It was unusual to see a deer. It was, 'Hey, I just saw a deer. Whoever heard of such a thing?' It's not that way now."

Morrison and the other members of his group—which was formed in 1995—
have spent years trying to get some kind of relief. Several organized archery
groups in the area work with private property owners. Arnold, who allowed hunting on his land, expressed hope that the archers could somehow gain access to the
park, too. Hudder was less keen about allowing public hunting in the park, but
even he wanted some kind of control, be it contraception or sharpshooters. "As
long as it's humane," Hudder said, just before his wife picked up another phone,
said her husband was done talking, and hung up on me.

Morrison, who would also be okay with giving archers a chance to shoot some
deer, said that if that's not acceptable to park officials they should consider a deer-
control program like the one run by their counterparts at Gettysburg National Military Park. Gettysburg uses "qualified federal employees" from that park and the
Eisenhower National Historic Site to shoot deer. The goal is keep deer numbers
low enough that they don't affect the ability of the park to tell its story. Gettysburg's
deer control program did not come easy, though. It developed only after ten years
of research and a victory in federal court.

Officials at Gettysburg began looking for a solution to their deer problem when
they documented that the animals were altering the crop fields and woodlots
important to understanding the history of the park, says public affairs officer Katie
Lawhon. The field where Confederate Major General George Pickett led his infamous charge and the woodlot where his soldiers took refuge just beforehand are
still there, for example, just as they were in 1863. They might not look the way they
did then, and do now, if deer hadn't been brought under control. "If those woods
were gone or the crops were gone, you wouldn't be able to walk through and experience the park as it was," Lawhon says. "That's why controlling the deer was very
important."

A 1995 environmental impact statement had set twenty-five deer per forested
square mile as an acceptable deer density within the park. That left the park with a
lot of work to do, considering that a 1991 population survey counted 1,441 deer on
3.2 forested square miles, a density of 450 deer per forested square mile.

Officials considered several deer management options—public hunting, reloca-
tion, sterilization, and sharpshooting by park employees. They chose sharpshooting, though their plan allows for the use of contraceptives should that technology
"become viable in the future," Lawhon says. Sharpshooters operating primarily at
night, when the park is closed, and on roads that were blocked off shot ninety-five
deer in 1996 and ninety-six in 1997. That started to bring the deer herd down.

A coalition of animal rights organizations and individuals sued the park to prohibit the hunt, though, effectively stopping it for about eighteen months, until the
U.S. District Court in Washington, D.C., handed down a decision on December 31,
1998, affirming the park's right to shoot deer. The court ruled that the shoot was
acceptable because park officials had "considered a full range of reasonable alternatives" and complied with all relevant regulations.

While the case was being considered, deer numbers climbed back to about
sixty-three deer per forested square mile. That number was back down to fifty-
eight in 2000 and has since dropped further. And the hunting will continue. "We
are going to have to continue to remove deer from the park. We are not going to be
able to get to our goal and then stop," says Lawhon. "This will have to be an ongoing management objective."

The program has resulted in no injuries or accidents and all of the venison is
donated to local food banks. Personal experience tells Lawhon the program is
working. "When I started working here in 1993, it was not unusual to see sixty
deer in a field when I was driving to work. It looked as if this were a cattle operation. There were deer everywhere, and it wasn't quite natural," says Lawhon. "It's
not like that any more. You still see deer occasionally, but it's not like it was."

Morrison would like to see a similar program at Valley Forge. He may yet get it,
and sooner rather than later.

Arthur Stewart, the superintendent of the park, wasn't ready to commit to any
program designed to remove deer from the park the first time we talked, which was
in late summer of 2000. "When we get to the point where we're seeing cultural
landscape recommendations, that's when we'll know what we have to do with the
deer. Until then, we just don't know," Stewart said then. "We're not here to take care
of the deer this season, or even next season. We're here to perpetuate this for people
a thousand years from now. So we're not going to just do anything willy-nilly."

By fall 2004, things had changed. The Penn State study—by then completed—
had determined that the park's deer "threaten human life or livelihood," "depress
the densities of favored species," "are too numerous for their own good," and have
pushed the system of plants and animals "off its equilibrium." If such things are
allowed to continue, "then wildlife management will shift from conservation to
pest management mode. This shift will not only weaken the support the American
public has traditionally invested in wildlife conservation but also diminish . . . the
respect, wonder, and awe with which many people in modern society presently
regard wildlife," the report read.

To get a handle on just how many deer Valley Forge had, researchers ear-tagged bucks, does, and fawns to monitor survival and determine how much time they spend in the park.

A natural resources inventory of Valley Forge conducted by park staff concurred, finding the impact of deer on the park equally serious. It showed that deer are altering the park landscape in a way that affects both the ability of the park to convey its history and the survival of the park's preferred shrubs and trees.

"What we are faced with is not even deer management so much as vegetative management," said Stewart. "The base of the problem is that deer are eating the next two or three generations of forest. Yes, we'll continue to have forests, but the composition of those forests will change. Right now, you can stand at the edge of one of the park's wooded areas and see for a long way into the woods. It shouldn't be that way, especially at the edge. It's quite stunning when you stand there and look and say, 'My gosh, there's nothing growing under six or seven feet.'"

Park officials have been developing a new general management plan for the park. A final draft was expected to be ready for public review by fall 2005. As part of that process, they expected to recommend some form of deer control, though shooting was unlikely to occur before 2007.

Though he did not want to prejudge anything when we talked, Stewart said public hunting is probably not a good option, given the variety of people who use the park and the hours they are there. Several members of the Nigerian Olympic track team train at the park during the day, for example, while a couple of groups of local runners use the park between midnight and 6:00 A.M. Contracting out with the USDA's Animal and Plant Health Inspection Service or someone similar to shoot deer seems more viable, Stewart said.

Even once the decision is made to shoot deer, and the "who" of the shooting is decided, there are other details that have to be worked out, like how many to kill. Stewart said he doesn't yet know the answer to that question. He is sure that once the shooting starts it will have to continue every year; otherwise "you're just removing deer temporarily and creating space for new ones."

"It's an interesting problem. It's an interesting equation, with a lot of parts to it," Stewart said. "We always have the threat, if you want to use that word, from the group that says if you control deer we're going to sue you, and from the group that says if you don't control deer we're going to sue you. We have to have all the bases covered for when, not if, we get sued," Stewart said. "It's a pretty rough course you have to cover before you get to the point where you can do it."

Valley Forge's problems, serious as they are, are on some level simpler than the deer problems facing the state's forests, particularly when it comes to the big woods country of the northern tier. Few could argue that Valley Forge has "too many" deer. The question of what constitutes overabundance in Pennsylvania's state, national, and even private forests is much more difficult to answer.

The search for a definition of what overabundance really means in those circumstances drew me to Allegheny National Forest one April day. It looked to be an interesting trip. It's not every day that you get the chance to become a "certifiable deer poopologist." That's what Tim Pierson was offering, though—the chance to tromp through the woods and count fecal pellets.

Pierson is a Penn State Cooperative Extension forester and a member of the Society of American Foresters' deer-forest committee. In 1998 he developed a "deer density and carrying capacity workshop" designed to show landowners and hunters how to estimate the number of deer on their property or on the land where they hunt. He and other extension foresters have hosted a few of the workshops each spring since. To keep things light and fun, Pierson gives out diplomas at the end of each course, proclaiming "graduates" poopologists.

I drove up to the Bradford Ranger District office near Marshburg to participate in one of the seminars. In talking to Pierson beforehand, I'd asked him if it had been his experience, as it had been mine, that people get very fired up when talking about deer numbers. Everyone wants to know, how many deer does Pennsylvania have? How many deer does it have per square mile? How many can it have or should it have?

Pierson said he knew all too well what I meant. In fact, he said he knew of several people planning to attend his workshop specifically to challenge him on the issue of deer density numbers. "Carrying capacity refers to the number of deer that the land can support, or carry, and still yield a healthy habitat for forest regeneration and biodiversity," he said. "The healthier the habitat, the healthier the white-tailed deer population.

"When we do these workshops we don't make any statements about how many deer a particular habitat should support. We just present the facts and let people make up their own minds. But I already know of four sportsmen or landowners who are coming loaded for bear, so it could be interesting," Pierson said.

It was. The kind of numbers Pierson and Dave deCalesta, a retired USDA Forest Service research biologist who helped present the workshop, talked about that day when defining what an "overabundance" of deer looks like were very different from the situation at Valley Forge. Pierson began the session by explaining just what the workshop was designed to do: teach us to estimate deer densities and examine forests for evidence of deer impacts. We began by going to the parking lot and measuring our pace—a pace being two steps—to determine how many paces were in one hundred feet. We then stepped into the woods to learn how to count pellets.

Knowing those two things, Pierson said, the trick is to walk one mile, always heading due south, along a designated route, stopping every hundred feet. At each stop, counters use a pole—in this case a converted ski pole marked off with tape at four feet—to examine a circle with a four-foot radius. Any collection of at least ten pellets is counted and recorded as one group.

The technique is not designed to come up with exact deer population numbers. But by using a formula that takes into account the number of times, on average, a deer defecates each day, the number of days since leaf off, and the length of the walk, biologists can come up with a reasonably good approximation of how many deer have been along that route, deCalesta said. Walking a number of parallel routes in a defined area then provides an idea of deer densities per square mile. The counts are also relatively inexpensive to do, quick to accomplish, and cover enough ground to approximate a deer's home range. "We feel pretty good about the accuracy and precision of our counts," said deCalesta.

Examining deer impacts involves checking what deer are eating. At each spot where you stop to count pellets, you also look for evidence of deer browsing. This means looking at trees, shrubs, and other vegetation within a "deer feeding zone" that measures from six inches above the ground to six feet above the ground inside the four-foot radius circle. You look for highly preferred species like sugar maple and red maple, moderately preferred species like hemlock and black cherry, and nonpreferred species like striped maple and beech—"what deer eat, what they might eat, and what they don't eat"—deCalesta said. Evidence of browsing is then categorized: no browsing, light, moderate, heavy, severe.

To get a handle on what hungry deer are up against, walkers also carry a pair of clippers and a plastic grocery store shopping bag. An adult deer will eat a bag's worth of browse in a day's time, nibbling a little from this plant and a little from that one rather than eating any one plant completely. We were challenged to see how much browse we could collect in the couple of hours it would take us to do our walk.

Educated in what to do and how to do it, we then drove out to a site in Allegheny National Forest to follow routes already done by experienced poopologists. Divided into teams, with each team assigned a guide to make sure we stayed on course and counted pellets and browse according to the guidelines, we began.

We took turns doing different jobs. One man counted paces and plotted our course on the compass. One carried the shopping bag and a pair of clippers, snipping off pieces of browse as we went. A third carried the ski pole. At each hundred-foot stop, he would put the pole six inches off the ground, near his ankles, and rotate it around him in a circle. We would count pellet groups and examine browsing within that circle, while one person recorded our data on a chart.

It didn't take long to realize that finding browse—especially of preferred species—was pretty tough to do. When you could stand on a hillside bench and see a hundred yards in every direction, as we could in several places, with lots of big trees towering overhead, no shrubs in sight, very few seedlings more than ankle high and all of them cherry and birch at that, you wonder how any deer live in big woods like these.

That's something hunters and others need to start thinking about, deCalesta said. Deer need four things for survival: food, cover, water, and space. Here in Pennsylvania, with millions of acres of public land and three times as much private open ground, space is not a problem. Water isn't either, nor is cover.

But food is a real issue. It can and does determine—depending on its relative abundance or scarcity—how many deer live in Keystone State forests. And right now, in many areas, especially across the northern tier, there's just not much food out there, largely because deer have eaten it all, deCalesta said.

MAST

What deer eat depends on the time of year and what's available. Mast—like acorns and beechnuts—is preferred, but deer also eat fruits like apples, pears, and berries and tree seedlings like sugar maples, tulip poplar, hemlock, oak, dogwood, apple, and cucumber tree. At certain times of year, the average adult deer might eat as much as eight pounds of food per day. How much is that? It takes six hundred new germinating sugar maple seedlings to make one pound, so even one deer can do a lot of damage to a forest, deCalesta said.

We talked about that when we got back to the ranger station. It was time to show how much browse we had collected. In short, it wasn't much. None of the groups came close to filling their shopping bags with woody stems and the like. Not surprisingly, then, when it came time to rate the deer impact on browse, it was rated moderate to severe in every case.

That shocked neither Pierson nor deCalesta. Sixty-three percent of the plots they had examined in their own studies showed no regeneration of key tree species. There were no plots that showed no evidence of deer impacts. "We've gone beyond the point where there's any regeneration of preferred species. Now we're seeing an impact on some of the less preferred species because the deer have nothing else to eat," deCalesta said.

As for deer density estimates, our four groups came back with different numbers. One group, at the low end, estimated the deer density along their line at 11.1 animals per square mile. At the high end, one group had 41.7 deer per square mile. The middle groups had 25 and 35.6 deer per square mile. Add that up and the average deer density per square mile in our study site was 28.35 deer per square mile, just about what the experts had counted themselves.

The problem was deciding what those numbers meant and what to do about them. One hunter who had been a part of the group that estimated the deer density at 35.6 admitted that the habitat he saw was severely degraded. In fact, he thought the deer density figure his group came up with was too high. "I'd be more likely to believe it if you told me there were only ten deer per square mile out there," he said.

problem is not density

What's also not unusual—and this is the problem for deer managers—was the solution the hunter offered. He suggested that if the deer population was down, the answer to bringing it back up was to quit shooting so many does. In that respect, Pierson and deCalesta said, the hunter missed the point completely. Not shooting does was the perfect way to increase the deer herd when it was small and there was plenty of unoccupied habitat left to be filled. The deer lived well, multiplied, and moved into new places.

When the available habitat is already saturated—indeed, when it's damaged from trying to sustain too many deer for too long—deer can hang on at some minimal level, surviving as best they can by giving birth to few fawns and devoting little energy to antler growth. Herds cannot grow, however, no matter how few you shoot, because they have no habitat to support them. It may seem counterintuitive, Pierson said, but the way to fix that and have more deer, or at least a similar number of deer but deer that are bigger and healthier, is to shoot more does until the habitat can rebound.

Pierson and deCalesta are among those who are trying to prove this point. The two men are members of a twenty-eight-person team that has been using the pellet-counting system to estimate deer numbers and measure deer impacts on a 114-square-mile area—containing 74,250 contiguous acres—of northwestern Pennsylvania known as the Kinzua Quality Deer Cooperative. It encompasses land owned by the Bradford Water Authority, Kane Hardwoods, Allegheny National Forest, RAM Forest Products, and Forest Investment Associates.

The KQDC is a ten-year project started in January 2000. The idea is to see whether forest habitats can be made healthier—and the health of deer improved—by getting the herd under some measure of control. "That's the goal, to have quality hunting, quality deer, and quality habitat, all at the same time," Pierson said.

On the KQDC, volunteers survey hunters by mail and in small focus groups to record things like how they view their hunting experience. Did they enjoy their hunt? Did they see what they considered an acceptable number of deer? Will they be back? Are they locals or did they drive in to hunt? What education level have they completed?

They also man three check stations where hunters can voluntarily bring the deer they take from cooperative lands. All of the stations operate the first two days of the rifle deer season, with one open on the two Saturdays of the season. To give hunters an incentive to bring their deer in, volunteers give away raffle tickets good for the chance to win prizes, including a couple of rifles, at the annual KQDC banquet. Those who bring in a doe get two tickets, those who bring in a buck, one.

All deer are aged. Bucks have their points counted and the beam diameter of their antlers checked. Volunteers also collect deer body weights, and that may be the most interesting data collected.

Biologists can monitor the health of a deer herd by examining the size of individual animals. Unfortunately, the poor habitat of the northern tier has led to poor-quality deer. Weights of deer harvested in the KQDC area showed fawns averaging 55 to 60 pounds, yearling bucks 105 pounds, and adult bucks 115 pounds. The biggest buck weighed 160 pounds, which is an average weight in areas of good habitat.

"These animals are not getting enough to eat," deCalesta said. "They should be a lot heavier." "Our habitat, across the entire KQDC, is yelling with a megaphone, there are too many deer for even the deer," added Pierson.

One young hunter at the workshop I attended, who said he was studying to become a biologist, suggested that the way to create habitat was to get out the chainsaws and level large sections of forest, as was done in Pennsylvania at the dawn of the twentieth century. He even volunteered to lend a hand.

But Pierson said that wouldn't work. There's not enough forest in public ownership to sustain large numbers of deer for very long, so even if you could cut all the trees, that would be a short-term fix. What's more, the state's other 11 or 12 million residents, who share ownership of the forests, aren't likely to approve cutting them all down in the name of "habitat" simply for the sake of deer and deer hunters. The only practical solution, Pierson said, is to lower deer densities to some reasonable level. But how many deer is that? People—notably hunters—have always wanted a number.

The problem with the whole debate over numbers, Pierson said, is that it misses the real point, which is the number of deer in relation to their habitat. So long as the habitat is good—lots of browse, say, mixed in with mast and agricultural crops—one area might be able to hold thirty deer, Pierson said. They could exist without having much impact on the forest around them. Another area of similar size but with degraded habitat might hold only ten deer. That doesn't mean that it needs or can handle twenty more, though. It may in fact need fewer. If the habitat is degraded, hunters might need to knock that population down to eight animals—or seven, or five, or three, or whatever—for a while to allow the forest to heal, Pierson said. When that happens—but not before—the deer herd can be allowed to build back up.

Instead of going into a woodlot and wondering how many deer it has, Pierson said, hunters need to go in and ask, does it have the right number of deer? "We need to get away from numbers, because numbers will kill you," agreed Merlin Benner, biologist for the state's Department of Conservation and Natural

Big deer and big bucks common in the state's big woods country into the 1930s and '40s are now rare there. With much of the habitat destroyed, deer with smaller racks and lower body weights are more typical.

Resources, which manages state forests and parks. "And numbers are really irrelevant. What's relevant is the condition of the habitat and the condition of the deer." The DCNR is hoping to prove that point, ironically enough, by using the latest technology to count deer on state forest land. The idea is to count deer, then relate those numbers to what's growing in the forest, as determined by a study of vegetation being carried out in those same places.

In March 2005 the DCNR contracted Susan Bernatas, president and founder of Vision Air Research, based in Boise, Idaho, to count deer on 281,000 acres of state forest land using forward-looking infrared—known as FLIR—technology. To use FLIR, Bernatas mounts a camera to the underside of an airplane's wing to count deer by sensing the heat their bodies give off. With the help of her pilot, Charlie Gay of Tunkhannock, Wyoming County, she flies in a grid pattern, working most often at night but also during the day when it's cloudy.

Experimental at best in the early 1990s, FLIR technology has advanced to the point that it can be very effective in monitoring wildlife populations, Bernatas said. The pictures it produces are detailed enough for a viewer to differentiate between, say, a deer and a coyote or a deer and a person. "We can see dogs, we can see a deer's ear, we can tell what's a puddle, what's a stick, what's a rock," Bernatas said. "If you fly over it and can't tell what it is, you have to redesign your survey."

There are three keys to making the equipment work: flying low (in this case, about a thousand feet above the ground), flying slowly (sixty to sixty-five miles per hour, or just fast enough to avoid stalling the plane), and pointing the camera at the right angle. Even then, the technology is not perfect. "There is no way, ever, unless you nail their little feet to the ground, to see all of them," Bernatas said of deer. "There's an equal opportunity for animals to walk into or out of your transect. There's always the potential for missing them, or possibly double counting them." But by flying in winter, when there's little leaf cover on the trees, biologists can generally detect 83 to 84 percent of the wildlife in a particular area, Bernatas said.

Going into the count, Michael DiBerardinis, secretary of the DCNR under Governor Ed Rendell, had said the numbers FLIR would produce were of "absolute importance" to the entire debate about how many deer the state has and should have. Hunters and others focus on numbers, so getting a count and showing how it relates to forest health is critical, he said. "Anecdotal evidence isn't going to cut it any more. This is too big."

What the count revealed—as many have said—is that the notion of too many deer is not necessarily the same as having lots of deer. There were lots of deer seen in some areas. A flyover of the Promised Land area of Delaware State Forest, for example, found 23.69 deer per square mile. That's 40 percent higher than what the Game Commission says the population should be in winter. The Denton Hill area of Susquehannock State Forest had 20.29 deer per square mile, which is 31 percent higher than the Commission's overwintering deer goal.

Other areas of state forest had far fewer deer. The portion of Tioga State Forest located near Arnot had just 10.91 deer per square mile, or roughly 27 percent fewer than the Game Commission's goal. The Cedar Run area of Tioga State Forest had just 9.64 deer per square mile, and the southern portion of Sproul State Forest had just 8.63 deer per square mile.

What hunters need to realize, Benner said, is why those areas have so few deer. DCNR has a rating system it uses to categorize the available habitat on any section of state forest. The habitat on the Sproul and Tioga State Forests is rated as "poor" at best, and as "very poor" at worst. That's why there are few deer in those places, he said—they simply have nothing to eat. "High-quality habitat, healthy habitat, and a healthy deer herd are absolutely connected," agreed DiBerardinis. "I think the numbers bear that out."

Robert Beyer, assistant director of wildlife and heritage services for the Maryland Department of Natural Resources, said wildlife managers can't stress that point enough. In charge of big-game management in Maryland, Beyer has overseen the use of infrared to count deer. The Maryland DNR has used FLIR to good effect, he says, largely to identify deer populations in urban and suburban areas and then develop management plans for those places. But you have to put the data FLIR gives you into some kind of context, he added.

"It's a very good tool. It's as accurate as anything that's out there," said Beyer, who grew up in Pennsylvania and graduated from Penn State University. "But what I always tell people is that it's one moment in time in one area. If you looked at the roads around Harrisburg at rush hour, you'd think, my gosh, there must be 61 million people living there. But if you look at those same roads at 2:00 A.M., you'd think there were only forty-one people living there."

More important, FLIR can't tell you whether the number of deer detected is the right number for the habitat. The "missing link" hunters have to grasp is the relationship between the number of deer counted and the quality of their habitat. "It doesn't matter how many deer you have. It's how many deer can the habitat support," Beyer said.

That's the same message Jeff Krause has been carrying to hunters and others. Krause is a wildlife biologist for the U.S. Army Corps of Engineers at its Raystown Lake property in Huntingdon County. The Corps conducted an infrared survey of 20,616 acres at Raystown in November 2004, using the same technology and the same firm—Vision Air Research—being used to count deer on state forests.

Raystown's property was separated into two-square-mile compartments before the study was done. Deer were then counted in each compartment. The survey revealed 1,636 deer in 518 groups. The compartment with the fewest deer had eighteen per square mile, while the one with the most deer had eighty. Across the entire Raystown property, the average was fifty-two deer per square mile, or more than double the Game Commission's goal for wildlife management unit 4A.

Krause notes that these deer are not distributed evenly across all of the compartments, or even within any individual compartment, however. In the compartment that had eighty deer per square mile, the deer were bunched in groups, with a three- or four-hundred-acre section in the middle of the compartment barren of even a single whitetail. It's quite conceivable that a hunter could spend all day in that section of woods and not see a deer, despite the fact that there are a lot of them overall, Krause says.

Interestingly, the heaviest concentrations of deer were found in the same areas that are most accessible to hunters. The compartment with eighty deer per square mile is bisected by a five-mile-long road that's been kept open for the two weeks of rifle deer season every year for the past fifteen years. "We count eighty-nine to a hundred cars parked along that road every year on the first day of deer season," Krause says. By comparison, the Terrace Mountain portion of Raystown—which is less accessible, harder to hunt because it's so steep, and therefore a seeming safe haven for deer—had just twenty-eight deer per square mile.

A study examining the amount and kind of browse available at Raystown, developed by Theresa Laurie of the Student Conservation Corps, was carried out on the same plots surveyed using FLIR. It found that the big woods areas of Raystown, which had the fewest deer, offered the least for deer to eat. The mature forest of Terrace Mountain, for example, supplies only about one-eighth the browse that can be found within recent clear-cuts, Laurie said. The point is that the one thing that most determines which areas have the most deer is the quality of the available habitat, Krause says. It's not access, it's not soil quality, it's not hunting pressure: it's habitat.

"It's no surprise there aren't as many deer in those areas, like Terrace Mountain," says Krause. "There's nothing for them to eat. If you could put a fence around that area and stock it with deer, and keep all hunters out, the deer would starve to death before winter was over because there's just no food." Krause has heard from plenty of hunters who believe the solution is to simply cut Raystown's big woods and create habitat. The Corps does some of that and would like to do more, with the goal of benefiting deer and other wildlife, he says. The problem is that the Corps can't timber its old forest without first being sure it can grow a new one. And there's no evidence that it can right now because deer—which exist at overabundant levels—browse the seedlings of preferred trees like oaks into oblivion before they can grow. If that's allowed to continue, twenty, thirty, and forty years from now Raystown will be left with a forest of species like striped maple, which is good neither for lumber nor as a source of food for wildlife.

It would be irresponsible to let that occur, Krause says, so the Corps has no choice but to fence deer out of the limited cuts it does or not cut at all. "Foresters are taught to look at the forest that's at their feet before they cut the forest above their heads because that's the forest of tomorrow," he adds. "None of us are arguing we have more deer than we've ever had. We all hunt here, and we all know deer numbers are down over the last few years. But that doesn't mean they're where they should be. Our message has been that you have to look at the habitat and the carrying capacity of the land."

Game commissioner Russ Schleiden gives the same message when hunters ask him how many deer the Commission thinks are in their county, or how many they could have. Numbers have their place, Schleiden says. For decades the Commission has estimated deer populations and densities to use in setting harvest goals, and it will continue to do so. But even Commission officials have to start thinking of deer in terms of impacts rather than numbers.

"I've been at sportsmen's clubs or banquets or meetings of that sort, and I've had hunters come up to me and ask me to give them some number in regards to where our deer population is or should be going. And I understand that," Schleiden says. "But I tell them I don't know what that number is and I don't really care either. I tell them I'm going to walk outside and take a look at your habitat. If your oak tree seedlings are healthy and growing, then okay, your habitat seems okay, and maybe you have just the right number of deer or could maybe even support more. But if I find out your oak seedlings are all browsed down to nubs, that habitat is not healthy and you've got too many deer, no matter what that number is.

"It all comes back to the habitat on the ground. That's what will tell the tale. That's what we've got to focus on," Schleiden says.

Mere numbers don't really mean a lot when it comes to what hunters should expect to see in the woods anyway, says Pierson. Average deer densities in the KQDC have varied from a high of twenty-two to twenty-eight deer per square mile. Individual plots checked using the pellet count method, though, have recorded densities from a low of 6.8 deer per square mile to a high of fifty-nine deer.

"People say, 'Wow, fifty-nine deer per square mile, I should see a deer behind every tree,'" says Pierson. "That means almost nothing when it comes to hunting season. When deer disperse over a growing season, they spread out, but not evenly. You may hunt two days in the wrong spot and not see deer, but that doesn't mean they aren't out there.

"The deer density goal for most northern counties, meaning those north of Interstate 80, for the last twenty years has been twenty deer per square mile. What does that look like to a hunter? Well, there's 640 acres in a square mile, so a density of twenty deer per square mile means one deer for every thirty-two acres," Pierson continues. "But most people have no concept of a square mile. A lot of guys might not hunt a hundred acres in a day. And if there's no one in the part where the deer are to move them, guys may never see them. I know guys who see ten deer in a field on a property that's only thirty acres, and they're not happy. Well, what's ten deer on thirty acres? It's hundreds of deer per square mile. You can't have that."

DeCalesta agreed, noting that all across Pennsylvania, deer populations as of January 2003 were already two and sometimes three times as high as the Game Commission's own winter deer density goals. If even those high populations seem too small to hunters—if they're saying they can't find deer—they need to remember that deer are not spread evenly across the landscape. Deer home ranges, which are about one square mile on average, are irregularly shaped and fluid. Deer found most frequently in one portion of their home range in the spring might spend most of their time in another part in the fall. A number of variables, from food availability to the season of the year to habitat changes, can determine which portion of its home range a deer uses most within a particular season. The point is that just because hunters can't always find deer doesn't mean they aren't there. "Seeing is believing, to most of us," agrees Kelly, the former Game Commission biologist. "Still, having a record population of deer doesn't mean there will be one behind every tree or that you'll see more while hunting or driving around."

Sam Dunkle, former president of the Game Commission board, agrees that deer density estimates don't tell the whole story. That said, those numbers can serve as a benchmark that the average hunter can look at and understand. They can give hunters some idea of how many deer they might expect to see in the future compared to what they're seeing now.

That's why he once asked the Game Commission's biologists to provide deer population estimates for each wildlife management unit in the state. "If we don't know where we're going, how are we going to measure our successes? Only numbers tell us how we are doing," says Dunkle. "That needs to be laid out so that we know where we've been, where we're going, and how we're going to get there." He also suggested that the Commission hire an outside entity to review the agency's method of tracking deer harvests and deer populations. That, he says, might put the debate over numbers to rest.

Game commissioners ultimately chose not to go that route, though, confident in the work of their biologists. Chances are that faith is well founded, says Scot Williamson, vice president of the Wildlife Management Institute. The institute has reviewed other states' methods of counting deer and has always found that, while there's always room for improvement, most systems for counting deer are pretty accurate.

Those who would suggest that game agencies do whatever is necessary to improve their methods of counting deer need to remember, too, that counting deer, especially in the heavily forested northeast, is costly. While deer hunting accounts for most of the revenue many states bring in, there's no way game agencies can spend a proportionate amount on studying or managing deer, Williamson says. They just have to do the best they can. "The have to decide how much accuracy they can afford," he says. "I'm not sure it's realistic to expect agencies to spend much more on deer than they already are, given the increasing pressures they're facing today. I think they just need to do things smarter."

The Game Commission is trying to do that. Its deer population estimates are based on deer harvests, which in turn are based on two things: the report cards turned in by hunters who are successful in killing deer and visits to butcher shops around the state.

By law, hunters who kill a deer are required to report this to the Game Commission using the postage-paid card that comes with every license. The reality, though, is that fewer than half do. Biologists say they can work with that because their checks of deer turned in at processors, cross-referenced with the cards that are submitted, give them a statistically accurate vision of how many deer have been killed.

They are looking to improve harvest reporting rates, however, since even biologists admit that monitoring deer populations is critical to making sure that management strategies are doing what they are supposed to. One thing that may help is a new law that in the future will allow hunters to report killing a deer via a telephone number or some sort of online system. "The current system serves its purpose, but we can always improve our reporting rate," says Chris Rosenberry, Alt's successor as head of the Game Commission's deer management section. "And this is one way hunters can have a say in deer management."

Even then, though, the key to managing deer properly will be managing them based on their impacts on habitat, says Steve Horsley, a plant physiologist at the

USDA Forest Service's northeastern research station in Irvine, Warren County. "Rather than get stuck on numbers, you need to look at the condition of the vegetation," says Horsley. "If all the browse is nipped, it doesn't matter if it was ten deer per square mile that did it or fifteen or twenty or thirty. Whatever the number is, it's too many deer for the vegetation to handle. A healthy deer herd needs a healthy range, and to have a healthy range we need fewer deer."

It's important, too, he says, that hunters remember how deer populations work. Imagine, he said, drawing an upside down U. You can insist that deer populations be managed for the maximum number of animals—the peak of the U—and even sustain those numbers for a while. Unless you continually manipulate the habitat in dramatic ways, though—like continually cutting down all of the state's forests—you can't maintain that peak. Since large-scale timber cutting isn't realistic—witness the opposition to any cutting on federal forests from environmental groups—the only option is to manage deer at some level below the peak of the U. There are two ways to do that.

One way is to manage deer in a fashion similar to what Pennsylvania has done for decades. Deer populations are brought to the peak, right to the brink of habitat destruction, then maintained there for as long as possible. When the habitat is destroyed, deer numbers decline, sliding down the right side of the upside-down U, Horsley says. The population settles in at some point where deer can hang on but do little more. The population never crashes completely unless there's a terrible winter, but it never gets any bigger, either, because the habitat won't support it. Deer tend to be small, with small racks and few offspring.

A herd of ten deer under that scenario, for example, might include one buck and seven adult does that give birth to two fawns that survive to fall. Because such a system has generally been accompanied by hunting seasons that focus on bucks over more plentiful does, the habitat is continually denuded by large numbers of deer trying to survive over winter.

The other option—which is based on managing deer in proper proportion to the available habitat—puts deer on the left side of the U. The number of deer never quite reaches the peak of the U, but it can be every bit as large as the population on the right side of the U. It is made up of much healthier deer, however, according to Horsley. In that scenario, a herd of ten deer might include two bucks and two adult does that produce six fawns, half of which are the next year's crop of bucks.

Because doe hunting is a staple of managing populations that way, Horsley says, populations reach their peak in fall and hunters have just as many deer to hunt, but the habitat has to carry fewer deer over the winter. Such a system makes better sense from a food standpoint, according to deCalesta, because deer herds peak in fall and shrink to their lowest in winter. That follows nature's pattern.

In fall, the energy demands of deer are lowest. Temperatures are still mild and food is at its peak of abundance, which allows the animals to build up fat reserves. Winter begins the downward slope in terms of food. Sometimes deer go long periods without even feeding in winter because to do so burns more calories than they can take in. Spring is the hardest time for deer. Food is at its scarcest because nothing's growing and all of the mast has already been eaten. And deer have used most of their fat reserves.

Simply put, better habitat can support more deer, says Brian Murphy, executive director of the Quality Deer Management Association, based in Watkinsville, Georgia. The key is to manage deer so that their numbers peak in the fall, when hunters enter the woods, and minimize their numbers in winter. When that doesn't happen, and you try to carry too many deer through winter, body weights, antler development, and fawn recruitment all decrease. "Once you get to a certain point, any incremental increase in deer does not mean an incremental increase in fawns," Murphy says. "They're just not surviving.

"It's not how many fawns are in a doe's stomach if you cut her open during pregnancy. You could have a herd of a hundred does on poor habitat and only have forty fawns survive. By comparison, fifty does in good habitat might produce seventy-five fawns that survive. The number of deer available to hunt is almost exactly the same, but, by shooting does, you actually get more fawns and more bucks, all of which are bigger and healthier."

The focus on numbers and "overabundance" might not be such a problem were it not for the fact that some confuse "overabundance" with exceedingly large numbers of deer. That leads to problems of perception and expectations.

State officials did not do a very good job of explaining what they meant by overabundance early on, says Tom Buzby, a member of the DCNR's Conservation and Natural Resources Advisory Council. Many areas of state forest have too many deer. That's why large areas of state forest and even some state park lands are enrolled in the Game Commission's deer management assistance program.

DMAP, as the program is known, allows owners of forested and agricultural properties to apply to the Game Commission for antlerless deer "coupons" at varying rates. Forest landowners can get one doe coupon for every fifty acres of forest, while farmers can get one coupon for every five acres in agricultural production.

Additional coupons can be had if landowners submit a written deer management plan for their property and have it approved by the Game Commission's Bureau of Wildlife Management.

The Game Commission sends DMAP coupons to approved landowners, who in turn hand them out to hunters. Hunters redeem the coupons with the Game Commission for a doe license good only for that specific farm or forest site. The idea is to "micromanage" those areas by directing hunters to the places where deer are causing the most problems, says Gary Alt, former head of the Game Commission's deer management section.

One landowner, for example, might be okay with having fifty deer on his property. Another with the same size piece of ground might want no more than twenty-five. There's no way a statewide deer management plan that sets seasons and bag limits across sixty-seven counties populated by different people with different land-use goals can address their concerns equally. With DMAP, though, different landowners with different goals can use hunters to take more or fewer deer from their property.

"It gives landowners a say in managing deer on their property. It gives them a say in determining how many deer their land can support while still allowing them to grow crops or trees or do whatever else they want to do," Alt says. "And it puts hunters right where the deer are, which goes back to what we said our goal was all along—to get the right number of deer of the right sex and age killed in the right places."

Hunters benefit in that they gain additional opportunities to hunt deer, said Marrett Grund, formerly a biologist in the Game Commission's deer management section, when the program was developed. That's because DMAP coupons are offered in addition to the statewide doe license allocation. A hunter who might be willing to take, say, four deer a year, but who was only able to get two regular doe licenses before, can now get two regular licenses and two DMAP licenses. That's going to be important to agencies like the Game Commission if hunter numbers continue to dwindle and fewer hunters have to shoot more deer each year just to keep population levels stable. "Without something like this, once the baby boomers start to move out, we're going to have a very difficult time managing Pennsylvania's deer herd," Grund says.

The problem, Buzby says, is that hunters have equated DMAP lands with places that are overflowing with deer. That might be the case on some agricultural properties, but it's not the case with most of the DCNR lands enrolled in the program.

On state forest DMAP sites, there may be too many deer for the habitat, but not necessarily large numbers of deer. In fact, some state forest DMAP lands probably hold relatively few deer, just because there's nothing to sustain them. The habitat is so far gone that it can't support much of anything. That's why deer numbers need to be decreased even further. Yet when hunters go to those places expecting to be run over by deer and then aren't, this leads to anger and confusion.

"If the habitat is already impoverished, it only takes a handful of deer to keep the regeneration down, so perhaps we should recast the program or these areas as habitat restoration areas," Buzby says. Merlin Benner agrees, adding that the DCNR needs to be "very careful" in how it promotes the need to reduce deer densities and the opportunities available to hunters willing to help get that job done. He's already heard some negative feedback from hunters who went to DMAP land expecting to see lots of deer and came away disappointed.

That's not to say there are no deer in those places. Interestingly, some of the highest hunter success rates on DCNR DMAP lands in 2003—up to 7.43 percent— were achieved in some of the least-hunted areas. But hunters need to know up front what they're getting into.

"They can't expect to go to an area that we identify as needing a reduction in deer and expect it to be a big park with hundreds of deer standing around where you just go shoot one as they walk by," Benner says. "This is a major, severely overgrown habitat. There are low deer densities in most of these areas. You're not going to see many deer. It's hard to get in there and it's a different experience than most hunters are willing to encounter."

"It's not like deer are falling all over each other," agrees Bob Merrill, district forester for Moshannon State Forest, which has land enrolled in DMAP. "But they are above the carrying capacity. And we may have to knock them down further."

Michael DiBerardinis addressed this issue the very first time he spoke before the game commissioners. "To our hunters who say they are seeing fewer deer in some areas, I say, 'you are right.' But the reason has more to do with the habitat being destroyed to such an extent that even small numbers of deer are sufficient to prevent any forest regeneration," DiBerardinis said.

It's important that expectations meet reality, too, Pierson says, because hunters are critical to controlling deer in places experiencing real problems with habitat and regeneration. The problem is that most hunters are used to seeing more deer. Pennsylvania has a hundred-plus-year-old tradition of always trying to grow more deer. Trying to shrink the herd is something new.

The change has not been an easy one to accept, and it shows. There's been a noticeable decline in the number of hunters traveling to the northern tier to hunt deer in the past decade, Pierson says. That's probably due to a combination of things: more deer in the agricultural areas closer to the state's population centers, changes in work and play schedules that have left people too busy to be able to get to the big woods for days at a time, and expenses like the cost of gasoline.

Those involved with the KQDC try hard to get hunters to come their way. Packets providing information on things like lodging, access, and maps are available from Allegheny National Forest, local tourism outlets, and even online at www.allegheny-vacation.com. But is that enough?

"If all of a sudden there are fewer deer, will hunters have the same fidelity to the area they hunt? Will they spend as much time in the woods as they once did?" Pierson asks. "From a management standpoint, those are all questions that are critical to answer."

Being honest with hunters about what they can expect in terms of deer numbers—whatever that population is—will be key to keeping them satisfied, says Williamson, a native Pennsylvanian from Cumberland County. "Agencies like the Game Commission have to be very clear about what hunters can expect to see in the woods. You can't have people going out expecting to see a ten-point behind every tree if the goal is to lower deer populations, because there are just going to be fewer numbers of deer. They need to say, 'Here's what you can expect.' I don't think they can do enough of that." Benner agrees, and says that the DCNR will in the future base its requests for things like new deer seasons not only on deer numbers but on hunter expectations.

If the FLIR counts reveal an area has few deer but still no regeneration, for example, the DCNR might ask for fewer DMAP permits but longer seasons in which hunters can use them. That would be preferable to sending large numbers of hunters with little time to hunt into areas with admittedly few deer and "making a whole lot of people unhappy and unsuccessful," Benner says. "We don't think that's the way to go."

Gilford believes that hunters of the future can adjust to seeing fewer deer. In his day, the expectation was that he could milk the cows on his dairy farm in the morning, go shoot a deer, and still have time to get to work as a schoolteacher. He never had a problem meeting that goal, either. His grandson, by comparison, can see as few as a dozen deer in a day and come home feeling he had a good day.

DeCalesta is not convinced that hunters will ever get deer populations down as low as perhaps they should be, but if they can get close, that may be good enough.

And perhaps the next generation of hunters will be okay with that. "I don't think we're ever going to go from thirty deer per square mile to fifteen. I'm hoping that if we can get it to twenty or twenty-five for a period of ten years, people will think that's the way it's supposed to be. If it goes down slowly enough, maybe folks will get used to that and think that's the way it's supposed to be," deCalesta says.

Pierson believes there's some hope for the future that way. With KQDC lands enrolled in the Game Commission's DMAP program, hunters are taking a few more does than they once did, along with bigger bucks. Thanks to antler restrictions, the average buck now has seven points, compared to three just a few years ago, with the average antler spread going from ten to fifteen inches. If hunters can fine-tune those numbers even more—say, get to the point where they're harvesting one buck for every two does—the habitat on the KQDC may really start to show some improvement, says deCalesta.

Getting there will mean making adjustments. Pierson says his daughters and the other hunters of tomorrow will hunt in different circumstances from what today's sportsmen are used to. But that doesn't have to be a bad thing. "They're going to hunt in a different environment. They'll have to find the food. They'll spend as much time still hunting as they do on stand," Pierson said. "When there are fewer deer in the field, there's a lot to hunting them.

"We're going to go through a couple tough years, for sure. But I'm optimistic. I'm optimistic hunting is going to continue to be good in Pennsylvania. And that includes the habitat. If I need to become even more skillful at hunting, then that's what I'm going to do," Pierson says. "And that's what I'm going to teach my children as well."

3

WHEN YOU CAN'T SEE THE FOREST FOR THE DEER

John Dzemyan is tall and lanky, with a loose-jointed, limb-swinging gait. The first time I saw him walking across the parking lot of the Game Commission's maintenance building near Ridgway, he immediately reminded me of Shaggy, Scooby Doo's laid-back sidekick. Like that cartoon character, he was friendly, easygoing, quick to smile and laugh. When he took off his hat, revealing a bald spot that he said back in college was covered with thick hair that hung down his back in a ponytail, the image was complete. I could just picture John cruising around campus in the 1960s in a brightly colored panel van, hanging out with the gang.

Unlike Shaggy, though, John's no jittery follower. There's iron in him, a resoluteness forged by years of standing in the heat cast by Pennsylvania's deer wars. This was evident one day when Greg and I met Dzemyan for a tour of state game lands 44 in Elk County.

Game lands 44 is located in the heart of Pennsylvania's big woods country. At the dawn of the twentieth century, when the great timber cuts that leveled the state's forests began, the woods of Pennsylvania's northern tier were the first to be cut down. Fortunately—in a move that ranks as one of the greatest conservation legacies in the state's history—the Game Commission and Bureau of Forestry began buying up that scarred land at tax sales. Trees were planted, the land was allowed to heal, and the hardwood forest we have today—among the most commercially viable in the world—took root.

Those northern tier forests were also the first places in the state to be restocked with whitetails. When the deer populations skyrocketed, hunters followed, so many camps springing up that they seemed to match the number of trees and deer. It quickly became tradition for generations of hunters—grandfathers, fathers, sons, uncles, and brothers—to trek north every fall to hunt deer. Over the next half-dozen decades, places like game lands 44 served as the backdrop for countless grainy black-and-white pictures of men and boys of various shapes and sizes, all standing or sitting or kneeling in front of the camp meat pole, an impressive bunch of deer strung up behind them.

But somewhere along the way, things began to change. Deer became harder to find. Big-racked bucks, especially, seemed to disappear. Slowly, almost imperceptibly at first, other parts of the state became better places to hunt deer. By the 1990s, the ten-county southwestern corner of the state surrounding Pittsburgh, the state's second-largest city, was Pennsylvania's new hot spot for deer. That remains the case, as this area—not the big woods of the north—has topped the state in both buck and doe harvests for more than a decade.

As a wildlife conservation officer in the northern tier and later as a land manager there, Dzemyan has taken a lot of abuse because of that. From verbal beatings at sportsmen's clubs to letters published in newspapers, the Game Commission and its officers, including Dzemyan, have been ripped for allowing the big deer herds of the past to disappear from the state's northern forests. Many hunters have blamed the decline on the overharvest of does. In fact, Dzemyan says, the exact opposite is true. The Game Commission hasn't allowed hunters to take enough does over the years, and the state's forests—and the deer that live in them—have suffered for it.

"Some sportsmen say that we're shooting too many deer because the timber companies are having too much influence on deer management, or that farmers are having too much influence, or that the insurance companies are having too much influence. Those are the three biggest lies that have ever been told around this state," Dzemyan said. "The problem is the deer themselves. Deer are a prey species. They need predation to stay in balance with nature, and there's only one critter left in Pennsylvania that can do that. That's humans. That's hunters.

"Deer are just like monstrous rabbits. If you've ever had a garden, you know rabbits can just decimate it. Well, deer can do the same thing to a forest ecosystem," Dzemyan said. "The key to Elk County, the key to all of Pennsylvania, is to harvest more does to allow the forest to regenerate. We have to bring them into balance with nature itself, and we've never done that."

The consequences, he says, have been serious. Deer have drastically changed the makeup of Pennsylvania's forests. Instead of a diverse system—where trees sprout, mature, and produce seedlings that grow to replace them, where the understory is thick and varied, where grouse, songbirds, salamanders, and snowshoe hares thrive in the layers of vegetation that grow between ground level and the treetops—much of Pennsylvania's forest is made up of seventy-, eighty-, and hundred-year-old trees reaching toward the sky, lots of hay-scented ferns blanketing the forest floor, and little in between.

Blackberries try to grow there. So do teaberries, young oaks, crabapples, Juneberries, sassafras, and wildflowers. The problem is that hungry deer nip them off as soon as they break through the soil, unwittingly destroying the very plants that might sustain them and their offspring for generations to come.

Challenge Dzemyan to prove his point and he'll take you to visit some of the many deer "exclosures" that exist on game lands. The exclosures are small plots—sometimes a few acres in the middle of a larger timber cut, sometimes just a few hundred square feet—that are fenced to keep deer out. The Game Commission erected its first exclosures in the northern tier in the 1950s at the behest of Roger Latham, though new ones are put up all the time all over the state.

What makes the exclosures so remarkable is the difference between what you'll find inside a fence—where deer can't go—and what you'll find immediately outside it, where deer are free to roam. Dzemyan illustrated that when he took Greg and me to visit a few exclosures on game lands 44.

He parked his truck in a small lot and led us through ankle-high grass to an exclosure formed of eight-foot-high woven-wire fence. The fence, one of several at this particular site, had been erected following a timber cut done in 1990 that covered about fifty to sixty acres in all. Nothing had been planted inside the fence or out, and no pesticides or lime or fertilizers had been applied anywhere. Nature was left to take its course.

The differences were startling. Inside the first fence we examined, an oak stump had sprouted, sending new shoots fifteen feet or more into the air. Teaberries were growing at ground level. Grape vines twisted and wound their way up young tree trunks like lace webbing. Outside the fence, the mature trees left standing to serve as seed sources were still healthy and growing. There were red and white oak, sugar maple, and cucumber trees, among others. What was missing—almost completely absent, in fact—were any young trees taller than midcalf

Blaine Puller of Collins Pine Company explains that foresters have to fence deer out if they hope to help the forests of tomorrow get a start today.

height. The area looked less like a forest than like a soccer field in need of a good mowing.

There can be no explanation for that lack of regeneration other than an over-abundant deer herd that's keeping the forests of tomorrow from growing, Dze-myan said, bending down and parting the grass just outside the fence. Hidden there, still wet from a sprinkling rain, was an oak seedling that stood just four or five inches tall.

"This oak is probably just as old as that one," Dzemyan said, pointing to a tree inside the fence that was about six feet tall. "But out here, deer keep everything browsed back so it never has a chance to grow. They can't get at what's inside the fence. Inside the fence all of the things deer need to survive are growing in abun-dance. Outside, it's a biological desert for deer and other wildlife."

Fences like the ones Dzemyan showed us are a fact of life in Pennsylvania's forests today. The Game Commission requires timber companies that cut state game lands to erect exclosures at each site, not only to serve as demonstration areas but also to assure that regeneration of key species can occur. The Pennsylvania

Department of Conservation and Natural Resources has deer exclosures all over its property, too, for the same reason. The DCNR's Bureau of Forestry even has to fence deer out of its nursery if it wants to grow seedlings for new plantings.

All told, it costs the DCNR about $2 million annually to maintain the more than eight hundred miles of fence that were on state forest land in 2004. "That is almost equivalent to having an eight-foot fence run from Philadelphia to Pittsburgh, up to Erie, over to Scranton, and then back to Philadelphia," says DCNR secretary DiBerardinis.

Private property owners also know all about how hard it is to get new trees to grow. Robert Ackerman, president of the Westmoreland Woodlands Improvement Association in southwestern Pennsylvania, says he hasn't seen any natural regeneration on his property in more than a decade because of an overabundant deer herd. The understory common in his forest years ago—black cohash, rattlesnake plant, and American ginseng—has disappeared, too, taking much of the wildlife that used to be there with it.

"My efforts to establish manmade regeneration—by planting close to fifteen thousand tree seedlings during the early 1990s—have been close to a failure. Of the tree seedlings that I planted, not more than two hundred survive," Ackerman says. "My woodland property is in a crisis situation, with natural regeneration of valuable Allegheny hardwoods at a standstill and my artificial tree regeneration program virtually a failure. If this condition is allowed to continue much longer, it will result in irreparable harm to the quality of my woodlands, the understory, and the associated natural wildlife habitat."

Blaine Puller, a lands manager with Kane Hardwoods/Collins Pine, expressed some of the same concerns one morning while we were touring some company lands in McKean County. Kane is a 150-year-old lumber company that owns about 125,000 acres in Pennsylvania, enough to make it the third-largest private landowner in the state.

Puller, who speaks with a hint of a drawl, is a tall man with a full head of neatly combed white hair who looks at home in his jeans, boots, and button-down shirt. It's what he wears when he testifies before game commissioners at their Harrisburg headquarters and when he meets Greg and me at a McDonald's in Bradford. He had promised that if we made the trip to northwestern Pennsylvania he'd show us "browse lines," areas of forest where it looks as though a professional tree pruner has clipped every leaf from every tree to a height of about six feet. These lines—common throughout the northern tier—appear when deer, in a desperate attempt to find food, stand on their hind legs to get to every conceivable morsel of food. Six feet is about as high as they can reach.

We drove out to a piece of Kane property. There, soaking up the summer sun on a day when every kind of tree and plant in the forest was in full bloom, I could see what he meant. Looking from the edge of the dirt road into what should have been a forest thick with trees of all ages, I could see far enough to drop two football fields between myself and the horizon. There were plenty of trees that stood close to a hundred feet tall and lots of ferns that reached to about knee level. There were few young trees poking above the ferns, though, and little in the way of brushy vegetation. That's troubling, Puller says.

"Foresters spend more time looking down at the ground than they do looking up there," Puller said, pointing toward the forest canopy. "We're not worried about the forest up there so much. We can make money on the forest that's up there. The deer are not impacting that. They're not eating the stuff way up there. They did that a long time ago.

"The forest we have now is not the worry. It's the forest we're going to have, or not have, in the future because of deer that we're concerned about."

This concern leads you to see some odd sights. We walked a few more yards up the road. There, on the right, was an area where an electric fence, run by solar-powered batteries, stretched into the distance. If a fence seems out of place in the middle of the woods, the tall plastic tubes—they look a lot like drain pipes—that were scattered about inside it were really strange. Tall and narrow, planted upright in the soil, open at the top to allow rainwater in, these tubes surrounded each young tree. They're used to keep trees safe from hungry deer until they're tall enough to survive on their own.

It's expensive to erect fences and tubes—cost estimates have ranged from $125 to $370 per acre. There's a lot of maintenance involved, too. Trees fall on the fence, holes have to be repaired, and the batteries in the solar-powered units have to be changed periodically. Foresters have no choice but to bear these costs, however, if they want their trees to grow out of reach of deer.

"One of our goals is to not have to fence," Puller said. "And we don't want all of the deer to die to make that happen. We have a better forest if we have some deer out there. They just have to be in balance with the ecosystem, and that's where they have not been."

If people haven't realized that—if they haven't realized that there can be such a thing as too many deer—that's not surprising, says Susan Stout, a research project

John Dzemyan talks about one of the plastic tubes used to allow trees to grow out of the reach of deer. Such tubes are costly to buy and install. But, like fences, they are a necessity if foresters want key tree species to regenerate.

leader with the USDA Forest Service's northeastern research station. Pennsylvania's white-tailed deer population hasn't been in line with the Game Commission's own stated deer density goals since the early 1940s, and then only briefly, she says. As a result, most of the state's residents today have never seen a healthy forest. "Nobody who's hunting today was ever hunting in a forest where deer were at the correct level," says Stout. "So we're talking about whole cultural changes, we're talking about making drastic changes, when we're talking about bringing deer numbers in line with habitat."

"You have to be able to see what's not there as much as what is there to know what impact deer have," adds Game Commission deer biologist Bret Wallingford. "You have to be able to know that this plant should be here and isn't. Where is it?"

But how many deer can a forest support while still allowing for regeneration? That's a question researchers in Stout's office, located on the edge of Allegheny National Forest, have spent a decade trying to answer. They erected four exclosures, then divided each of them into four subsections. Wild deer were driven out, then replaced with captive female deer in varying densities—equivalent to ten, twenty, thirty-eight, and sixty-four deer per square mile. The forest inside each exclosure was manipulated through clear-cuts and thinning to simulate full-size forests being managed on a hundred-year rotation.

The sites were then monitored for ten years, with vegetation sampled at periodic intervals, to measure the impact of deer on forests. The resulting study, published early in 2004, documented that whitetails can and do alter plant diversity and abundance, courtesy of their appetites. Impacts become noticeable as soon as deer populations reach about fifteen to twenty animals per square mile, with the most dramatic changes visible when deer densities jump from twenty to thirty-eight animals per square mile.

Deer, the study confirmed, prefer to feed on certain species, including sugar maples, pin cherry, black and yellow birch, and oaks. They don't find other species, like black cherry, as tasty. That finickiness determines what kind of forest grows around them. The study noted, for example, that test sites initially made up largely of maples, birch, and oak became cherry forests as the deer browsed their favorite species into oblivion. Black cherries dominated 19 to 31 percent of the forest understory when research began. Ten years later, in areas with thirty-eight deer per square mile, black cherry made up as much as 55 to 78 percent of the understory.

Ferns—another species deer do not like to eat—also increased significantly as deer numbers rose. Once ferns got established, they took care of themselves, too, shading out competitors and making regeneration even more difficult.

The thing hunters and others need to take from all this is that it's critical to make sure the right kinds of forests are allowed to grow, says Steve Horsley of the USDA Forest Service. Cherry forests, for example, have far less ability to sustain deer and turkey and bear than do acorn-producing oak forests. Just because a patch of woods looks lush and healthy and vibrant doesn't mean it's very good for wildlife. "Everything that's green isn't food," Horsley says. "It may be green and it may look like food, but it's not."

Forests with little understory other than ferns have little or no ability to sustain species like neotropical songbirds and other mammals, adds Cindy Adams Dunn, director of the DCNR's office of education, communication, and partnerships. There's no food for them and no nesting cover.

"To the unknowing, that type of open forest actually looks pretty good. There are a lot of ferns, there's an open forest structure, you can see forever. It's almost like a park. But really, that's an ecological desert," says Dunn, former director of the Pennsylvania Audubon Society. "The more astute observer notices the mid-story and sees what's not there.

"Just try to find spring wildflowers in April and May. Wildflowers are a good indicator of what's happening for the nonhunting public because they're in the same place, year after year. But where are the jack-in-the-pulpit, the trillium? In some places they're gone because of the deer."

Not everyone believes a deer reduction program of the magnitude Horsley and Stout and Dunn talk about is necessary, though. It's true that songbirds and wild-flowers have their place, says Charles Bolgiano, a director with the Unified Sports-men of Pennsylvania. But the people who want to use those species to drive deer

Open forests with no understory may look parklike, but in reality they are biological deserts with little ability to sustain deer or other wildlife.

numbers down below even the Game Commission's long-standing goal of twenty-one deer per forested square mile—people he calls the "kill all the deer crowd"—are going too far.

"The problem is not that hunters expect to see a deer behind every tree. Hunters do expect to see a reasonable number of deer," Bolgiano says. "The problem is the environmentalists and tree huggers want a goal of only ten deer per square mile. They want to bring Pennsylvania's forests back to the ecological state they were in when they were first settled by the Europeans."

There's no need to drop deer densities that low, agrees Woody Shields, also of the Unified Sportsmen. First, he contends that the state has, on average, the habitat to carry sixty or more deer per forested square mile—anything less is merely a "cultural carrying capacity." Second, hunters can handle higher numbers of deer and still promote regeneration if given the chance. The problem, he says, is that they're not always given that chance. "If hunters get access to an area, you don't see problems with habitat. If you make it all but impossible for hunters to get to an area, like behind locked gates in the Allegheny National Forest where Susan Stout does all of her studies, then yes, you see habitat problems," Shields says.

Commissioner Mohr thinks the Game Commission and Bureau of Forestry should worry less about killing deer and more about timbering if they want to regenerate oaks and tulip poplars and white ash and the like. Focusing on lands that he says might be deemed too inaccessible or "unsuitable for forest products" because of the type of trees growing there, the agencies should be doing timber cuts on a scale big enough to overwhelm existing deer populations.

"I weigh 338 pounds, but when I go to a smorgasbord, I can only eat so much. I'm not going to devastate that table," Mohr said. "It's the same with deer. They can only eat so much, too. You put enough on their plate and they can't effect one iota of regeneration."

Ron Freed, Pennsylvania Audubon's point man on deer issues prior to his retirement, doesn't think that kind of thinking will fly with the general public, though, or even with some hunters. "The key point I keep coming back to is that all of these people who keep talking about wanting more deer, they're not asking for more deer on private land. They want more deer on game lands and state forest lands.

"I can maybe see their point about game lands, in a way, because hunters bought and paid for them, although I have to wonder where that leaves the guys who want to have habitat for grouse and woodcock and pheasants. They all buy a license, too, and helped pay for those game lands, so what about what they want? But hunters who want more deer don't have a right to demand that on state forests. They are just one of a long list of stakeholders who use that land."

The real issue, says George Kelly, the retired Game Commission biologist, is that even if you could get everyone to agree to manage public land solely for deer, there's no way you could ever cut enough timber to stay ahead of deer forever. Eventually, you'd run out of trees to cut and then you'd be right back in the same situation: too many deer and not enough habitat to support them.

"Sometimes you'll see a guy with a nice buck and you'll say he must have had a good day. He'll say, well, no, he saw two bucks and shot one, but he only saw four deer total. He wants to be able to shoot that same buck but see eighty deer a day.

"Well, I guess you can do that, but at what expense?" Kelly asks. "At the expense of our forests, for us and future generations. To restore that habitat, you have to bring that deer population under control and let the forest heal itself. And it will."

Forests—public and private—can sustain more deer than are out there now, though, according to Wayne Haas, a director of the Unified Sportsmen. The problem is that the forest industry doesn't want to deal with deer, he says. Foresters are pressuring the Game Commission to knock deer numbers down, and they are winning that fight. "We've seen a reduction in the herd since 2000, and it ain't over yet. It's going to go down ever further. They've got the hammer and they're using the hammer," Haas says of foresters public and private. "They don't want to have to deal with deer on regeneration. They think that if the deer are gone they won't have to put up fences and they'll save money. I believe that's the whole motivation behind all of this, the forest industry."

It's true that the forest products industry is a big part of Pennsylvania's economy. In the 1920s, when much of the state was timbered, the forests were made up largely of softwoods such as pines, hemlocks, and conifers. When they were cut down, less shade-tolerant species, like the hardwoods common today, grew in their place.

The industry that grew up relying on those species is now the fourth-largest segment of the manufacturing economy in Pennsylvania, generating about $5.5 billion in sales each year. It supports twenty-eight hundred to three thousand companies statewide. These logging and sawmill operations and furniture makers and paper mills employ about ninety thousand people spread across every county.

Pennsylvania exported $760 million worth of wood products in 2003, at least partly because the state is considered home to the largest, highest-quality concentration of black cherry in the world. Louisville Slugger, which provides 80 percent of the bats used by Major League Baseball, gets three-quarters of its ash from Pennsylvania, too.

"It's obviously a renewable resource that, if managed properly and harvested properly, will continue to be important to the state for quite some time," says Keith Craig, executive director of the Pennsylvania Hardwoods Development Council, a twenty-five-member arm of the state Department of Agriculture that was created by the state legislature and is a mix of private industry representatives, government officials, and academics.

If there's a problem, Craig says, it's that Pennsylvania's forests are "even aged," meaning they are all equally old. Most of that timber will be prime for harvest over the next ten years. That makes now the time to determine what kind of forest

Pennsylvania will have in the future. "If left to its own devices, the current forest would age and die and the new forest that would emerge would be a softwood forest again," Craig says. "That's just the way it would be. It's not that that's a death knell, but it would be a dramatic change."

If people don't want that to happen—if they want to maintain a hardwood forest, not only because the timber is more valuable but because acorn-producing oaks are better for wildlife, including deer—now is the time to act.

"That regeneration is not currently occurring. We have this beautiful forest, so we're in good shape that way, but regeneration is not occurring, so we've got a problem," Craig says. "We're at a serious juncture in our history. We're not facing an irreversible crisis, but we are facing a crisis of opportunity that needs to be addressed in the next couple of years."

"We all know that the commercial harvest of our forests is increasing as it reaches maturity, so we don't have a lot of time to get this recovery process under way," agrees Stout.

Certainly the DCNR, which manages about 2.4 million acres of state forest and state park land, has no intention of catering solely to hunters or deer. The agency was for a long time one of the Game Commission's toughest critics, largely because of fears that deer are jeopardizing the state's standing as managers of a certified forest.

Pennsylvania became the first state in the country to have its state-owned forests certified according to Forest Stewardship Council standards in 1998. Its 2.1 million acres of state forest still rank as the largest tract of certified forest in North America. That certification is meant to convey that the state's forests are operated in a way "in which timber products are produced in a manner that sustains the timber resource, maintains the forest ecosystem and meets minimum financial and socioeconomic criteria."

Being certified carries certain tangible benefits, says Dave Wager, director of forest management certification for Scientific Certification Systems, the California-based company that examined Pennsylvania's forests. It provides access to markets—like the U.S. Green Building Council, Home Depot, and the City of Los Angeles—that buy strictly from certified producers. Certified forest products can, in some cases, also bring premium prices.

When the DCNR received certification for its state forests in 1998, it came with a warning: do something about the deer population that was threatening the sustainability of the forest. In a two-hundred-page report, Scientific Certification Systems singled out white-tailed deer as a serious problem within state forests, one that has "modified both managed and unmanaged forest communities over the last 70 years."

"Overabundant deer have, through selective feeding, altered this region's forest structural diversity; shifted species dominance and equability; reduced, altered or eliminated advanced forest regeneration; and eliminated or reduced other wildlife species as a result of competition or habitat alteration," the report said.

The DCNR's response at the time was to partner with the Wisconsin-based Sand County Foundation to implement quality hunting ecology strategies on a couple of forest demonstration sites—the Quehanna Wild Area in Elk State Forest in southern Cameron County and Tioga State Forest in Tioga County. The theory behind quality hunting ecology (QHE) is that, given the chance to reduce deer numbers, hunters can repair degraded habitat for all kinds of wildlife, says Kevin McAleese, program director for the Sand County Foundation.

Under QHE guidelines, a lot of "baseline" monitoring goes on, McAleese says, like counting deer by age and sex and taking inventory of forest plants and animals. Given that starting point, biologists can then measure things like how many deer an area can support and still have a diverse, healthy ecosystem. Hunters benefit because those kinds of forests support bigger, healthier deer. "Those are the real issues. It's not antler development or glandular secretions. It's really the ecology, the way that things interact, that we don't know enough about yet," says McAleese.

The foundation's home, the Aldo Leopold Reserve in Madison, Wisconsin, is the first place quality hunting ecology was put to work, beginning in 1989. Hunters at the reserve have to kill two does to "earn" the right to shoot a buck. That changed the nature of the harvest. Whereas hunters used to take one and a half to two bucks for every doe shot, they were shooting five does for every buck at the start of this century. "But the buck kill has stayed about the same," McAleese says. "We're not shooting off all the deer. They reproduce to fill that void. But our doe kill is way up."

At the same time, the forest ecosystem on the reserve is healthier. While it's not perfect—the reserve is small and surrounded by farms that don't practice QHE, "so I'm not sure if we can claim victory yet or if we ever will," McAleese says—there have been signs of success. The reserve is seeing bigger, dominant bucks and bigger does. Body weights are up about ten pounds on average for each. And the forest understory is coming back.

No one can say whether quality hunting ecology could have worked on state forests. The DCNR dropped its support for the program after about a year and threw its resources behind several Game Commission research projects—namely, the fawn mortality study and buck study—that promised to make managing deer statewide a more precise process. Those studies, together with policy changes like concurrent buck and doe seasons, an October doe season for muzzleloader hunters, an October rifle doe season for junior and senior hunters, and higher doe license allocations, have all been positive steps, says Merlin Benner, the DCNR biologist. But that doesn't mean the DCNR's deer problems have gone away. In fact, when Pennsylvania's state forests were recertified in 2003–4, it was with the caveat that it continue to press for reductions in the deer herd.

While the DCNR has made some progress since the release of the first certification report, a lot of work remains to be done, Wager says. Deer continue to affect the vegetation in state forests, and if that issue is not addressed, future certification of the state's forests could be at risk.

The report recognized that the DCNR does not have the authority to set deer seasons or bag limits on its lands, however. "That's really part of the conundrum, that there's only so much they can do," Wager says. "And, as you can imagine, it's certainly a monumental task to turn deer numbers around. But it needs to be addressed. We do expect more is going to be done over the next five years of this certification."

To bring about change, Wager's report recommended that the DCNR develop and institute—prior to a late 2004 audit—a "corrective action plan" outlining "earnest and aggressive strategic, public advocacy, and political actions aimed at liberalizing hunting regulations in ways that reduce the deer density on state forests."

It didn't take long for DCNR officials to start this process. Shortly after the report came out, DiBerardinis put a halt to the practice of giving grants to conservancies interested in buying land destined to be turned over to the Game Commission for state game lands. The moratorium was never put into writing and the DCNR's own Citizens Advisory Council did not know about it, according to two members of that board, LeeRoy Vatter of Indiana and Bill Mifflin of Philadelphia.

"I'm not a hunter, but I know, particularly from my experience in Philadelphia and Fairmount Park, the need to control deer. It's a very grave issue in a lot of Pennsylvania," said Mifflin, who serves as director of operations and landscape management for the City of Philadelphia. "It's unfortunate, and I can understand the secretary's position, but no, I did not know about the moratorium."

If the DCNR's advisory council was not aware of the funding ban, conservancies around the state had "all heard about it," according to Carol Witzeman, president of the Central Pennsylvania Conservancy, based in Harrisburg. "There was nothing official sent out, but the word sort of got around," added Renee Carey, executive director of the Northcentral Pennsylvania Conservancy in Williamsport. "Everybody knew that was the way it was." DiBerardinis said he had no choice but to institute the ban, given that an overabundance of deer is the number one threat to the future of Pennsylvania's state forests.

An ongoing study known as the "Pennsylvania Regeneration Study," a five-year project begun in 2001, seems to back up that assertion. Conducted by staff from the DCNR's Bureau of Forestry and the USDA Forest Service, this study consists of examining five thousand plots across the state, looking for evidence of tree seedlings—and particularly oaks—as small as two inches tall. They're also being categorized by seedling source and height class. The research that's been done to date showed that as little as 50 percent of state forest sites studied had sufficient seedlings and saplings to replace the existing forest with a similar one.

"In other words, if disturbed, such as through a windstorm, insect or disease outbreak, or timber harvest, half of Pennsylvania's forests are at risk of failing to regenerate," reads a report from the Bureau of Forestry. "And that's optimistically looking only at stands that have enough light," adds Bill McWilliams, a Forest Service scientist coordinating the project. "In stands without adequate light, it's even worse." In one-third to one-half of all timber stands, the only way to prevent this lack of regeneration is to turn to some costly form of remediation, like herbicides or fencing, says McWilliams.

The top priority, the one thing that must be done to change that, DiBerardinis says, is to get control of a deer herd that is about twice the size it should be. He instituted the moratorium as a way of driving that point home.

He didn't leave it in place long, however. Six months or so after the moratorium went into effect, and following a private meeting with several game commissioners, DiBerardinis lifted it. He credited the decision to "a sincere willingness to find new ground on deer reduction measures, and a commitment to continue high-level discussions around land management and recreation concerns of interest to both agencies." Hunters, he says, had done a good job of managing deer, considering the tools that had been given them. Now it's up to the Game Commission, with help from the DCNR, to put more tools at their disposal.

To that end, DCNR officials have pushed very heavily over the past few years for changes to the deer management assistance program, or DMAP. The DCNR received about twenty-five thousand DMAP coupons for the 2004–5 hunting seasons, good for more than 720,000 acres of forest and park land.

DMAP

With a limited number of hunters to work with, though, and restrictions on how many deer they can take, DMAP still can't work as configured, he says. In 2003–4, for example, hunters bought 10,654 of the 16,312 coupons available for DCNR land, killing 2,343 antlerless deer. That resulted in an average reduction in the deer herds on DMAP areas of 3.3 antlerless deer per square mile. That was good, but hunters could probably have taken more deer, DiBerardinis says, if they'd been allowed to take more than one deer per DMAP site or to use rifles during all seasons on DMAP lands. The DCNR had asked the game commissioners to approve those changes in time for the 2003–4 deer seasons, but they did not.

DiBerardinis would also like to see party hunting allowed on DMAP lands. Under that scenario, a single hunter within a group would be able to fill all of the tags held by his party. If ten hunters were hunting from a camp, for example, and one of those hunters had the opportunity to kill six deer, he could do so, tagging them with his partners' tags, so long as everyone in the party agreed.

In the meantime, DCNR officials are looking to make changes on their end, too. The agency has not been able to sell all of its DMAP tags during the first two years the program has been in place, according to Benner. Coupons good for remote forest tracts, like some of those for the Algerine and McIntyre wild areas in Tiadaghton State Forest, were especially hard to give away. Knowing that, the DCNR is looking to develop new ways of better directing hunters to areas most in need of help in a "moving window of management."

One idea that's been bandied about internally is to give outfitters special access to some areas to market remote hunts. Another option might be to give individual hunters an extra incentive to hunt those hard-to-reach places. The DCNR might, for example, require hunters to shoot a certain number of does in an area before they could take a buck. That might keep the number of hunters down overall, but it might also draw dedicated hunters willing to remove a few does in return for the chance to shoot a trophy buck. The DCNR might also take areas in and out of DMAP.

"Knowing that the number of hunters is a limited resource, we have to find a more effective way to use that hunting energy," Benner says. "As some areas start to show reductions in deer numbers, we might take them out of the program and try to concentrate hunters on those areas that need more help."

There's even been some talk that, if all of those efforts fail and it becomes clear that hunting can't do the job in some places, the DCNR may have to turn to sharpshooters to kill deer. That, though, would be a last resort. "Hunters haven't had the opportunity to actually manage deer because we've treated deer like a fragile resource instead of the resilient one it is," says Benner. "We need to give them that opportunity. We need to give them as many tags as they are willing to fill."

"We don't want to dictate to the Game Commission," adds DiBerardinis. "We think that they've made progress, but certainly not enough. And we know that we have a burden to meet as well. But our hope is that through active dialogue, by sending some proposals we have to the commissioners, we think we can come up with some ways of reaching our goals."

What some would like to see the DCNR—or anyone, for that matter—also talk about are the other factors that might be responsible for the lack of regeneration common in Pennsylvania's forests. Sam Dunkle, the former game commissioner, is one of those who believe that deer are a problem, but not the only one, and maybe not even the major one. He said as much when he took the unusual step of testifying—as a sportsman—at a meeting he was presiding over as board president in mid-2004. "Make no mistake, the reduction of the Commonwealth's deer herd alone will not restore forest habitats to their former productivity," he said.

Dunkle says there are four stresses affecting the state's forests: acid rain, disease and insects, nutrient depletion, and deer. Acid rain may be the worst offender. It was found to be a problem in the state's streams as long as forty years ago, he says, killing trout in some places and making it impossible to stock fish in others. Tree ring data from red oaks in those same watersheds show that they began experiencing growth declines at the same time.

Dunkle thinks the Game Commission needs to acknowledge this and to balance deer herd reductions with efforts to apply acid-neutralizing dolomitic lime to timber harvest areas at a rate of two tons per acre. It should also initiate an interagency taskforce "that recognizes the importance of acid deposition in wildlife habitat destruction with the primary objective of achieving a coherent and coordinated policy to reduce further damage and remediate the considerable losses in quality habitat that have already occurred."

One Penn State University professor of forest hydrology, Bill Sharpe, would also like to see acid rain given more emphasis. Sharpe has spent more than twenty-five years studying acid rain in Pennsylvania. The problem, he says, is that the state is downwind from the Ohio Valley, "the greatest industrial complex in the world." Acid precipitation that originates from coal-fired generating plants in Ohio, Indiana, Illinois, West Virginia, and western Pennsylvania has been falling on the state's forest soils for decades. The result—as determined by a blue ribbon international team of acid rain researchers Sharpe assembled in 1998—is that acid-affected forest conditions are as bad in Pennsylvania as anywhere else in the world.

It's no coincidence, Sharpe says, that so much of Pennsylvania's forest understory has become dominated by hay-scented ferns in recent decades. The state's northern tier forests in particular have little natural buffering ability and hay-scented fern is very tolerant of acidic soil. It's not just young trees that are suffering from acid rain, either. Older trees of some species—like red oak—are dying sooner than they should, and that, according to Sharpe, can't be blamed on deer.

Like Dunkle, Sharpe believes that public and private forest owners should be applying lime to their lands right now to mute the effects of acid rain. If they're not, he hopes a study he's undertaking will persuade them to change their minds.

Sharpe, with a few others, has received funding to perform a study at two sites in Moshannon State Forest. He will lime the sites, then monitor them to record any changes in vegetation, forest floor–dwelling birds, water quality, brook trout populations, insects, and quantity and quality of deer forage.

Sharpe does not expect the study to show that deer are not affecting forest regeneration. He has no doubt that they are. But researchers need to determine the relative roles of deer and acid rain and other factors in preventing regeneration so that the proper treatments can be undertaken. "It's an emotional issue," he says. "Certainly the people who are worried about shooting too many deer have latched on to acid rain as an alternative theory. I have always told them we need to keep deer numbers at sensible levels, too.

"But when I look at all of the news releases and see what I read in newspapers and newsletters and it's deer, deer, deer, to me, that's a very myopic view of the world. If we continue to reduce deer numbers as low as we can with the tools available, but don't do anything about acid rain, I think we will still look back in 15 years and say we still don't have any red oak regeneration or white ash or sugar maple or hickory regeneration. What happened?

"I may not be around to see it, but I believe that's what's going to happen," Sharpe says. "This is something we need to get going on, and get going on it soon."

Sharpe admits that he's in the minority when it comes to his theories on acid rain. Most scientists, including the majority of his colleagues at Penn State, believe deer are the main issue.

There's good reason for that, according to Horsley. A recent study of the impact of liming on four sites in north-central Pennsylvania's Susquehannock State Forest

Forests with no brushy vegetation force deer and other wildlife to rely on mast crops to survive from year to year. In years when the supply of things like acorns, grapes, and beechnuts is poor, the deer have nothing else to fall back on.

showed that while some species—like sugar maples—respond to liming with increases in survival, seed production, and crown vigor, at least in the short term, many other species, like birch, beech, striped maple, pin cherry, and black cherry, do not. Nor do oaks, the most critical tree species for wildlife because of the mast they produce each year. "The point is that only a few species, at least in the northern hardwoods, seem to respond to lime," Horsley says. "I don't think it's a cure-all."

Horsley and some of his colleagues in the Forest Service are taking a closer look at the acid rain issue, too, however. From the spring of 2004 through the fall of 2009 they'll be studying the response of northern red oak seedlings to liming at several state forest sites. Four plantings will be done inside deer-proof fences; four will be planted outside the fences. The seedlings will be measured every fall to see if the trees inside the fence outperform those outside.

Horsley doesn't want to prejudge the study, but he says that past experience with other research projects indicates that deer, more than acid rain, will determine which seedlings do best. "The only factor, when we were looking at fencing, lime, herbicides, the only factor that had a long-term effect on regeneration was fencing, which is the exclusion of deer," he says. "That isn't to say there aren't other factors that may have some effects. But in the thirty-some years I've been here, if we wanted to study those other factors we had to do our studies inside a fence. You have to keep the deer out or you can't even get regeneration to begin those studies."

Other scientists say the solution may be not to lime the state's forests but to burn them. The Game Commission already does some prescribed burning on state game lands to maintain warm-season grasses, says Scott Klinger, director of the agency's Bureau of Land Management. Some recent research indicates that burning could help spark regeneration of key species, especially oaks, if carried out in forests, too.

Periodic, slow-moving, low-intensity surface fires that stay on the ground rather than getting into the forest canopy can burn away leaf litter and burn off shallow-rooting competitors, agrees Marc Abrams, a professor of forest ecology at Penn

State University. That leaves deep-rooted, thick-barked oaks to thrive in the less shaded forest that's left behind. Fire doesn't lead to overnight regeneration—controlled burns over a twenty- to thirty-year time frame are needed. But there's plenty of evidence to indicate that the forest community's long-standing policy of suppressing all fires has, however unintentionally, changed the composition of Pennsylvania's forests. "If you look at the forests that have been burned regularly since the 1960s, they have a strong oak component," Abrams says. "Those that haven't are primarily maple.

"The whole 'Smoky the Bear' mentality is what we're trying to change, the idea that all fire is bad. That's the major difference from twenty, thirty, forty years ago. Foresters who went to school then were taught that any fire had to be put out right away. Now we're trying to teach students just the opposite, that we're probably not using fire enough as a management tool."

Indeed, Native Americans commonly used fire to manipulate habitat in the Appalachian region prior to European settlement, according to research by Mary Ann Fajvan, a USDA Forest Service research silviculturist in Morgantown, West Virginia. These days, there are two fire management techniques being tested to see if fire should again have a place in eastern forests.

One technique involves setting fires in early spring or after leaf drop in fall. Once oak seedlings are established, the mature trees can be harvested. The other technique involves removing 50 percent of the overstory as a first step. Several years later, after oak seedlings have gotten a start, one or more fires are set to burn off competing young vegetation. With young oaks dominating what's left, the rest of the mature trees can be cut.

Klinger says the Game Commission hopes to get more involved with burning, possibly at a couple of study sites. "Ecologically, fire has a place. And we want to do what we can to ensure we have a healthy forest producing acorns for deer and turkeys and squirrels and other wildlife fifty years from now, not just this year," he says. "We're just on the cusp of this."

Pennsylvania could be on the verge of undertaking some more groundbreaking research, too. In April 2001 the Pennsylvania office of the National Audubon Society and the Pennsylvania Habitat Alliance, a consortium of sportsmen's groups, conservation organizations, wildlife professionals, and others, asked a group of professionals to look at deer management from an ecosystem perspective. The result was a group known as the Deer Management Forum. "We wanted to come up with a sort of blueprint for ecosystem management," says Audubon's Ron

Freed. "The idea was that if someone wanted to manage deer from an ecosystem perspective, they could look at this report developed by experts to see how to do it."

Those experts—scientists and policymakers from all over the country—first convened in October 2001. They spent the next three years looking at how best to manage deer and conserve biodiversity at the same time. Their report came out early in 2005. It said that deer populations, out of control for decades, have caused ecological havoc and that solutions to that problem are needed.

"I've never seen a hobblebush in Pennsylvania in my lifetime, except on a cliff where deer can't reach," said Roger Latham, a plant ecologist from eastern Pennsylvania—and the son of the Game Commission biologist Roger Latham—who was a member of the forum. "Hobblebush used to be superabundant in northern hardwood forests like you find across Pennsylvania, but it's just plain gone. Deer love it. It's deer candy, I guess. The thing we looked at is what you have to do if you want to save those species."

Fixing Pennsylvania's forests will require human intervention to keep "deer populations below levels that severely alter the composition and diversity of forests" forever, according to the report. Forum members recommended using an adaptive resource management, or ARM, approach to do that.

ARM is a sort of "learning-by-doing" approach that involves five steps: setting a resource goal based on values that stakeholders agree on; identifying competing theories and their management recommendations; implementing what is determined to be the best combination of management actions, like reducing deer to a certain goal and avoiding the use of herbicides; making predictions about the results of various management actions and then comparing the predictions against data collected at regular intervals; and updating management based on which theories performed best.

Forum members suggested a two-tier ARM approach. Some management strategies would be adopted on a statewide basis, while others would be applied to multiple ten-square-mile forest treatment areas in all major forest regions of the state. On some of those sites, deer numbers might be allowed to remain at existing levels as a sort of control, while on others deer numbers would probably be drastically reduced. Things like vegetation composition and soil acidity would be measured at each site to examine the relative importance of deer browsing vs. acid rain, for example.

There are at least two potential roadblocks that must be overcome to test the forum's ARM plan. First is the question of whether hunters will participate. Drastically

reducing deer densities across the state in a short period of time could be problematic if hunters aren't inclined to go along, the report's authors admitted. Second,
for the forum's recommendations to be put into play, multiple agencies—namely,
the Game Commission and the Department of Conservation and Natural
Resources—would have to agree to implement and pay for it. Benner, one of the
report's authors, says the DCNR "wasn't buying into" the report as a whole, but
would build some elements from it into its deer management strategy.

Certainly, though, many people might be interested in getting the answers to two
of the biggest, or at least most anticipated, questions the deer forum study proposed
to look at—namely, how long will it take Pennsylvania's forests to recover, and how
many deer can they sustain once they're healthy? No one is sure what the answers
are, but many suspect that the recovery period will be measured in decades.

"It's not a quick thing. It's not going to be a quick recovery," forester Bob Merrill
predicts. "This isn't a fast food place where you drive through and order your food
and out it comes. This is nature. It takes time. People are going to have to be patient."

"People ask me how long it might take for the habitat to recover and how long
we might have to keep deer numbers down. Well, we have to get the habitat fixed
before we can even start thinking about how many deer we can have and when,"
adds Blaine Puller. "When we have the habitat, we can have more deer, but we've
got to have the habitat first. And I don't think anyone knows how long that is going
to take."

The Deer Management Forum report touched on expected recovery times, as
well, and was equally adamant about not expecting too much too soon. Woody
species may recover fairly quickly, but soft species may take longer to come back.
Even erecting fences for six to seven years, as foresters who want to spark regeneration do now, "does not provide long-term protection for vegetation in the lower
levels of the forest," even when deer numbers are extremely low, the report said.
"Although there are indications that the regrowth of forest understories can occur
in a few years following the reduction or exclusion of deer, full recovery of the
structure and function of forest ecosystems will likely take decades and perhaps
require active intervention beyond the mere reduction of deer numbers."

It's possible that the 1.6 million acres of forest older than fifty years could show
partial recovery within five years, the report said. The average time for recovery of
some species and some forests might range from five to eighty years, though, and
that's if the recovery begins right now. "The longer Pennsylvanians wait to reduce
deer densities on non-industrial private land, the more stands will pass into a state

that is highly resistant to recovery, brought about by intense deer pressure and, in many cases, a third diameter-limit cut," according to the report.

Keith Craig, of the Pennsylvania Hardwoods Development Council, believes it will be important to see additional policies aimed at controlling deer put in place within the next five years, and he's not alone in thinking that way. "Our forests, in terms of mature trees, are fine as is. But if we want to regenerate them and perpetuate them for the future, we've got to address this. We're really at a crossroads," says McWilliams. "I think it's taken a while for this to catch on, that deer are really abundant, but that's finally where we're at. Now, the 'what are you going to do about it?' has started."

"We've got a real small window here," Puller agrees. "We've got a real bad situation on our hands. We can't wait forever to do something."

Horsley referred to a study of the Hearts Content Natural Area in Allegheny National Forest as proof of the need to act. That study was carried out in the 1920s to document the diversity and abundance of plants there, species like hobblebush, yew, and azaleas. When scientists returned to those same plots and studied them again just a few years ago, they discovered that "much of that whole shrub layer is gone," says Horsley. "While we found most of the same species present, their abundance was dramatically different. Plants that were once abundant had been reduced to specimens, which is to say individual plants.

"If you don't control deer impacts, many of the species that are there now will be lost without heroic efforts, like planting or bringing in an outside seed source. If we don't get regeneration of these species now, the seed supply goes away," Horsley says. "In our lifetime we may not see a healthy herbaceous supply. Woody vegetation can come back more quickly. But the longer we wait, the harder it is. That's why it would be a good thing to do this now.

"It doesn't matter why you want to have the forest. For hunters to have healthy deer, for people who like wildflowers, who value all kinds of wildlife, for people who like trees or rely on them commercially, all of those folks need to care about having too many deer in the woods, and need to care about the deer themselves."

John Dzemyan is doing his part to bring about change. He offers public tours of places like game lands 44 and its deer exclosures when given the chance, with the goal of showing hunters and others just what impact deer can have on their own habitat. Ultimately, he would like people to realize that controlling deer—not eliminating them completely, but controlling them—will lead to a healthier forest with the potential to grow more and different plant and animal species, along with bigger and healthier deer. "Ninety-nine percent of the people see this and they say, 'Wow, I wish I'd known about this twenty years ago.' So it does work," he says.

If Dzemyan is right, the very hunters who have been upset with the lack of deer in the big woods could be the people to benefit most. The ultimate good of controlling deer properly is that it will position hunters as society's best conservation stewards, the people who saved a forest ecosystem that was in danger of collapse, in the words of Kevin McAleese of the Sand County Foundation. And they'll get tangible rewards as a result. "Hunters will be able to stand up and say they're working to restore ecological balance, promote forest health, and say 'Oh, by the way, we're going to grow bigger deer,'" says McAleese.

"That's the future of hunting," agrees Bryon Shissler, president of Natural Resource Consultants, Inc., a Somerset County–based natural resource consulting firm that's helped various clients figure out how to manage deer on their property. "It's about building partnerships with landowners. You watch out for them and they watch out for you. And we together recognize the natural role of predation in the ecosystem. It could change the image of hunting."

"If we can go into one of those areas where overabundant deer have just destroyed the forest ecosystem and use hunters to turn that around, it's a win-win," agrees Gary Alt, former head of the Game Commission's deer management section. "Hunters get the deer they want and the hikers and bird watchers and campers who just want a healthy forest learn that hunters are their best tool for getting those things. What a breakthrough that would be."

4

TOO MANY MOUTHS IN THE GROCERY AISLE

It was almost perfect, really, in a twisted sort of way. We were standing at the edge of a cornfield on Sheldon Brymesser's farm in Boiling Springs, Cumberland County. The corn was green and lush, row after row of stalks taller than my six foot one. The woods beyond the field, the grass sprouting from the tractor tire–rutted dirt where we had walked, the farmhouse lawn in the distance, all were just as luxuriant. After three hot, dry summers in a row, we had finally gotten some rain, and everything was responding. A light, gentle mist was falling even today, and everything seemed fresh and vibrant.

A closer look, however, revealed some troubling signs. Examining individual corn stalks rather than the field as a whole, we saw some that were bent or broken. Everywhere, there were telltale tracks in the dirt.

"They're never going to get any higher than this, they're never going to get an ear, they're never even going to be any good as silage," said Brymesser of the damaged stalks. "The deer take a bite and fold the stock over and that's the end of the corn. It never grows back. We've been lucky, they haven't really been able to keep up with the corn this year, so we'll probably get away with losing about 10 percent of our tonnage. Last year, no way. With the drought, things were slow to grow and the deer just killed us."

Even among the stalks still standing tall there was evidence of deer. Brymesser was showing us how many of the ears had been nipped by hungry whitetails. They had moved from stalk to stalk, sampling a little here, a little there. Brymesser, who farms about eleven hundred acres, counting what he owns and leases, was holding one of the rough stalks in his calloused hands when something funny happened. As he was talking, Mike Pechart, now an executive assistant in the Pennsylvania Department of Agriculture, motioned toward something over Brymesser's shoulder.

We all looked. As if on cue, a white-tailed deer had stepped out of the corn about eighty yards away. She stopped when she saw us, her tail held at half mast and her ears swiveling around to catch any sound. She was too far away for me to see it, but I could imagine her nose twitching, too, as she tried to catch our scent in the air.

Behind the doe, still half obscured by the first row of corn, was a fawn. It stopped, following its mom's lead. Was there a second fawn, we wondered? Maybe even a third? Twins are common and triplets aren't unheard of in areas of good habitat, and Brymesser's farm certainly offered that.

We never got an answer. After a few more seconds the doe, her body language betraying her impatience with our presence, turned and silently melted away into the corn, taking at least that one fawn with her.

"We have two hundred acres of ground here that's in woods, and if the deer could all stay there, that would be fine with me," Brymesser said, staring toward the spot that had held two deer just seconds earlier. "But they surely don't. And there's been a definite, substantial increase in the number of deer in the immediate area. I've seen as many as fifty-two deer at a time in our fields. And that's at any time of day. Any time you look around out here you can see them. It used to be you'd only see them in the early morning or right at dark. But now it's all the time. It upsets my wife because she'll look out to the fields and she'll see them here all the time."

We were visiting Brymesser's farm to get a firsthand look at the damage people like Pechart describe when talking about the need to control deer in agricultural areas. The problem is large and very real.

Alice Wywialowski, senior wildlife biologist with the U.S. Department of Agriculture's Animal and Plant Health Inspection Service, pointed me to a study released in 2002. It determined that annual crop losses from wildlife totaled $619 million nationwide, with the loss of fruits, nuts, and vegetables costing another $146 million. Deer alone accounted for 58 percent of the field crop losses and 33 percent of the fruit, nut, and vegetable losses. Both numbers were up from a decade ago and were worst in northeastern states.

That means a lot in Pennsylvania, where agriculture is the state's number one industry. Pennsylvania has, according to the state's Department of Agriculture, one of the largest rural populations in the nation, with fifty-nine thousand farms, and ranks first in the nation in the number of acres of farmland preserved for agricultural use. It probably also ranks near the top in deer damage, though firm numbers are hard to come by.

Penn State University researchers tried to put a dollar figure on the destruction wrought by deer. They conducted a study in 1997 that determined deer caused about $76 million of crop damage to Pennsylvania's farms each year. That was probably a conservative estimate, though, Pechart said, given that a 1999 survey of the Pennsylvania Farm Bureau's 33,400 member families estimated wildlife-related losses at between $7,000 and $9,000 per farm. A similar survey of Pennsylvania Vegetable Growers Association members pegged their losses at $6,320 each, on average.

"And that's really, for the most part, bottom-line losses," says William Troxel, executive secretary of the Growers Association. "If farmers lose that much, they just have that much less to live on that year. It is rather significant for them."

Doug Gilbert, a Crawford County farmer and chairman of the Farm Bureau's state wildlife committee, had told me much the same thing one evening while we talked on the phone. Given all the other challenges facing agriculture today, deer can be the wild card that tips the scales toward profitability or ruin, he had said.

I had wanted to talk to Gilbert some more, so Greg and I made a trip to northwestern Pennsylvania to see him. We wanted, too, to get a look at the land that is among the state's best for raising deer. Crawford County, like most of the counties on the state's western edge, offers great living conditions for deer. Dark, rich soils support quilt-like patches of crops across the landscape. Those fields of corn and soybeans and alfalfa give birth to lots of deer that reproduce quickly and grow fast. The living is so rich that bucks, research has shown, grow bigger and better antlers and do it faster here than just about anywhere else in the state.

I was more than a little intrigued by Gilbert's situation. The year before we first talked, having as many deer on his property as he did could have worked to Gilford's benefit. A group of New York hunters had offered to lease his property in exchange for exclusive rights to hunt whitetails there. The group of twelve to thirteen hunters said they would buy all the seed he'd need to plant corn and alfalfa in the spring—he plants fifty to sixty acres of each, so that was equivalent to about $3,000 to $3,200 in cash—if they and they alone could hunt his farm the first week of buck season. Gilbert said no. "You're going to see more and more of this in Pennsylvania," he predicted, "but I don't want to get into closing it [his property] to the public." That doesn't mean deer aren't a serious problem, though, Gilbert said.

Greg and I made the two-and-a-half hour trip to Gilbert's house to talk about that. Arriving there was like taking a step back in time, if not to the nineteenth century then at least to an era that seemed made for black-and-white television. Gilbert had told me that he had a generations-long connection to farming and this land, working the same fields his family had since 1818. It wasn't hard to believe.

Knocking on the wooden screen door on the wraparound porch of the old farmhouse, I almost expected an Aunt Bea–type character to answer and maybe offer us some lemonade or a slice of pie. Instead, Gilbert came to the door, shirt off and a toothpick in his teeth. He left us long enough to put on a T-shirt, and then we sat on the porch and talked, he in a rocking chair that creaked whenever he shifted his weight to make a point. I sat in another, while Greg leaned up against the railing. Gilbert's pickup truck was sitting under a tree in the yard, his tractor a few yards away in the background. There were a few dairy cows in the field behind the old barn, and waist-high corn growing in fields beyond some other outbuildings and across the road. Only the digital camera slung over Greg's shoulder seemed obviously to be from the twenty-first century.

Pastoral and peaceful as this life is, it's not an easy one to live. Gilbert's brother realized that years ago and left the farm for a less land-dependent career. Gilbert stayed with his parents—they were both in their eighties and still living on the farm when we visited—and was trying to make a go of things with a few cows and fields of corn, alfalfa, and soybeans. He plants the 125 acres of his 385-acre spread that are tillable, along with seventy-five acres on a neighbor's farm.

A nonfarmer—even my long-standing plans to put in a vegetable garden had yet to be realized—I asked him just how severe the deer problem really was. I admitted that, like everyone else, I had heard stories about what deer can do to a crop, and about how tough farming is in general. But driving along any of the country roads around home, with fields of corn growing just out of reach beyond the window that separates the air-conditioned car from the summer heat outside, everything looked fine. So long as there was corn on the supermarket shelf or in the back of some farmer's wagon alongside the highway, with a homemade sign offering twelve ears for $3, everything seemed normal.

Gilbert said that this was a common perception, but not necessarily an accurate one. "People just don't believe how bad farming is in this country, and I can't blame them. You go into a supermarket and the shelves are just overflowing with everything you can imagine," he said. "But the margin in farming today is such that you can't break even on anything. We haven't been able to break even on beef in seven years. And, usually, if the price of alfalfa is down, corn is up. Now, unless you've got a big enough operation that you can spread your costs over a large area, you can't break even on anything."

Compounding the problem—or at least the nonfarming public's understanding of the problem—is that not all deer damage is obvious, says Troxel. Anyone can understand that if a farmer grows ten ears of corn and deer eat three, he's out that much corn. What's less clear to the casual onlooker is that, for the vegetable growers whose market is human consumers, deer cause problems when they eat just a portion of a farmer's product.

"If deer nibble off the top of an ear of field corn, which deer tend to do, or if deer get in your hay crop, you may be able to salvage something," Troxel says. "There's no real way to salvage sweet corn that's been nibbled unless the grower has animals himself that he can feed it to, but most increasingly don't.

"Nobody is going to buy an ear of sweet corn that's had the top nibbled off by deer. You may still have some corn on that ear, but realistically it has no market value. And the same is true with other vegetables, like tomatoes and cabbage."

Dairy farming—Pennsylvania's number one agricultural activity—is affected by deer, too. Not only can deer eat the crops a farmer grows to get his own herds through the winter, they can spread disease. Farmers should be able to vaccinate their cows just once a year, says Dennis Wolff, secretary of the Pennsylvania Department of Agriculture and owner of a six-hundred-acre dairy farm in Columbia County. In areas with lots of deer, however, they might have to vaccinate their cows four times a year.

Things can get so out of hand that, on occasion, farmers have to go to the time and expense of planting extra crops just to account for deer, says Bedford County farmer Fred Claycomb. Claycomb doesn't blame the deer for being hungry. Their numbers have been allowed to get so high in some places, like his Bedford County, that many of the natural foods they should be able to find in the woods are gone. The deer have eaten themselves out of house and home. Their numbers could have and probably would have plummeted already were it not for the fact that the deer are staying alive by eating farm crops intended for other uses.

"Our alfalfa fields, our hay fields are helping to sustain these deer artificially. If you somehow fenced off all of the farms, you'd see the deer population crash because there's nothing for them to eat in long, long stretches," Claycomb says. "For me, that means that when I plant, I plant one fifteen-acre plot two times, and five to six acres of it a third time, just to keep the deer off the forty acres I hope to get a crop from. If I don't, I don't have a chance."

Talking to Bob Kieff really pulls things together if you want to know what trying to farm in a deer-rich state means. Kieff farms in Wayne County in northeastern Pennsylvania. He knows all of the million-dollar deer damage figures that get tossed around, and he's got his share of stories about big herds of deer in his fields. What makes him so interesting is that he's a meticulous record keeper and a bit of a tinkerer, too.

His farm, to hear him describe it, is made for deer. He's got some woods—80 percent of them the acorn-producing oaks that deer love—and open fields. Once home to a dairy herd, those fields are now used to grow crops, mostly hay, but also some corn, clover, and alfalfa. His property is surrounded by private hunting clubs, too, "so naturally my fields were just an unending dessert plate" for the area's deer, Kieff said.

Losing a portion of his crop has always been a part of the cost of doing business. About ten years ago, though, Kieff decided to figure out exactly how much of an impact deer were having. He installed high-tensile electric fence—six strands spaced out to a height of six feet—around twenty-five acres of cropland. "For me, it was a trial," Kieff said. "The idea was to train deer not to go into the crops surrounded by the electric fence."

Kieff planted his crops inside the fence, worked them all summer, just as he had before the fence went up, then harvested them. When he compared his yields from the acres inside the fence to what he had taken off the same plots a year earlier, he was shocked.

"I had one five-acre field that would just be brown with deer. It might have forty deer on it at any time. I seeded it and took two small loads of hay off it. I reaped about six to eight tons without the fence," Kieff said. "Then I fenced the area. The deer tried to get in. They'd walk the outside of the fence, looking for a way in, but eventually started to avoid the area. That year, I took twenty-eight loads of hay off that field. I got more than seventy tons."

Fencing off a five-acre plot to grow corn produced equally stunning results. Before the fence went up, the site had never yielded more than thirty-eight bushels of corn to the acre. The first year after the fence went up, the site yielded 155 bushels to the acre, an increase in production of more than 400 percent. "The amount of crop I took off that field was unbelievable. I realized that what I had been doing all those years was fertilizing the ground for deer. Not for me, for deer. I was absolutely amazed. The economic gain for me was fantastic."

It's probably not fair to say that each and every farm in the state suffers that kind of damage, Troxel says. There are indeed growers who just don't have many problems with deer. Such people are few and far between, though. "It certainly is a significant problem for a lot of growers," according to Troxel.

There's not a lot of help to be had, either. In Pennsylvania, livestock farmers who lose sheep or cattle or other animals to coyote depredation receive some money from the state to make up for at least a portion of their losses. If a black bear causes a farmer problems, getting into crops or beehives, Game Commission officers will often try to trap it and move it to a more remote area.

There are no such programs to address deer damage. Though there's occasionally some talk in the state legislature of paying farmers for losses attributable to deer, there won't be checks in the mail any time soon because no one's sure where that money would come from. There's no way to move deer, either, and nowhere to take them if there was.

One option farmers do have is to shoot whitetails for crop damage. The first deer they kill that way is theirs; all others must be reported and saved for collection by the local wildlife conservation officer. Several farmers I talked to said they were afraid to shoot deer, though. They had heard rumors of people threatening to shoot livestock in retaliation, or threatening to burn barns down. Whether those threats were real or just barroom talk passed on from one person to the next, no one could say. But no one was eager to find out, either. "We heard rumors of guys threatening to shoot one cow for every deer a farmer killed," Gilbert said.

Anyway, shooting deer is not much of an option for farmers, Kieff said. Shooting even one deer is work; shooting enough to slow the crop losses they're causing would take way too much time from a farmer already pressed to get his chores done each day. "I just don't have time to go out and shoot deer. It's impossible. By the time I have to shoot it and haul it and clean it and get it ready for the wildlife conservation officer, I just don't have time to do it," Kieff said.

This doesn't mean that farmers hate deer. They certainly don't want them all dead, as some might think, Wolff says. Many farmers are also hunters, and a good portion of those who aren't at least enjoy seeing deer on their property. What farmers can't afford to do, though, is stand by and be driven out of business simply because some people want more deer at any cost, he said. That's the issue. "We do not have a deer problem. We have a deer population problem," says Wolff. "Farmers do not want the deer herd eliminated. They just want the deer herd controlled."

"We love deer. Farmers love deer. But there are too many of them," agreed Pechart, himself a deer hunter who grew up on the family farm. "Farmers are just trying to make a living and deer are certainly not helping. If you have a bushel basket full of shelled corn and you reach your hands in and take a scoop out, that's the farmer's profit. If you have deer eating that, it's going to make an impact.

"The biggest thing is getting deer under control. We're all willing to live with some deer," Pechart said. "But farmers can't be expected to feed all of the state's deer out of their own pocketbooks because there's not enough food in the forest for them to survive. That's too big a load to bear."

"It's not that we don't like the deer," agreed Brymesser. "I hunt myself, and I enjoy the sporting side of it. I think what farmers are looking for is some say in deer and deer management."

That hasn't necessarily been easy to come by. In early 2000, the Farm Bureau was one of several groups considering suing the Game Commission for failing to manage deer properly. More than a few people—including some in the Game Commission—thought they might win, too. "We've always had a tough relationship with the Game Commission. Their concern is the sportsmen who just want more deer and not the farmer," Pechart said.

Ironically, the problem has never been that sportsmen or Game Commission officials don't believe that farm country holds lots of deer. Rather, the strain has always largely been over one issue—control. Hunters say they can and will control deer if given access to the lands where they are causing problems; the farmers who are having the problems want hunters, but they want them—at least to some degree—on their terms.

That leads to problems, says Thomas Boop, a game commissioner from Northumberland County. Farmers who don't allow hunting, or allow only very limited hunting, are in effect creating refuges for the very deer they are concerned about. "Show me an area with a deer problem and I'll show you an area with an access issue," Boop said. "If there were no access problems in Pennsylvania, a lot of our problems would go away. We don't have problems with too many deer in those places where hunters can hunt."

"We hear all the time about these farmers with too many deer, but they don't want to let anyone onto their property," adds Greg Levengood, a director of the Unified Sportsmen. "They seem to want to have their cake and eat it, too. If they would make their property more accessible, I'm sure there are hunters who would be willing to take some of those deer."

Former game commissioner George Venesky agrees. He believes that many farmers are to blame for their own problems. It's true that something like 85 percent of the state is in private ownership and "we ask a heck of a lot of private landowners in Pennsylvania," Venesky says. But farmers and other private landowners haven't shown themselves to be overly willing to accept what help is offered them, either. As proof, he pointed to the Game Commission's public access programs, the farm game and safety zone programs. Both are designed to keep private property open to public hunting. Farm game is open to contiguous farms and other properties totaling at least a thousand acres, while the safety zone program is made up of properties of at least fifty acres. There were 21,546 farm game agreements with landowners across the state in 2004, keeping more than 2.4 million acres open to hunters. The safety zone program had 8,824 agreements and more than 1.4 million acres of land.

That looks great on paper, Venesky says. The problem is that neither farmers nor the Game Commission do a very good job of telling hunters where those properties are. Some signs get put up around accessible properties. The Game Commission has regional maps that identify, in general terms, open properties, too. Green-colored areas represent state parks and forests. State game lands are an orange-brown, and private ground is yellow.

That's not much help, though, at least compared to what some other states do, Venesky told me. When he hunted pheasants in South Dakota, that state's game department provided him with a booklet that listed the names, phone numbers, and addresses of landowners whose property was open to public hunting. That brings the people with the game together with those who would like to get some of it.

"Here [in Pennsylvania] is a public access program, and we're keeping information the hunter needs away from the public. It's almost bizarre. It's like a guarded secret," Venesky says. "It's not very progressive, in my mind. You look at one of those maps you can get of each region of the state, and you look for lands in the farm game program, and all you see is a blob of yellow. What's that tell you? Not much, except in the most general terms. You might drive out there and see some safety zone signs that tell you someone there is in the program, but that's it. That's not right."

Farmers and other private landowners are to blame for that and, as a result, for their wildlife problems, he says. The Game Commission, working in cooperation with the Farm Bureau, gave landowners the chance to provide details about where they are located and how much game they have and how many hunters they want. The idea was and is known as the LINK program.

LINK was meant to direct hunters to farms with wildlife problems, primarily deer damage issues. Landowners who sign up for the program—developed in 1999, it still exists—do not have to guarantee that their land will be open to public hunting, nor do they have to allow every hunter who asks permission to hunt on their land.

What the program does, however, is allow landowners to post information on the Game Commission's website about things like where their property is located, how many hunters they'll accept per day, and what species may be hunted. Hunters can fill out an "information and profile" form that can be mailed to the landowner. The landowner can then decide whether to allow a given hunter on his property.

The LINK program has not proved successful, in terms of either attracting farmers or getting hunters onto their lands. Only twenty-four landowners were enrolled in the program in 2004. Not all of those were people looking for help with deer, either. Some wanted hunters out after groundhogs and coyotes, for instance. That's okay, Venesky says, but then farmers have no right to complain about things like having too many deer. "The Farm Bureau doesn't have a leg to stand on," Venesky says. "They've been given all the tools in the world. If they don't take advantage of them, shame on them. They're not going to get any sympathy from me."

There's a perception among hunters, too, that public access areas aren't very visible, says Scott Klinger, who directs the Game Commission's Bureau of Land Management. With about thirty thousand private landowners enrolled in one of the Commission's access programs, and nearly 4.5 million acres—counting those in the forest game program—open to hunting as a result, Pennsylvania is among the leaders nationwide in providing sportsmen with places to hunt on private ground. You wouldn't always know it, though, to talk to hunters, according to Klinger. "As one hunter told me," he says, "we have this public access program, but it's a stealth program. We have this public access program, but if you call one of our regional offices and ask where these places are, we can't give you a map."

Access to private lands for public hunting figures to be a "critical issue around the country" in the twenty-first century, according to Klinger, who sits on an international committee studying the problem. In an attempt to rectify that—and address the deer damage issue in the process—Game Commission officials were, in late 2004, turning their attention to a new idea.

Using two grants from the National Shooting Sports Foundation, the Commission's Bureau of Land Management was developing public hunting maps, broken down by county. Each map would be available as a downloadable file on the commission's website, with some hard copies perhaps kept on hand, too. All would list the state game lands, state park and forest lands, and federal lands open to hunting in each county. More important, they would also more specifically identify where farm game and safety zone cooperators could be found.

The maps will not go so far as to include the names and phone numbers of cooperators, Klinger says. The plan is to survey landowners, though, to see how much information they would be comfortable providing, and whether they would consent to have more signs put up around their property.

Klinger warned, however, that even those things would cause some landowners to pull out of the access programs, fearful that they might be overrun with hunters. "We are going to lose some. I'm going to be honest with you," he says. "But this is going to be a true public access program. The entire goal of this is to let people know where these cooperators are."

Even then, farmers have to work with other farmers and other landowners to control deer, says former game commissioner Steve Mohr. It does a farmer no good to open his land to hunting if the landowners who surround him don't do the same. The owners of those properties—whether they are farms, municipal parks, housing developments with large lots, or something else—need to realize that they are causing part of the problem and need to become part of the solution by allowing hunting on their lands, too.

"Somehow we have to educate those people who harbor the deer how much damage can be done to everyone," Mohr says. "I mean, I feel for those farmers who are trying to make a living and his neighbors are harboring those deer. Somehow we have to make that guy who wants a hundred deer per acre but can't feed them either let us trim that herd or make him support them somehow."

Farmers don't buy the argument that access is the heart of the deer problem, though. It can be an issue, Gilbert said. Farmers who won't allow hunting are asking for trouble. "If they want to post their land, that's their right, and that's fine. But we don't want to hear them complain about deer damage."

But most farmers don't prohibit hunting. In fact, many encourage it, Troxel says. "If they are having problems with deer, I think most of them recognize the value of hunting, and are likely to open their land as opposed to posting it.

"Now, vegetable growing is something that can still be done in areas where hunting is tough to do because of the number of houses, or because the surrounding land might be posted, but I think growers are open to hunting where it can be

Doug Gilbert of the Pennsylvania Farm Bureau believes having farmers and hunters work together is the best way to keep deer populations in line.

done," he says. The only question seems to be who gets to do the hunting, and what type of hunting they're asked to do.

Ron Johnson runs a farm in Bedford County. He's got problems with too many deer, but he also posts his land. If that seems incongruous, it's really not, Johnson told me. His intent, he says, is to maintain some measure of control over the kind of hunters on the property. "I don't post my ground to prevent hunting. I post it to manage hunting. If you're going to help me knock the deer population down, you've got to apply for and fill some doe tags. A lot of people like to hunt bucks. One year I had nine people hunting my land and they were all hunting bucks. Only three shot does. If that's how you want to hunt, that's fine. Convincing people to shoot does is hard. But if you're not, you're not helping me. I need someone who will."

Brymesser likes to have a say in who hunts his farm, too. He's not opposed to allowing hunters on his property. His family has had its land enrolled in the farm game and safety zone programs since the 1950s. He had allowed forty-two hunters on his property the fall before we spoke, but he wasn't sure how many deer they had killed. Whatever the number, it wasn't enough, so he had considered "just

Sheldon Brymesser knows very well the impact of overabundant deer. Even in good years, deer eat 10 to 15 percent of the crops his farm yields.

opening the gates and letting them go," letting unlimited numbers of hunters on his property. He'd thought about doing the same thing before, though, and never been able to pull the trigger. A few bad experiences were the reason.

"What I'm afraid of is the wild shooting. I've had people shooting toward the house, shooting everywhere. Once the deer start running, they just don't care how they're shooting or where they're shooting. That's the person that concerns me," Brymesser said. "The guy that's a little more sincere in his hunting, that's the guy I like. But you don't know who that is if you don't talk to them first."

Kieff, too, welcomes hunters to his land, though he requires them to report any and all deer they take so he can monitor who is helping him and who is not. Finding good hunters who are willing to come back to his property year after year has made a difference.

"Just having a hunter around will deter deer to some degree," Kieff said. "They don't like the noise or the disturbance or whatever, and will sort of move back out of the area. I find it very successful if you can have a hunter come in and harvest a deer, especially if he can do it while my crops are still standing."

Farmers also need hunters who are willing to hunt—really hunt, long and hard—said several of the farmers I talked to. Many felt that that kind of hunter has become increasingly rare.

Ron Ambrose is a farmer in Westmoreland County, in the state's southwestern corner. He lives on the county's eastern edge, not far from the Laurel Ridge, not too many miles from what passes for big woods in that part of the state.

Forty-three years old, Ambrose was born and raised on his 168-acre farm. He runs a dairy operation, growing—or rather trying to grow—corn and hay for his own livestock. His problem is that he's surrounded by property owned by a private shooting preserve that has never been and will never be open to public hunting. That preserve harbors all manner of deer, deer that hide out on the posted ground by day and raid Ambrose's crops by night. Nine to ten months a year he has to buy feed for his cattle to replace his own crops that have been gobbled up by deer. He's seen as many as eighty deer feeding in one of his fields at a time, and spotting does with triplet fawns is not uncommon. "That makes the old population explode," Ambrose said. "They eat most of my corn. They get the most, and I get what's left. When we do shoot one, they have an inch of fat on their backs, the ones we get."

Ambrose allows hunters on his property, provided they stop to ask permission first. They shoot some deer, too, but not nearly enough. While the fact that the shooting preserve harbors deer is a big issue, another is that too few of the hunters who do hunt his farm really stick with it. "It used to be that you'd have guys come in as soon as it broke daylight and stay till dark. Now, by lunchtime they're gone," Ambrose said. "They come in for a few hours a day and then they're gone. They're all out riding the roads. And then you don't see anyone until Saturday.

"I tell guys, if you see a deer early, you better shoot it because by dinnertime you're not going to see anything anymore because nobody's in the woods. Nobody's pushing the deer around. I know part of it is that the deer hide out on the posted ground or only come out after dark," Ambrose said. "But years ago, guys would work for deer. Back ten to fifteen years ago, guys would drive deer around or work together to find deer. They don't do that any more."

Ambrose has gone so far as to open roads on his property to make it easier for hunters to get around. He doesn't want them just driving where they please, maybe through his fields, but he's roped off parking areas, like the one he put at the top of a quarter-mile-long hill, so that hunters could drive right up to the woods rather than have to make the trek on foot. "Some of the guys who hunt here are a little older, so I'm trying to make it easier for them to get around. I'm trying to do whatever I can to get guys out there," Ambrose said. "Where I'm at, I'm sort of limited. I've got to do something because the deer are taking over."

Hunters don't necessarily expect landowners to go that far, but they do seem a bit spoiled these days, Gilbert agreed. Maybe the incredibly high deer numbers of years past made some hunters lazy, he said, since they could routinely see deer without having to do much preseason scouting or in-season walking.

Jeff Grove, director of local government programs and wildlife specialist with the Pennsylvania Farm Bureau, says he suspects that is the case, based on what farmers are saying. "I'm hearing farmers saying they're having a hard time getting good hunters out there. Hunters don't seem to be willing to drive deer any more," he says. "When I was a kid, hunting used to be a real skill. Now, with the way the working man has to work, I'm not sure those skills are as honed today. Driving around at night with a spotlight doesn't tell the true story. That's not real scouting.

"The thing that I find amazing is that I've been confronted by hunters who say there are no deer in an area, when the concern that I'm still hearing with farmers is that they still have too many deer. They are experiencing too many deer. We would much rather have hunters utilize and benefit from the resource than address the deer issue any other way, but they've got to be able to do it," says Grove.

It's tough to say what it might take to change that, or even whether it can be changed. If many hunters don't like to work hard to find deer, or if they don't have the skills to find deer now, when populations are still relatively high, will they put the time and effort into finding deer if and when the size of the herd is reduced? That's a big question.

Clearly, though, everyone wins if partnerships between deer hunters and farmers plagued by deer can be established, says the USDA's Alice Wywialowski. Hunters get their sport and farmers sustain less crop damage. "Deer populations have gone through the roof, and the more that hunters are allowed to harvest deer, the more deer populations and the damage they cause will be reduced," she says.

Building partnerships takes work on both sides, though, and if there was one encouraging thing Greg and I encountered in talking to farmers and hunters about farmers, it was the apparent willingness on both sides to look for common ground.

We spent one early Sunday morning talking to the Pennsylvania Deer Association's Jim Seitz, standing in his front yard, the sun of a July morning burning the dew off the grass. Seitz said the vast majority of hunters are conscientious sportsmen and conservationists. They are good, safe hunters. The world is changing, however, and those hunters have to change with it. Farmers need to provide access to their ground, yes. But hunters need to reach out as well, he told me.

In the future, it's not going to be okay—if it ever was—to just pull to the side of the road and start hunting in the neighbor's woodlot. That doesn't mean hunters can't still hunt those places, but they're going to have to build some relationships first, Seitz said. "Hunters should be visiting farmers now," he said. "Shoot some of their groundhogs. Put a few bales of hay away. You're going to get a place to hunt. And it's surprising how easy it is, if you're willing to make a little effort. It's not the farmer's responsibility to track hunters down and tell them they've got deer. It's the hunter's responsibility to find his own place to hunt and establish that relationship with a farmer, with a landowner."

Gilbert also talked about working with sportsmen to control deer. He's been involved in a sort of pilot project in the northwestern corner of the state that brings together farmers, sportsmen, and Game Commission officials to seek solutions to deer issues. Such cooperation was often lacking in years past, he said.

Farmers who were seeing deer wreak havoc with their crops couldn't get people to understand what they were going through. Hunters suspected that farmers who shot deer for crop damage were just using that as an excuse to shoot big bucks before hunting season opened and everyone had a fair shot at them. Even some Game Commission employees seemed unconcerned at best, or openly hostile toward farmers at worst, according to Gilbert. That's all changing now.

"This lets everybody see we aren't the bad guys we were portrayed to be, and sportsmen aren't the bad guys either. We're in this together," he said. "I really like what I'm seeing now, I really do. We've got to be able to sit down and communicate. We can all sit down together, we can get to know one another, we can talk to one another. We as farmers can explain what we need in terms of wildlife control. We can hear the wildlife conservation officers tell us what they need in terms of law enforcement. We can hear what the sportsmen want," Gilbert said. "That's what we need, communication."

To take things a step further, in the fall of 2004 the Farm Bureau's wildlife committee was kicking off a voluntary pilot program designed to link farmers with new deer hunters. "We intend to 'adopt' a junior hunter and his parents, inviting them to the farm to give the new junior hunter a positive hunting experience their first time out. We are interested in starting a program to encourage young first-time hunters to continue the tradition," Gilbert said. "We feel that a positive experience will help everyone interested in this important tradition and sport."

Farmers can shoot deer for crop damage, but most don't have the time or energy to do so. They prefer that hunters do the job.

If there's a dark cloud remaining on the deer-farming front—and many farmers say there is—it's one that comes back to that same issue: control. Farmers not only want a say in who hunts their land, they want a say in how many deer should be killed. Who better to decide what size deer herd is acceptable, at least on a specific property, than the person who owns that property? Pechart asked.

It falls to the Game Commission, he said, to give farmers and other landowners the power to make some of those decisions, at least in cooperation with biologists. Until that happens, things like increasing public access to private ground, asking hunters to hunt harder, and adopting junior hunters amount to little more than "a band-aid to the overall problem. The problem is that there are too many deer and too much damage and not enough control," Pechart said.

John Dawes wonders how willing the Game Commission really is to share its decision-making authority. Administrator of the Western Pennsylvania Watershed Program, Dawes is also a longtime Angus breeder in Huntingdon County. He is not a hunter, but he allows his son, brothers-in-law, and others to hunt on his three-hundred-acre farm. He's had his land enrolled in the farm game program for thirty years, too, yet says he's seen the profitability of his farm go down every year for a decade or more.

Dawes doesn't blame that on hunters. He has seen a growing willingness on the part of at least some sportsmen to shoot does, and he knows of dozens of females that were taken from his farm in 2003. Still, the herd is much too large.

"I see groups of twenty-five deer at a time moving around my farm, mostly does with young fawns. That presents a big problem," Dawes says. He really began to notice a problem six years or so ago. The season's first cutting of alfalfa would show evidence of browsing by deer. By the time the second cutting came off, he could see where as many as forty deer had been bedded in the field. The problem didn't stop there, either. When a professional forester visited Dawes's property, he pointed out that there was little or no regeneration going on in Dawes's woodlots. That has not changed.

Dawes believes the Game Commission can turn that situation around and get the deer herd under control for the benefit of everyone, but only if commissioners listen to the recommendations of their own biologists and press for further reductions in the deer herd. That is not always easy, he admitted. Hunters—who, unlike himself, pay for wildlife management in the state—and others who have grown used to seeing lots of deer might not always support efforts to reduce the size of the herd. Commissioners must remain steadfast, though, and keep focused on the bigger picture. They must have the political will to do the right thing, Dawes says. He's not sure that will happen.

Comments like those made by Mohr at the April 2004 meeting worry him. Mohr voted against Gary Alt's recommendation of 1,039,000 doe licenses for 2004–5—the largest allocation in the state's history—not because he felt it was improper from a biological standpoint but because he worried it would turn off some of the very hunters the Commission needs in order to operate. "If you think everyone's happy, you're under a rock," Mohr said then. "Scientifically, that's great, but socially and politically, we're going to pay hell for those allocations."

The allocation was adopted and almost all of the licenses sold, but Dawes wonders if commissioners can or will do the same thing year after year, in the face of pressure, if that's what it takes to solve the deer issue. "I wish I could be more hopeful," Dawes says. "But I sense some cynicism on the part of some commissioners. I'm saying that with the full recognition that time spent on the Commission board is not a paid position. They want to do the best thing for the resource, but they're not necessarily following through with the recommendation of their professional biologists.

Game commissioner Roxane Palone doesn't disagree with Dawes in terms of just how serious the situation is. She believes, though, that commissioners are in fact committed to a deer management plan that is intended to balance the deer population with the available habitat. Change may come slowly, it may take time, but it will come, she says. "I think we've come a long way already," Palone says. "It's true we have more work to do, but I think we're committed to doing it. I know I am and I think the majority of the other commissioners are, too. We just have to keep moving forward and working together to get to where we need to go."

As proof of the Commission's willingness to change and adapt, she pointed to the development of its deer management assistance program, or DMAP. It's been somewhat slow to develop but is helping to control deer where that control is needed most, she says.

There was some concern among sportsmen and game commissioners initially that DMAP would lead to more posting. The fear was that landowners would cry about deer damage just to get additional licenses that they and their family and friends could use on their posted ground. "I understand why people post their land. There are a hundred reasons, and ninety-nine of them are legitimate," said former game commissioner Bob Gilford. "But I don't want to create private hunting preserves. This can't just be something for Uncle Bill and his grandkids."

The result was that in 2003, DMAP's first year, commissioners restricted it to landowners whose property was also enrolled in one of the agency's public access programs. That drew a lot of fire from the Farm Bureau and others who felt they were being blackmailed into trading deer-hunting opportunities for deer damage control.

Craig Sweger, a farmer from Washington County and a member of the Pennsylvania Farm Bureau's wildlife committee, said he opens his property to hunters, provided they ask permission first. He's had too many bad experiences with hunters, though—cut fences, hunting in safety zones, people shooting over others—to just throw open the gates to everyone. Requiring public access would keep most farmers from enrolling in DMAP, he warned.

Sweger is right. Largely because of the public access requirement, only 176 landowners controlling 695,396 acres—or about 2.5 percent of the state's land mass—enrolled in DMAP the first year. More telling, only 28,769 of those acres were not already open to hunting before DMAP came along. A total of 32,783 coupons were issued to landowners.

A year later, when commissioners dropped the public access provision as a requirement for being a part of DMAP, 696 landowners controlling 1,707,969 acres were approved for enrollment in DMAP, good for 47,366 coupons. "DMAP is about managing habitat," game commissioner Russ Schleiden said, in explaining the Commission's change of heart. "It's a part of the big picture. It's not about posted land. It's not about private land. It's not about Game Commission programs."

While much of the growth in DMAP from the first year to the second, in terms of acreage, was attributable to more state forest being put into DMAP, the growth in terms of participants was tied directly to farmers' joining the program once the access requirement was dropped. The percentage of farmland in the program increased from 35 percent to 42 percent and the percentage of coupons available for use on private land jumped from 11 to 21 percent.

And how is DMAP working on the ground? It seemed to be off to a good start, albeit in need of some tweaking. In the program's first year, a few more than one in four DMAP coupon holders actually shot a deer. The highest harvests actually occurred in the two wildlife management units in the north-central part of the state, 2F and 2G, where the habitat is the worst and deer damage the greatest. That would seem to indicate that DMAP was successful in directing hunters to those lands where landowners wanted additional deer removed.

DMAP had a few problems, too, though. In its first year, only about 80 percent of the hunters given a coupon redeemed it for a doe license. What's just as bad is that some of the hunters who redeemed their coupon for a license never used it. Ron Ambrose, for example, has been in DMAP from the start, but it didn't do him much good the first year. He handed out all twenty-one DMAP coupons he was given for his farm and was hoping at least half of those tags would get filled. By season's end, though, only two of those coupons had been used to harvest a deer.

Part of the problem, Ambrose said, is that DMAP tags are not transferable between hunters. At least five of the hunters who had his DMAP tags had planned to hunt his farm during the post-Christmas flintlock deer season. All ended up shooting several deer each at other sites before Christmas, however, and lost their interest in taking any does from his property.

"They never even showed up here," Ambrose said. "They had already killed deer elsewhere, so they never even showed up. I can't blame them in a way. You can only use so many deer. But I'd like to see it where the guys can give me the DMAP tags back so that I can give them to someone else. It would be the same as the red tag program. I don't see why they couldn't do it," he said. "Right now, once guys get that tag, they can't give it to anyone else. That's their tag. But I'm dependent on them. I'm the guy taking a beating."

Gary Alt hopes that in the future hunters will gain a better understanding of just what DMAP is intended to do and will realize that they need to fill their tags on those lands. DMAP tags offer hunters a chance for some additional recreation. But the program is also about building better relationships between hunters and landowners and controlling deer numbers. If hunters don't pay attention to those two things and harvest some deer, they're not getting the job done. That's not a position they should want to put themselves in.

The number of hunters is in decline nationwide, Alt points out. While everything possible should be done to reverse that trend, hunters have to act now to convince landowners and society at large that they are the best tool for managing the state's wildlife and wild lands, and that they care enough to fill that role. "We should not do it because we are forced to do it. Hunters should lead the charge," Alt says. "As hunters, we need to tell society what we can do for them."

As for the red-tag program Ambrose mentioned, it's an older Game Commission program also aimed at thinning deer numbers in agricultural areas. It provides farmers—Gilbert is a participant—with a set number of red deer tags, based on acreage. The tags are given directly to farmers, who in turn hand them out to hunters. Each tag allows a hunter to kill one antlerless deer. Hunters can hunt from February 1, after the close of the last regular deer season, through September 28, days before the next earliest season begins.

Farmers can ask that hunters who don't kill a deer by the end of the day return the tag to them so that it can be given out to another hunter. That's what Gilbert does. It's helped, too. Gilbert's had his farm in that program for a number of years and said it's played a role in bringing deer numbers down to a level that's tolerable. "I'm happy with the way things are now. It's like it was twenty or twenty-five years ago. There's still damage, but I can live with it," Gilbert said.

Troxel admits that he wouldn't have thought a few years ago that the Game Commission would ever agree to anything like a red-tag or DMAP plan. Add to that antler restrictions, concurrent buck and doe seasons, and an October doe hunt for junior and senior hunters, and it's amazing just how far the agency has come in terms of opening up deer management.

The Game Commission board deserves credit for the progress it's made, Troxel says. Now the challenge is to keep the pedal down, even as those tools start to work, deer numbers drop, and complaints about that fact grow loudest. "I think, in general, as an association we see most of the changes undertaken by the Game Commission as helpful and positive," says Troxel. "But this is one of those things where it's going to take time to see real changes at the farm level. We haven't seen any dramatic changes yet in terms of the amount of deer damage on the ground. We are hoping that, in the long run, we will see a positive impact on the farm level from less deer damage, but we're not there yet. Deer management is quite a divisive issue, we all know. But our position, I believe, is to ask them to stay the course."

Only time will tell if the Game Commission board will indeed continue to follow the recommendations of its biologists, says Jeff Grove. He worries a little when he hears some commissioners say that they don't want to trim the herd so much that hunters lose interest in the sport. But he's never expected the deer debate to be a quiet one, either. "Very seriously, this is an issue that has always been a priority," says Grove. "I've been here thirteen years and I've never seen it get less vocal. I have not seen it cool down. I have only seen it get more emotional and I think that's because the pressures are increasing. It's harder than ever to make a profit at farming, and when you see a big deer herd out there, it can make the difference between paying your bills and not paying your bills."

"All we've ever wanted was to get the deer herd down to where we could live with them," Gilbert said. That figures to be an ongoing challenge, according to George Kelly, the retired Game Commission biologist. Pennsylvania's landscape is changing. At the dawn of the twentieth century, most of the forests had been leveled. When they started to grow back, covering mountain after mountain with brushy cover, that's where the deer were. Now those forests have matured. They still hold some deer, but not as many as they did. The deer have moved, settling in farm country.

"The high deer populations used to be in the more mountainous regions of the state, the north central, the northeast, the south central to some degree. When we hunted in the 1950s and 1960s, that's where we hunted," Kelly says. "I grew up in Westmoreland County, but the deer population was just growing there back then, whereas it had already been high in the north central for more than thirty years. Things have shifted now, with the southwest and southeast and northwest being the best deer habitat."

Brymesser knows all about that. He was about at the end of his rope that late summer day that we talked. Dusk was approaching as we took one last lap around his cornfield. The edge of the field closest to the woods, as you would expect, was the hardest hit by deer. We walked along a deer trail at the corn's edge that was, in Brymesser's words, "pretty much like a cow path." There were deer tracks, made when the ground was muddy, collecting dust, along with some fresher ones.

Brymesser believed he would be okay that year. The summer's rains had prompted some exceptional growth—enough that his crops, like Pennsylvania's forests a hundred years earlier, had overwhelmed the deer herd. The deer had eaten well at his expense, to be sure, but they hadn't been able to keep pace with the crop that summer.

He worried, though, what the next summer might bring. If there's one thing a farmer knows, it's that you can't count on rain. "I've never shot a deer out of season for crop damage, and every Tom, Dick, and Harry, and everyone else, asks me why I don't. Well, I want to be able to shoot a ten-point buck in the regular hunting season the same as everyone else. I want to be able to go out and hunt deer the same as everyone else. That's the fun of it," Brymesser said. "But every year I'm getting more and more tempted. There needs to be some type of control and we don't have that now. It's not going to be far in the future when I may have to get my rifle out."

"Farmers don't want anything but what they work so hard to produce," says Pechart. "But agriculture is in a serious state of affairs in Pennsylvania. Some farmers are close to hanging it up because of deer damage. Farmers certainly need help controlling deer."

5

AT HOME IN THE 'BURBS

It was the reference to "Mad Dog," I remember, that surprised me. Michele Clarke is a middle-aged mother of two who stands a hair shy of five feet, I'd guess. Dressed in business-casual clothes and the kind of shoes that I think my wife refers to as "flats," she had led me down a carpeted hall flanked by clean white walls to her office. It's one room in a nice building with big glass doors, a woodlot to its rear, and a perfectly manicured golf course across the street.

Now we were sitting on opposite sides of the desk where she works as director of parks and recreation for the municipality of Murrysville. A community of 18,872 located on the western edge of Westmoreland County, just twenty miles from Pittsburgh, Murrysville is close enough to make working in the city convenient, but far enough away to offer lower property taxes and a quieter lifestyle. As such, it is a community of two worlds. Home to transplanted city dwellers, home-grown suburbanites, and farmers, Murrysville is about 50 percent rural and 50 percent developed.

The developed half of the community is cut by one major highway, Route 22, which is destined to go from four lanes to six in some areas. Strip malls, sixteen-pump gas stations, and chain restaurants are its hallmarks. The other half of the community is made up of woodlots interspersed among housing plans and golf courses and twelve hundred acres of parks.

Clarke spends her days making sure that Murrysville's residents have something to do with their time. She coordinates a spring egg hunt and playground activities for children, a swimming program for families, and yoga and fitness classes for seniors. There's even a winter snowman contest. In that role, you wouldn't think she'd have much need for a man like Michael "Mad Dog" Maddy. Yet on this day, that was the name that came to her lips. She didn't call him Michael, or Mike, or Mr. Maddy. Just Mad Dog.

Hearing her say it—particularly in such an offhand way, like someone might talk about Harry or Fred or John—struck me as funny. But having to deal with an overpopulation of white-tailed deer like Murrysville's can forge some strange partnerships, I suppose, like this one between a public servant and a deer hunter. "I've lived here twenty-five or twenty-six years and I've never seen so many deer," Clarke says. "You drive along and they're just standing there."

There's a price to be paid for having all of those lovely deer, and Murrysville has been paying it. Two of the four drivers in the Clarke household, for example, have hit deer with their vehicles. Michele's husband has contracted Lyme disease, an illness that's carried by ticks that in turn spread by parasitically attaching themselves to deer.

Bob Schlemmer, chairman of Governor Ed Rendell's Advisory Council on Hunting, Fishing, and Conservation and a Murrysville resident, can also attest to just how many deer live in Murrysville, albeit using another kind of proof. Schlemmer, who has seen as many as eighteen deer in his yard at one time, needs only to walk up his driveway to see evidence of the overpopulation of deer.

"I've got a browse line on my house," Schlemmer says. "I've got ivy growing up the walls, but there are no leaves from about five feet down to the ground. And I haven't had to trim my shrubs in ten years. The deer take care of that for me. We've got a lot of deer in Murrysville."

Murrysville councilman Ted Mallick once hit two deer at the same time with his vehicle as he was coming home from work. He regularly sees other deer—basking in the glow of the security light he installed, thinking it might scare them away—doing their part to keep his lawn clean. "They like apples, I can tell you that. When they fall from my tree, I don't need to worry about them being on the ground too long," Mallick said.

If some Murrysville residents like living among all those whitetails, there are others who do not. In his role as councilman, Mallick hears from the people who have just had enough of deer. It's anger induced by frustration that boils over the phone lines from their homes to his ears. "When someone gets $5,000 worth of shrubbery eaten up in their yard, we start to get calls," Mallick said. "I don't blame the deer. I wish we could move them up to Cameron County or somewhere, but we can't. And unfortunately, it's to the point that, for many people, deer are becoming little more than pests."

Murrysville is not unique in this way. Deer are highly adaptable creatures that thrive in what might be called "edge" habitats. Given the right mix of woodlots, crop fields, and housing developments where they can find little places to hide and lots of food—from wild sources like acorns and beechnuts to delicacies like ornamental shrubbery and apple trees—their numbers can explode. Unfortunately, these conditions are often found most perfectly in Pennsylvania's urban and suburban neighborhoods.

"I've got places all over my district just like that, where deer come out at daylight and dusk to eat and move around. Then during the day they retreat into their little refuges and hide out until it's time to feed again," said Rod Ansell, a wildlife conservation officer in the heavily populated southern third of Westmoreland County. "They get pretty thick in those places, believe me."

Controlling deer in such places is far from easy. In fact, it might be the trickiest aspect of deer management facing the Pennsylvania Game Commission this century—and not because of the deer so much as because of the people sharing space with them. "Controlling deer in the big woods is tough," says George Kelly, the retired deer biologist. "It's doubly tough if you can't get guys in there to hunt. But I think it can be done. When it comes to deer in urban and suburban areas, though, it's really about education. Everybody wants their acre in the country, but they're not really aware of the processes that are going on out there. We're really going to have to work hard in the future, as biologists and managers, we're really going to have to work hard to control deer," Kelly said.

Game Commission biologists are working to develop an urban/suburban deer management strategy that specifically targets deer living around people. It may well have to be a plan with many subsections, says Marrett Grund, another former deer biologist with the Game Commission who has worked on controlling deer in urban settings in places like Minneapolis.

Much of suburban southwestern Pennsylvania is a mosaic of woodlots and roads and communities, and may require one type of plan. Philadelphia and the rest of southeastern Pennsylvania, which has more people per square mile than any other part of the state and is in some ways more like New Jersey than the rest of Pennsylvania, might require another. The private gated communities in the Poconos region in the northeastern part of the state might require a third, Grund said. Clearly, though, some master plan must be created, and soon.

"It's going to be a big challenge, but we have to do it," says Cal DuBrock, direc-tor of the Game Commission's Bureau of Wildlife Management. "We absolutely have to tackle it." The question is how. The saying "the devil is in the details" cer-tainly applies to urban deer management.

In rural Pennsylvania, where those people who haven't shot a deer themselves probably have a family member or neighbor or friend who has, the answer to control-ling deer is hunting. Things aren't so simple in the suburbs, however, where hunting is as foreign to some people as it is familiar to others; and this presents new chal-lenges. With no final version of an urban deer management plan in place as of late 2005, communities around the state are dealing with deer in different ways.

Murrysville has been dealing with deer for a quarter of a century. That's where Clarke and Maddy come in. Clarke has been tasked with getting a grip on the number of deer in Murrysville and she's using Maddy and other hunters that he recruits into a regimented, organized unit to do it. The municipality allows hunting—albeit strictly controlled hunting done under rigorous guidelines—in five of its publicly owned parks. It had been doing that for twenty-five years as of the 2004–5 hunting seasons.

"We don't have a lot of wolves around here to eat deer. Or cougars," Clarke said matter-of-factly. "What we do have is an overabundance of deer. And we have hunters who are willing to eat them. So we're using hunters to balance nature."

The Murrysville parks open to hunting are the Kellman Nature Reserve (56 acres), Townsend Park (160 acres), Duff Park (148 acres), Murrysville Community Park (300 acres), and an undeveloped parcel known as the Pleasant Valley tract (262 acres). In the Kellman Nature Reserve and Townsend and Murrysville parks, hunting is limited to those using archery equipment. In the other two parks, hunters can use bows or muzzle-loading rifles.

What no hunter can do is just show up, walk into the woods, and proclaim him-self ready to start shooting. Maddy requires that hunters pass a proficiency test first. Archers have to be able to put three arrows—one shot from a distance of fifteen yards and two from twenty yards—into the vital organs on a three-dimensional deer target. Muzzleloader hunters have to be able to group three shots on a paper target from fifty yards away. Hunters who pass these tests are then assigned to a specific park. They have to report when they are going to be hunting, mark their arrows with their name and address, and report any lost arrows. Hunters also have to report all deer killed and any that might have been wounded and lost. They also get a dashboard plate for their vehicle and a back tag for their coat so that police know who's parked in the parks before daylight and who's dragging a deer out after the sun is up.

At Kellman Nature Reserve, which is surrounded by housing developments, hunters are also required to bag and carry out the insides of their deer—commonly called "gut piles" when encountered in the woods—when they leave. "A lot of people who live in the houses that surround the reserve on three sides let their dogs out the back door. We don't want those dogs to drag the gut piles home," Clarke says. "We don't want to offend anyone while we're doing this."

All hunters in these parks must hunt from elevated tree stands so that any missed shots bury themselves harmlessly in the ground. They also have to have at least one antlerless deer permit to get into the program. They don't always have to shoot a doe first; on the opening day of a particular season, they can shoot a buck if one walks by. After the first day, though, they are encouraged, if not required, to shoot antlerless deer, since controlling doe numbers is the key to controlling a deer population.

Hunters have to be diligent about hunting, too. If they're assigned a park and then don't at least try to remove a deer or two, they might get bumped in favor of someone on a waiting list with more time or desire. "Our object is to shoot deer," Maddy says. "If you don't kill a deer, but you're in there trying, that's going to be a plus for you. But we're not going to put someone in there if they're never going to hunt. We need people in there to cull the deer."

Clarke agrees, noting that Murrysville does not allow deer hunting in its parks just to provide recreation for those who aren't interested in her softball and tai chi programs. Murrysville allows deer hunting because it has a deer problem and hunters who are able and willing to take a few animals offer a solution. If hunters enjoy hunting and can use the deer they kill, that's fine. But do the job they must.

"The municipality's main goal is not just to offer recreational opportunities. It's about culling the deer population first," Clarke says. "But if we have hunters, citizens, who are willing to shoot the deer, we're solving the problem without costing any of the other citizens any money. We're a state with a lot of hunters. Why not use the resources that are out there?"

Clarke's goal, her hope for Murrysville's hunting program, is that there will come a day when hunters kill more deer in the parks than motorists do on the roads. In that regard, work remains to be done. Drivers kill more than two hundred deer annually on the community's roads. Hunters killed seventy-five in 2003–4, and that was the most they'd ever gotten up to that time. The number of hunter-killed deer has increased every year the community has allowed hunting, however. And Murrysville has been liberalizing its program over the past few years in an attempt to help hunters do even better. It's opened new parks and allowed new firearms, like those muzzleloaders.

Murrysville also closes several of its parks for a few days each fall to make it easier for hunters to get deer. News releases sent to local newspapers announce the closings and explain, for the sake of nonhunters, why they are necessary. Interference from hikers, dog walkers, and other park users unfamiliar with hunting made that a necessity. "When you're getting around suburban areas, people have no clue about hunting," Clarke says. "We put signs up telling people there's going to be hunting and when. But it's hard to kill deer if you put a hunter in a stand and he waits all morning and just as the deer are coming in someone walks through talking or laughing or letting their dogs run without a leash. Or you get guys like the one who went in with a flashing red lamp on his head because he didn't think the hunters would be able to tell him from a deer."

Maddy has harvested as many as fifteen deer in a single season, hunting in suburban settings, seven of those deer coming from Murrysville alone. None went to waste, either. What Maddy and his family couldn't use was given to food banks or neighbors or friends.

Not every hunter in Murrysville is taking as many deer as Maddy. The number of deer being removed overall, though, is high enough that residents are noticing. Some of the homeowners who were initially wary of allowing hunting in their community at all have actually asked to have hunters on their own property so they can get some relief.

"I think we're a prime example of partnering, the very kind of thing they're talking about all around the state," Schlemmer says of Murrysville's hunting program. "Our citizens who are hunters and nonhunters are working together to control the deer harvest. I think every year it gets more successful."

Mallick would like to give the program a real boost and allow hunters to shoot deer with modern rifles. There need not be any safety concerns, he said, so long as rifle hunters are required to pass a proficiency test comparable to the ones the archers and muzzleloaders take now.

The difficulty, he said, lies not in finding qualified shooters. There are plenty of those out there. Murrysville, in fact, is home to a competitive rifle club, many of whose members are also deer hunters. The problem lies in educating the public about how safe rifle hunting is and how important it is that the municipality use it.

"Remember, we're not doing this for the sake of sport," Mallick said "We're trying to thin the herd. And if you're trying to thin the herd, you should try to be as efficient as possible. We need to be looking for ways to let hunters take more deer. In the hands of a competent marksman, a high-powered rifle can be a very surgical tool."

Not everyone in Murrysville loves the idea of shooting deer, though. Joan Kerns, like Mallick a member of Murrysville's council, has lived in the community for more than twenty-eight years. Her home is less than a mile from Townsend Park—one of the places where hunters are trying to thin deer numbers—yet she feeds the deer in her yard.

Kerns has seen as many as eighteen or nineteen deer on her lawn at a time, and she admits that the animals can be hard on landscaping. She considers herself a supporter of the hunting program, too, albeit a reluctant one. There have never been any hunting-related accidents in Murrysville's parks, but she worries that there may be, someday. More than that, though, she worries that all the emphasis on killing deer, rather than teaching people to live with them, devalues the animals.

What's particularly disturbing is that some of the people who don't like deer and want them removed are like the same ones who move to Murrysville and then complain when they occasionally get a whiff of manure from the farm next to their new housing development, she says. "Farmers can't put diapers on their cows. Likewise, deer are a fact of life and you learn to deal with them. We move into the deer's neighborhood and then we plant salads. People move here because there's lot of green and trees, then they don't like it when the deer eat their plants. If you plant something you want to save, screen it off. This is their natural habitat. You can't move into an area like this and then say you don't want deer in your yard."

"I think it's necessary to have some type of control," Kerns says. "But I don't think you have to eradicate deer to live with them."

No one believes Murrysville's deer hunting program will eliminate deer-vehicle collisions altogether, or make ornamental shrubs perfectly safe, or keep anyone from getting Lyme disease. If hunters can at least get to the point where they're taking a hundred or more deer every year, though, they may bring all of those things down to more acceptable levels.

Maddy, for one, thinks they can do it. "The people who live here, they know there's a problem. If they see one or two deer in their yards, that's one thing. If they see twenty to forty, there's something wrong," Maddy says. "But they're seeing that I can put two or three hunters on their property and we can remove deer. We can do that. All in all, I think we're on to a solution that can help out. From what I can see, it's going to take quite a few years to get things in check, but we're helping to alleviate the problem a little bit."

The people of Fox Chapel Borough in Allegheny County think they're on the right track, too, using a combination of hunting and sharpshooting to control deer. They did not arrive at answers quickly, however.

Fox Chapel encompasses eight and a half square miles, nearly half of which are wooded. It is home to about five thousand people in single-family homes, three churches, one private school, and community parks; there are no businesses within the borough. Less than ten miles from downtown Pittsburgh, it is an affluent community, where an undeveloped one-acre lot will sell for a quarter-million dollars or more.

Fox Chapel is also an oasis for wildlife, more than partly by design. According to the borough's website, "Our wooded hills and uncrowded residential developments are a valuable regional asset. Fox Chapel is a classic example of what can be done to preserve openness and spaciousness in the very midst of urbanization and industrialization. This example must not be destroyed."

Indeed, the borough has an environmental advisory council that makes sure residents toe the line. For example, residents have to secure a permit before removing any tree—healthy or diseased—that has a diameter of six inches or more at a height of fifty-four inches above the ground. Deer can't read, so you have to forgive them if they didn't get the word about not altering the landscape. As early as the 1970s, white-tailed deer were the biggest violators of the borough's environmental policies, as they destroyed the very habitat they themselves relied on. In those early days of deer overabundance, it fell to residents themselves to figure out ways to keep the deer at bay.

"We tried all the rumors," says Jerry Cecil, a member of the borough's Environmental Advisory Committee. "We tried soap. We tried dried blood. We finally bought a system that made noise and blinked lights. All that did was keep us up at night. After thirty days, the deer would come in and pay no attention to it, so the lights and sirens were going off all night."

By the 1990s the problem had become what Cecil refers to as "an ecological disaster." The most visible evidence of that was the community's landmark Trillium Trail. A footpath famous for being blanketed by those wildflowers, it had become more like the No-Trillium Trail, as the oversized deer herd ate every flower as soon as it poked through the ground.

The shrubbery around individual homes also commonly fell victim to hungry deer. "We were constantly getting calls from people wanting to report vandalism,"

David Laux, the borough's police chief, told me one afternoon while sitting in his office. "We'd go out to the house and they'd be pointing to their shrubs, which would be decimated. But it wasn't vandalism. We'd point to the ground and say, 'See these. These are hoof prints from deer.' They'd just be everywhere."

Deer-vehicle collisions were so common that they became a running joke around town, Laux said. If you believed the stories police heard, you'd think that no one ever crashed after having a bit too much to drink, or taking a corner too fast, or sliding on snow or ice. Anytime a motorist had to call police because he'd driven off the road or hit a pole or wound up in a ditch, his defense was the same—he'd swerved to miss a deer.

To get an idea just what they were dealing with, borough officials commissioned an infrared aerial survey in 1992 to see how many deer lived within the borough. Considered experimental technology at the time, it revealed 270 deer, says Ernie Wiggers, a wildlife biologist with the Nemours Wildlife Foundation in Buford, South Carolina, who did the count as part of his thesis. Subsequent estimates put the population three times that high, or about 103 deer per square mile.

Officials surveyed residents to see what they wanted done. Eighty-seven percent wanted the deer controlled in some way. Deer contraception was considered first but was ruled out as too ineffective and too experimental. Trapping and transferring the deer was likewise eliminated as an option because no one else wanted the deer. Ultimately, borough officials settled on a plan that relies on hunting—something that 78 percent of residents surveyed called for—and help from the police thrown in to control deer.

As in Murrysville, Fox Chapel's hunt is strictly controlled. The borough used a zoning map to plot sites where hunters might potentially be set up. If a resident would like a hunter, police visit the site. If hunting is viable there—as is the case with nearly 70 sites right now—a hunter will be assigned. If a site is too small, or surrounded by residents opposed to the hunt, it isn't hunted. Police personally introduce hunters to the property owner whose land they will be hunting, and if that owner isn't comfortable with that particular hunter, the hunter will be moved to another site. Hunters can hunt only the site assigned them.

Hunters have to show they can meet a minimum proficiency level with their equipment to get into the program. That's not been a problem. Seventy hunters had qualified when Laux and I spoke, with seven hundred more on a waiting list to test for the program. Hunters have to produce, too, if they want to stay in the program. They fill out log sheets throughout the hunting season that list the dates

Fox Chapel police chief David Laux uses hunters to control deer in that Allegheny County community. Hunters have not solved all of Fox Chapel's deer problems, but they have improved the situation.

they hunted, their times in and out, and the number of deer they saw on a particular day, sorted by age and sex. They are encouraged to shoot as many deer as they can, with the borough agreeing to pay the cost of butchering any they can't use. The meat is then given to the Greater Pittsburgh Community Food Bank.

"Early on there was a perception we had a huge buck population and that they all had huge racks," Laux said. "But my hunters are not buck hunting, they are meat hunting. If everybody brings in at least two, that makes my job easier. I have guys, though, that bring in ten. They're just machines."

Police sharpshooters also kill some deer. Laux says police work in teams—one officer acts as the driver and spotter, parking a police car on the edge of the road near a bait site. He also shines a flashlight at the bait. If he sees deer and no cars, a second officer in the back seat will shoot. All shooting takes place between 11:00 P.M. and 1:00 A.M., generally from December through January, so as to be as inconspicuous as possible. The high-powered rifles police use are equipped with suppressors to keep noise down, as well.

In the program's early years, hunters accounted for most of the deer removed from the borough. In 2002, for example, 255 deer were killed there. Hunters took all but thirty of them. "I'm very proud and very happy with the way the program is working," Laux said. By fall 2005, things had changed. Deer were learning which areas to avoid in order to stay clear of hunters. That fall, hunters killed 110 deer; Laux shot 137 at night. Still, he said, the borough needs its hunters. "I tell my hunters, 'You are my program.' It's not me, it's not the borough, it's the hunters. They can make me or break me, and they've been making me."

"You want archery hunters who are willing to come in and help solve a problem. And there are a lot of archers willing to do that if given the chance," said Dan Sitler, then a wildlife conservation officer in Allegheny County for the Game Commission. "That program Fox Chapel has is a model program. You could take it anywhere in the United States and be successful."

The early opposition to hunting—which took the form of picketers walking through the borough's parks, where there were no plans to hunt anyway, ironically, banging on pots and spreading human urine—has not gone away entirely. It's much less conspicuous, however, with police recording only about five complaints a year, usually from the same small group of people.

"The joke in town is that the people are separated between the deer huggers and the tree huggers, with the deer huggers being the people who don't want to do anything with them and the tree huggers being the people who want them all gone," Cecil said. Ask Laux about it and he says—without a smile—that he knows of two antihunters who would like to see him "stuck with an arrow." Another woman, a vehement antihunter who refuses to let hunters on her property even though deer cost her thousands of dollars each year by eating the shrubbery she pays to have planted, is equally adamant in her opposition to the program. She believes Laux and others want to eradicate all of the deer in Fox Chapel. That's not so, he says. "I tell her that's not my job. We don't want to eradicate them. We just want to control them. But she just wants to see them. Well, she's still seeing them and we're still killing them."

Police do try to keep the program out of sight and out of mind, though. Sitting in Laux's office talking about deer, I feel a bit like a crime reporter chasing down a story of murder and intrigue. Laux is friendly and courteous, but his bosses—council members and the people of Fox Chapel they represent—want their hunt kept very quiet, and Laux is careful to keep things that way.

He shows me paperwork detailing deer-vehicle collisions and deer harvests, but some areas of the paper are blacked out. The zoning map on the wall behind him is off limits, too. Greg and I can look at it, but I can't take notes on what I see and Greg can't take pictures of it, or even of the chief with the map in the background. He doesn't want anyone to look at a picture and know where hunters will be posted.

When I ask for the names of homeowners who either do or do not allow hunting, or of hunters who participate in the program, Laux politely declines to give that information out, either. I start to feel like I need a white-tailed version of Deep Throat passing me names after moving a potted plant to and from his window.

"It's not to be evasive, it's not to be clandestine in any way. That's just what our people want," Laux says. "Our residents don't want their names in the paper." What they do want is the deer herd trimmed, and that work will go on. "We're going to continue to do it," Laux says. "We can't stop. If we stop hunting today, we'll be back up to seven hundred deer in two years. I can't foresee any reason why we would stop it."

Hunting is not the answer—or at least not the main answer—for everyone with a deer problem, however. Upper St. Clair is a case in point. Another

Allegheny County community that's spent years wrestling with the issue of how to control its deer population, it relies on hunting in part. Township officials have looked at other options, too, ultimately ruling out one but opting for another.

Beginning in 2000, the township paid to have a series of aerial counts done of the community's deer herd. The counts—which some believe can give a snapshot of deer numbers but not count animals exactly—determined that there were 250 deer in Upper St. Clair in March 2000. A count done one year later found 125 deer, while a count in March 2002 found 190. Those were all prebirthing-season estimates, meaning that the summertime population of deer, counting fawns, might actually have been three to five hundred deer in those years.

To get a handle on those deer, the township, back in 1998, created an ad hoc citizens' committee to look for solutions. It came up with a broad range of recommendations, advising the township to develop a public education campaign on living with deer. Library materials were made available, the township's website has a deer management section and links to other sites offering advice on deterring deer from entering gardens, ranking ornamental plants by how much deer prefer them as food, and deer repellants, among other things.

At the committee's urging, the township also installed Strieter-Lites—reflectors designed to deter deer from crossing roadways—in a largely unsuccessful attempt to limit deer-vehicle collisions—and retained a biologist as a consultant. The committee also recommended that the township institute an archery hunting program in Boyce-Mayview Park, its main natural oasis. That program is run by Whitetail Management Associates South, a group of organized hunters.

I talked once with Rich Wingertsahn, who was then executive director of this group. Wingertsahn, who has since moved away from Pennsylvania, was confident that hunters could lower the deer population in Upper St. Clair, if given the chance.

While they have succeeded to some degree, the number of deer killed by vehicles in Upper St. Clair continues to outpace the number taken by hunters. In 1999, the first year there was hunting in Boyce Mayview Park, hunters killed 67 deer in Upper St. Clair, while motorists killed 130. In 2000 the numbers were 53 deer for hunters and 127 for motorists; in 2001, 47 and 130; in 2002, 44 and 136; and in 2003, 34 and 157.

"The problem is the places we're not hunting," Wingertsahn told me one evening over the phone, saying that most of the community's deer problems were centered in areas where no hunting is allowed. "It's a question of access and time. This overpopulation problem didn't crop up in a day. It's going to take years to fix this. But I think we're making a world of difference in the areas where we are hunting."

Township officials were not convinced—or at least not interested in expanding hunting opportunities—and looked at other options. In 2001 they asked the Pennsylvania Game Commission to make Upper St. Clair the first site in the history of the state to host a deer birth control demonstration program. They even brought Dr. Jay Kirkpatrick, director of science and conservation biology at ZooMontana and a leading expert in the use of PZP, or Porcine Zona Pellucida, the contraceptive of choice, to come and talk about the drug and how it works.

Kirkpatrick has worked with PZP for more than twenty years on a variety of animal species. He explained that the drug is a natural protein that allows boar sperm to attach to a sow's ova. When injected into females of other mammal species, PZP elicits antibodies against that animal's sperm-recognition protein, thereby stopping sperm from entering the egg. The Food and Drug Administration still considers the drug experimental because no one knows, for example, how humans who eat a PZP-darted deer might be affected. That's why it can't be used on deer within thirty days of any hunting season.

Testing of PZP—which has just one manufacturer nationwide, that being Kirkpatrick's employer—on free-ranging deer has occurred, however, most famously on Fire Island. A barrier measuring thirty-two miles by half a mile wide near the south shore of Long Island, New York, Fire Island has more than two hundred deer per square mile. It's also home to about four thousand homeowners, most of them affluent New Yorkers who maintain second homes there. The National Park Service also owns one-third of the island.

Working with the U.S. Humane Society, a national organization that describes lethal deer-control methods like hunting as "irresponsible," Kirkpatrick said he's achieved some success, even though only one of five separate deer populations on the island being treated with PZP had decreased by the time we talked. When I spoke to him a short while after his visit to Upper St. Clair, he told me what he told those residents then—that PZP can work in certain circumstances.

It can take a while for contraception to work, however. Deer have to be darted twice in the first year and once a year thereafter, and it's not easy to dart deer or to get every deer every time out. Using a "saturation bombing" theory, when you dart as many deer as possible in a three-week period, some deer might be darted twice and others not at all. Statistically, after five years the people doing the darting can be reasonably sure they've gotten every deer.

Even then, however, the program has to run continually, because PZP, as it exists today, is not a permanent contraceptive. "Is this easy? No, it is not easy. But is it doable? Yes, it is doable," Kirkpatrick said.

Representatives of the Humane Society, which advocates PZP research and use, visited Upper St. Clair one year or so after Kirkpatrick did to do their own analysis of whether the community might be a good PZP test site. They concluded it was not, and recommended against undertaking such a program.

Contraception programs have not worked quite as well as originally hoped, says Allen Rutberg, a professor at Tufts University and a member of the Humane Society's technical staff. Vaccinations administered with a dart are not as effective as those administered by hand, with the success rate peaking at 75 to 85 percent. Deer must be somewhat tame, too, or those armed with the dart guns have a hard time getting within twenty-five to thirty yards—the effective range of the guns—of enough deer.

Running a PZP program can be costly, as well. While Kirkpatrick said no Fire Island program ever cost more than $10,000 annually, Rutberg says the cost can climb to $25,000 or $50,000 annually, depending on the number of deer in an area and how much research, if any, accompanies the darting effort. "I think we came into [PZP testing] in 1993 with very high expectations, and it's proven to be more difficult than we expected. The big quest now is for a longer-acting vaccine," Rutberg says.

But the debate about PZP—as Upper St. Clair proved—is rarely about the drug itself, or its effectiveness, or the science of contraception on wild animals. Rather, it's more often a referendum on hunting, or at least on hunting in urban and suburban areas.

The Game Commission made its stance clear in responding to Upper St. Clair's request to become a PZP test site. The Commission didn't deny the request outright, but it attached so many conditions that there was no realistic way to actually make a test program a reality.

At the same time, Vern Ross, then executive director of the Game Commission, made clear the Commission's stand on hunting versus birth control. Ross said the agency could not support a PZP program because it is funded by hunter dollars. More important, he said, was that "we do not view contraception using PZP as a viable alternative for practical application in managing urban and suburban deer populations." Hunting, he said, is the way to control deer.

"This PZP technology is 100 percent effective in zoos, yes," added Jerry Feaser, press secretary for the Game Commission. "But that's an entirely different situation in Upper St. Clair and any other suburban setting in Pennsylvania. We believe

Some suburban communities have considered using birth control to manage deer populations, but this has never been tried in Pennsylvania nor proved successful elsewhere in the country.

there are other more effective methods, primarily hunting, that should be used first. The hurdle we must overcome in some of these kinds of places is the fear that archery hunting is not safe. Archery is in fact very safe, but we have to make more people aware of that."

Predictably, antihunters in Upper St. Clair took the opposite viewpoint. Resident Nancy Bellamy, who said she knew of an anonymous donor who was willing to fund the township's PZP program, said the fact the Game Commission is supported by people who buy hunting licenses "does not exactly make them an ally in the effort to control deer with more humane methods."

What's more, she is offended by statements, made by people like Wingertsahn, that hunters are performing a service to the community at large by hunting deer in the township. "They do it for free because they want the entertainment," Bellamy said. "And they would not do it if they weren't allowed to keep the meat. They pretend it's a public service, but it's not. Suburban deer management is not about furnishing more hunting grounds. It's about perceived problems with deer. I see no reason why we shouldn't apply to the Food and Drug Administration and see if we can get a permit for a PZP program."

A few others just don't think hunting works as an urban deer management tool. Township commissioner Gloria Smith admits that hunters do kill some animals, yes. But the number of deer they take has never reached the targets set, she says, and deer only reproduce faster when pressured. Township residents are affected by the hunt, too, as many avoid Boyce Mayview Park during hunting season out of fear for their safety. "This hunt is not very good as a deer reduction program," says Smith, who was the only commissioner I spoke to who felt that way. "That's why I'm definitely convinced a PZP program is the answer to urban and suburban deer management."

Connie Karis, another Upper St. Clair resident, said that while she's no fan of hunting, there are places where it may be appropriate. But urban and suburban settings like Upper St. Clair are not among them, in her view. "I believe, from the people I talk to, and maybe I just talk to the nicer people, that they want us to just keep going, keep going, in terms of pressing this issue. Now that we have PZP, hunting is absolute lunacy," Karis said. "But we're not threatening hunting in Pennsylvania. Pennsylvania has a lot of woods and they can go do their thing. This is just an effort to stop hunting in Upper St. Clair. We just don't want hunting near our schools, near our churches, in our neighborhoods, near our roads."

Such talk—from hunters and antihunters alike—is maddening, says Jay Kirkpatrick of ZooMontana. A native Pennsylvanian who is also a lifelong hunter, Kirkpatrick says PZP is not a replacement for hunting everywhere. Those who debate whether it is, or should be, are missing the point and wasting time. "This is not about hunting or antihunting. That's a red herring," Kirkpatrick says. "As a goal, we should be trying to turn that temperature down. It's a very emotional thing because it's perhaps symbolic. But it just isn't that big a deal because we're not invading the huntable population.

"The technology is not good enough to apply to Pennsylvania's deer, or even to Elk County's deer. It can work where lethal control is no longer legal, wise, safe, or publicly acceptable. This technology has limitations. But it is another tool you can use to do something where deer populations aren't huntable. This deer thing has

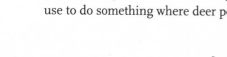

completely disgusted me. Just disgusted me," says Kirkpatrick. "I'm tired of the politics surrounding deer and with dealing with the animal rights activists, the bow hunters, and the politicians up for re-election."

Rutberg agrees. "We're not looking to vaccinate all of the deer in Pennsylvania. In rural areas, where densities are lower, that's just not practical," he says. "We see this principally as a humane tool for resolving conflicts between humans and animals. It's not a large-scale deer management tool. And I'm not sure that it ever will be." Still, he believes the day is coming—perhaps within ten years—when PZP and similar drugs will be available on store shelves for purchase and use by local police departments and animal control officers. On that day, PZP will be convenient and effective enough to be a reasonable alternative for dealing with urban deer populations.

And it will be preferable to hunting, Rutberg says. "Of course we'd prefer that [to hunting] for a couple of reasons," he says. "One is the humane issues of archery hunting. Second, bows and arrows probably don't work. They can kill some deer, but they can't effectively control the population."

Controlling the population, of course, remains Upper St. Clair's goal. And if hunting can't do the job completely, and PZP is impractical for this particular community or unsatisfactory to the Game Commission, something else needs to be done, says Frank Marsh, president of the township commissioners. That's why, with all other options exhausted, the township sought and received permission from the Game Commission to hire professional sharpshooters to cull deer.

Every major airport in the state and many of the smaller ones have permits to hire such people. They allow shooters to kill as many deer as they can, provided they report all kills to the Game Commission and attempt to see that all of the venison is given to food banks or needy families. It's not easy to get a permit, though. Communities have to do things like hire a wildlife consultant, study their deer situation for a number of years, develop a deer management plan, and show that hunting would be impracticable as a first option, at least in some parts of the community, says John Smith, law enforcement supervisor in the Game Commission's southwest region office. "It's not something, even across the state as a whole, that there's a clamor for," he says.

Indeed, on a governmental level, Upper St. Clair was just the third entity—behind Fox Chapel and Philadelphia's Fairmount Park Commission—to receive such a permit. It was a last, but a necessary, resort, according to Marsh. "We've got people who are seeing their shrubs being eaten, their gardens ravaged. I've got a deer path right through my own front yard. And when they eat the wrong thing and throw up in your yard, it's not a pleasant thing," Marsh said. "And we know we've got people hitting deer with their cars, so it's a safety issue. We're going to continue this program until we've accomplished our objective."

If Philadelphia's experience is any indication, however, the road to using sharp-shooters to kill deer in Upper St. Clair will not be without bumps. Philadelphia's Fairmount Park has two main sections, Pennypack Park and Wissahickon Valley Park. All together, the park is described by the city as "the largest municipally operated, landscaped park system in the United States." It's also a haven for white-tailed deer.

As far back as 1994, a study by Shissler's Natural Resources Consultants found deer to be "problematic and a threat to the long term health" of the park. Shissler's report said the Wissahickon, located in the northwestern corner of the park, should have about thirty deer; it had about 250 when an aerial survey using infrared technology was done. The area of the park known as Pennypack was even worse; it should have had about thirty deer, too, but had ten times that many.

Those numbers surprised no one, says Barry Bessler, chief of staff for Philadelphia's Fairmount Park Commission. Certainly, the number of deer-vehicle collisions seen in the city would suggest there are plenty of deer hiding somewhere. "The way we control the deer population now in Philadelphia is with vehicles," Bessler told me. "More than two hundred deer are killed on the highways in Philadelphia each year. If we kill that many on the roads, how many are in the woods?"

Those collisions have caused several human fatalities in recent years, including one in which a police officer died when he hit a deer while responding to an emergency. Having too many deer has hurt the park itself, too, Bessler says. There's been ample evidence for quite some time that having the large number of deer has led to some severe overbrowsing, affecting the composition of the park's ecosystem. "We're seeing mounting evidence that controlling the deer is necessary to save the future of the valley," Bessler says. "This is something we have to do. I have no choice."

"This" means the park's use of professionals to cull deer. Bessler was a little leery of talking about the program when I first called. Animal activists have called him a murderer and worse in public meetings, on TV, and at protests. "I've got children and they watch TV and they go to school and they hear these things," Bessler said. "It's kind of scary for them."

He ultimately agreed to talk, though, because he remains convinced that something needs to be done to keep Fairmount Park's deer under control. What he told me was that the park commission first turned to Tony DeNicola, owner of White Buffalo, Inc., a Connecticut-based nonprofit organization, to get a handle on their deer. A biologist with a doctorate in wildlife ecology from Purdue University, DeNicola and his employees travel the country shooting deer in municipal parks, on the grounds of large corporate headquarters, and at similar places. If all goes well, they remove deer quickly and quietly, then leave without most people knowing they were even there.

They shoot rifles loaded with .223-caliber ammunition of DeNicola's own design, formed on a lathe and shot into the skulls of road-killed deer to see how they fragment. He wants bullets that expand quickly upon impact, rather than pass through a deer and keep traveling, possibly toward houses or office buildings. He's got a suppressor on these rifles, too, for silence. Such "military countersniper technology," as he calls it, is required when you're shooting at night, often close to homes where people are sleeping. "We're shooting more rounds in a suburban context than the entire law enforcement community in one year," DeNicola said.

DeNicola hunts from tree stands at least thirty feet in the air, placed over bait he's maintained for two to three weeks before moving in. At other times he'll hunt those bait sites from his truck, shooting out the window. He's also shot from trees in household lawns and from the decks of houses.

Speed is of the essence. In twenty to twenty-five seconds, he has to be able to kill eight to ten deer from his truck or four to six from his tree stand. "It has to be quick. You generate confusion once you start shooting. If given time, that confusion will turn to fear, and you don't want that," DeNicola said. "It's critical to be extremely cautious in your shooting so as to manipulate deer behavior."

When the deer are down and dead, DeNicola and his crew put bags over the animals' heads—the only part of the animal they aim for—to keep any blood from escaping onto the forest floor. They next not only remove the deer—which are dressed off site—but also collect all of the leaves that may have some blood splatter on them. They're bagged and hauled away, too. Nothing is left behind to show that a deer was even there, let alone died on the spot.

Generally, DeNicola needs sites with deer densities of at least a hundred deer per square mile to be able to do his job. That's usually not a problem. Most of his clients have 150 to 250 deer per square mile by the time he's called in. One suburban Texas community that hired him had more than four hundred whitetails per square mile.

When deer numbers get that high, he and his crews can be very effective. In one ten-day period in Iowa City, he shot 360 deer, 103 of them in one day. He could have gotten more, too, but the butcher who was processing the deer for a local food bank couldn't take them—he ran out of room in his meat locker.

None of the deer DeNicola shoots go to waste; like those from Iowa City, all go to a food bank or other outlet serving the hungry. Food banks really benefit when he's in town, too. DeNicola says he's successful only in those cases where he's able to shoot very high numbers of deer. His goal is usually to reduce a deer population by 75 to 95 percent.

"If I get two or three out of twenty, what good does that do? I've got to get eighteen or nineteen out of twenty," DeNicola says. "You have to realize it's a lot like slaughtering cattle in a pen. It's not fun. It's not intended to be fun. It's highly stressful.

"Sometimes I'll meet a hunter who wants to know if he can tag along for a night. I always tell them this is not hunting. This is not what they know. We're using every illegal technique. And those techniques are illegal because they're not sporting, because our objective is not to be sporting. Our objective is to be as efficient as possible. I look at it as if we're almost a suburban farmer," says DeNicola. "Deer are a crop out there, and we're harvesting them to supply food banks."

Even DeNicola admits that there may be limits to where he can do his work, though. In the Texas community that had more than four hundred deer per square mile, for example, whitetails were living in housing tracts, visible at all hours of the day. There was no cover but there were no predators either, so cover wasn't really a necessity. Removing deer in such places is especially challenging, and not just because of the proximity of people and houses to the shooting.

"There were does bedded in the lawn, at noon, with people walking their dogs and with fawns, less than a week old, right there, too. That's unreal. How do you remove deer there?" DeNicola asked. "Can you do it discreetly? When the doe is content to bed down in Mrs. Jones's back yard, can you shoot it in front of Mrs. Jones? I don't know."

There are those who wish DeNicola and others like him didn't shoot deer anywhere. In Philadelphia, ironically, that opposition is shared by hunters and antihunters alike, though their reasons are decidedly different.

Greg and I met with a pair of vocal antihunters—albeit after a few stops and starts—one afternoon in Fairmount Park. Shug Davis and Bridgette Irons are cofounders of Friends of the Fairmount Park Animals, an animal activist organization. We finally got together on our third attempt at a meeting.

Davis had canceled our first meeting when she found out I was a hunter. She worried that I wanted to make fun of her and her organization. When I convinced her that this wasn't my intention, we arranged a second get-together. That time, though, Greg and I got lost on the way to the park, and by the time we arrived Davis and Irons had to leave. The Republican National Convention was in town, and they had protests lined up every night, this particular one centering on the use of horses to pull carriages on city streets.

We finally hooked up on our third try and were standing on a walking trail talking about deer. I knew that Davis and Irons has been urging the park commission to do a PZP test in Fairmount—even though Rutberg had told them it wasn't a very good site for the technology, as the deer in the park "are kind of wary" and able to move around freely.

I had a hard time asking questions about that or anything else, though. Both women were so passionate about deer that it was hard to get a word in. Clearly, they see no need for controlling deer. The wealthy homeowners who live adjacent to the park are the ones who need controlled, they said. "This is not about deer," Davis said, her face turning red as she gestured animatedly with her arms. "This is about rich people not liking deer eating their flowers. They don't want them eating their gardens. The deer are scapegoats."

Irons—who said she attends most of the park commission's public meetings carrying a sign that says "Secrets and Lies" that she holds up whenever officials "hide" the truth about deer—was less emotional, or at least a few decibels quieter. She was no less convinced that everyone should just leave the park's deer alone, however.

I pointed to a rhododendron bush near where we were standing, or what had once been a bush. Now it looked more like a tree, with every single green leaf from eyebrow level down to the ground gone. I asked if perhaps there wasn't a need to trim the deer herd that's causing that kind of overbrowsing. But Irons didn't see anything wrong with the bush or the deer's impact on the park. "They haven't destroyed anything," she said of the deer's impact on park plants. "They've sort of reshaped them, that's all. Leave them alone. Laissez-faire."

They hinted that they were less inclined to leave DeNicola alone. In his first year of trying to remove deer from Fairmount Park—starting two or three months behind schedule because of the timing of the city's getting its permit from the Game Commission—he got forty-three deer on forty-four shots in two nights.

The following year someone sprinkled all of his bait sites with bleach. Others ran through the park at night, when he was to be shooting, to disrupt his efforts. He had equipment stolen or damaged as well. When I asked about this, Davis and

Bridgette Irons, one of the co-founders of the Friends of the Fairmount Park Animals, does not like the idea of killing deer in Philadelphia using hunters or sharpshooters.

Irons would only admit to "serendipitous acts of civil disobedience." They did say, though, that the kind of killing DeNicola does is too random and all encompassing.

"It's not a cull. A cull is selective. They're not being selective," Davis said. "They're just coming in and mowing them down, male, female, fawns, everything."

Hunters don't want sharpshooters culling deer in Fairmount Park either, but only because they would prefer they be given the chance to do the job. "This put the fear of God into us because we realized that hunters have to do a better job, and that means killing more does to knock deer populations down," says Dave Laden, a Philadelphia hunter and president of the Pennsylvania State Fish and Game Protective Association, the state's oldest sportsmen's group.

Hunters can control deer in places like Fairmount Park, but only if they are given the chance, Laden asserts. There are areas of private property around the park that allow hunting. Such spots are intentionally hard to find. Property owners who don't want to be hassled by antihunting activists or neighbors are often reluctant to publicize the fact that they allow hunting. Likewise, hunters who find one of these "honey holes" are loath to brag about it and invite competition.

The only thing that makes those places different from Fairmount Park is that the people who live there have seen that hunting can help them and have chosen to accept that help, Laden says. "There's a cultural access problem. It's not physical, it's cultural. We really need to educate people about the need to open their properties. When you're dealing with people who are several generations removed from hunting, it's all about education."

Even the Game Commission—which granted the Fairmount Park Commission a permanent deer-culling permit only after years of wrangling and political pressure—long wanted the park's deer controlled by hunters. The Commission even went so far as to do its own examination of the park at one point, measuring the length and width of the Wissahickon and Pennypack valleys to see where hunting could be carried out around safety zones. It identified hundreds of sites where hunters—strictly archers, as Philadelphia does not allow rifles within city limits—could set up to shoot deer.

"We've said from the beginning we want to see them maximizing opportunities for licensed sportsmen to be a part of the overall strategy for managing deer in Fairmount Park," says Mike Schmit, deputy executive director of the Pennsylvania Game Commission. "The problem with hunting in any metropolitan area is that, when you get to the point of suggesting hunting as the solution to a wildlife management problem, you find out very quickly that many, many people are uncomfortable. They're not necessarily what we think of as an antihunter, but they're uncomfortable with hunting because they don't understand hunting. Is it humane? Is it efficient? Well, yes it is, but they don't know that and we need to explain that," Schmit says. "People need to be educated."

The Fairmount Park Commission wants no part of archery hunting, though, for three reasons, Bessler says. One, he says, it's never been proved that archers can consistently shoot enough deer to control a population. Two, hunting hasn't been allowed in the park for 135 years, and park commission members are reluctant to break that precedent. Third, and perhaps most important, allowing a hunt would cause "a huge public relations problem for us," Bessler says. "The last thing I need is a wounded animal with an arrow sticking out of its neck wandering fifty yards beyond our border and onto somebody's lawn or onto a playground.

"And nothing about this, from our perspective, is intended to be sport," he adds. "It's intended to be an animal reduction effort to help lower their impact on the forest. And nothing else. We can't have the slightest perception that this is anything about sport."

"This is not a hunting issue," Shug Davis agreed. "It's that there's no place in an urban park for bullets or arrows or any type of shooting."

All of those complaints and concerns aside, Fairmount Park's deer herd is being thinned, at least to some degree. Though DeNicola no longer works there, the wildlife services division of the U.S. Department of Agriculture's Animal and Plant Health Inspection Service has been contracted to cull deer. APHIS shooters killed more than five hundred deer each year in 2002 and 2003 and more than 160 in 2004.

There are no plans to stop the shooting, Bessler says. To do so would be worse than folly; it would be irresponsible. "This is a very daunting challenge for us," he says. "This is something we have to do. We don't have any choice. If we are going to be stewards of the forest and preserve this park for future generations, we have to do it. God forbid the child of some politician be killed or maimed when they're in a vehicle that hits a deer. All eyes are going to be on us and people will be asking why we didn't do something."

That is really what urban deer management comes down to: managing deer to the satisfaction of the people who live with them. Biologists can tell the residents of a particular community how many deer they should have, based on habitat, says Ernie Wiggers of the Nemours Wildlife Foundation. They may choose to put up with more, though, or ask for even fewer. Either way, so long as their deer program gets them to their target figure, it's a success.

In Fox Chapel, for instance, the deer population heading into the fall hunting seasons usually hovers around four hundred animals, according to Laux, the borough's police chief. That's much higher than it should be, perhaps, but a more or less manageable number. Deer-vehicle collisions are a third of what they were in 1993, and most residents seem pleased with the way things are going. "Deer-human problems have, if not totally disappeared, at least dropped below that threshold where people start to get concerned and want to talk about doing something," Wiggers says.

"We still cannot raise flowers. We had to erect a fence around our Trillium Trail. And we can't raise tomatoes in our borough at all without fencing them pretty far out," adds Jerry Cecil of the borough's Environmental Advisory Committee. "But we think our program is very successful. We've decided that hunting is really the only practical way we can manage deer, though we continue to work at it. We look at it as a long-term project that requires patience and persistence. It's a constant battle."

"Ultimately, we just want deer and people to coexist," says Wiggers. "We want to see how many deer we can have and still have an acceptable level of interaction between deer and humans. That could be two hundred deer or it could be fifty deer. I think that's for the community to decide."

Whether hunting can be a part of managing deer in other urban and suburban areas is also a community decision. Kirkpatrick believes that hunters are foolish to even try and gain access to places like Fairmount Park. The irony is that such demands might do more to kill hunting—in urban parks and elsewhere across the state—than any pzp program ever could. "I find the idea of walking into a suburban or urban park and shooting a deer that's habituated to people to be the antithesis of sport hunting," Kirkpatrick says. "If I were an antihunter, I'd be promoting those hunts. I think they're folly. I think they are one of the things that will bring hunting to its knees."

DeNicola disagrees, at least to an extent. A bow hunter himself, he said hunters may be able to gain access to some urban areas if they and the game agencies that typically cater to them become more flexible. He also offered a warning, though. Many of the areas where he's called in to kill deer are communities that are "fed up and want to do something, and may be ready for killing deer, but aren't comfortable with the general public doing the killing." Hunters, he said, have to be able to recognize that and know when to back off. "Sometimes they're in there for selfish reasons, to kill a trophy buck, and the public knows it," DeNicola said of some urban hunters. "With that portrayal, we're going to kill ourselves in the long run."

Gary Alt thinks much the same thing. He wants to use hunting to control deer wherever possible. He doesn't want to promise anyone what he can't deliver, though. If hunting alone cannot solve a community's problem—because of access or safety zone issues or community opposition—hunters need to be up front about that. "If we promise to solve their problem when we can't, we'll be found out pretty quickly and that will do us no good. We need to help wherever we can and step back and let them find other solutions where we can't," Alt says.

It was with those kinds of thoughts in mind that Alt, Bryon Shissler, and representatives of sixty-five organizations cooperating under the umbrella of the Ecosystem Management Project conducted a series of seminars around the state in the fall of 2005. They met with hunters, municipal officials, conservationists, and others to discuss the challenges of managing deer that live in urban settings. A list of recommendations resulted. Some ask the Game Commission—which was invited to participate in the seminars, but declined—to change its regulations to allow hunters to be more effective in urban and suburban areas. Others would make it easier for communities to deal with deer when hunting can't work.

For instance, on the hunting front, the groups suggested that hunters be allowed to shoot multiple deer at a time, rather than making them shoot one and tag it before going on to the next one. They also called for the legalization of hunting over bait. Changes that would allow hunters to take deer from DMAP properties outside of the regular hunting seasons, let landowners give DMAP tags directly to hunters at no cost, and create a two-week, any-tackle October doe season on DMAP lands were also suggested. Hunters on DMAP lands in particular should also be able to use rifles in all seasons and transfer tags between members of their party, the groups said.

Most interesting, perhaps, the groups suggested that the Game Commission start a hunter certification program. Under it, hunters who had achieved some minimum level of training in everything from skill with a firearm to hunter etiquette would be registered. Municipalities that wanted to invite hunters in to kill deer could pull names from that registry and be confident they were getting the kind of sportsmen that fit their needs.

If hunting can't work, landowners, community associations, conservancies, and other similar entities should be allowed to apply directly to the Game Commission for deer control permits, the groups recommended. Now, if a landowner wants to have a sharpshooter kill deer on his property, he has to get his municipality to apply for a permit for him. The groups participating in the seminars also asked that the Game Commission allow communities to trap and euthanize excess deer in some areas, and to sell the venison that results from sharpshooting programs elsewhere. That revenue could help offset the cost of removing the deer, the Ecosystem Management Project groups said.

Game Commission officials were given a copy of all those recommendations, and others. Whether they will lead to action, no one could say. What is clear is that, in the meantime, deer in suburbia will continue to be a problem. If hunters want to be a part of solving it—if they want to pursue their sport in postage stamp-sized woodlots as well as unbroken tracts of forest—they'll have to make some adjustments. That means accepting responsibility for making hunting more palatable and understandable.

That was the message Cal DuBrock, director of the Game Commission's bureau of wildlife management, gave me one day while we were in the heart of Pennsylvania's "big woods" country, at the Moshannon State Forest maintenance building, where successful elk hunters have to check in with their bulls and cows. DuBrock works in the state capital of Harrisburg and hunts in heavily populated Lancaster County, so he knows about hunting near people. "At one of my stands, you get up there and you can see about a dozen houses, people going to work, school busses. If I had binoculars, I could probably watch morning TV," DuBrock said.

He also knows that if hunters are going to hunt in such places, around people who did not grow up in a hunting atmosphere or know little about the sport, they'll have to become educators. Connie Karis, for example, says she's had hunters come up to her front door dressed in their orange and camouflage hunting gear asking for permission to hunt her property. Hunters have to be smarter than that, DuBrock said.

"It takes a special kind of hunter to want to hunt under those conditions. We'll always have this kind of hunting," DuBrock told me, pointing to the big woods outside the Moshannon State Forest building, "and that's good. But we're going to have more of that kind of urban and suburban hunting, too, and that's something very different. If those people wear a shirt and tie to work, you have to wear a shirt and tie to meet them. That's what they're used to, and you have to meet those expectations. They don't have relationships. All they have is stories. Hunters have to work to build those relationships, and that takes patience," DuBrock said.

Dave Laden agrees that hunters must be politely aggressive in looking for new places to connect with deer. They need to spend less time looking for farms and other areas traditionally thought of as hunting country and start seeking permission to hunt the deer they drive past each day on their way out of town. "I just hope hunters pick up the ball and start asking people they maybe wouldn't think of asking for permission to hunt. You have to look around for a house with a big enough yard to get around the safety zone issue and then knock on some doors," says Laden. "Nobody likes it. It's sort of like cold calling. You might get ten rejections for every success. But once you're in, you're in like Flynn."

Indeed, when relationships do form, they can become strong. Laux talks of how many of the homeowners who are involved in Fox Chapel's hunting program now look forward to having hunters control deer in their community. "If hunting season starts and one of our homeowners doesn't see the hunter assigned to his property soon enough, I'll get a lot of people calling and saying they haven't seen 'their' hunter," he says. "Then I call the hunter and say, 'where are you, why aren't you hunting?' Our people want them in there. As for the hunters, hunting here is a different type of challenge. For a lot of our hunters, it's a cool thing to hunt in an urban environment. Hunting is challenging anyway, but this is a new type of challenge for them."

Michele Clarke, too, is ready to work with hunters, be they named Mad Dog or anything else. Murrysville needs help controlling its deer and if hunters are willing to provide it, everyone wins. "We're getting more hunters, we're getting hunters to know our parks better, we're getting hunters and nonhunters to know each other, and they're all working together," she says. "You need that community support. You need hunters who know the parks, who know their neighbors, and who the neighbors know.

"I think that in this state we've gone beyond the time when hunting exists only as recreation or sport."

6

BAMBI VERSUS THE BUICK

The first time I tried to set up a meeting with Lou Calandrella, he turned me away. It wasn't that he didn't want the company, he said. The rejection was for my benefit. The muggy heat of August—when corpses swell, flies buzz, and maggots crawl—is not the best time to play sidekick to a professional roadkill collector.

Those aren't quite the words Calandrella uses to describe what he does for a living. The business cards he hands out to potential customers when he's stopped in church or along the side of the highway use much more antiseptic language, referring to his business as "LC Deer Disposal." But make no mistake, dead white-tailed deer are Calandrella's stock in trade.

Calandrella is an independent businessman who contracts with the Pennsylvania Department of Transportation to collect dead deer along eleven hundred miles of state roads in Westmoreland County. If you suggest that his job is one that not too many other people would want, no matter the pay, Calandrella won't disagree. The looks he gets from fellow drivers, the curses they hurl his way, the gestures they make that might make your mother blush, all are testimony to what people think about even having to share the road with him.

"You have to have a sense of humor with this job," Calandrella said. "Sometimes when the weather's warm I'll pull up to a red light, and I'll have half a dozen deer in the back that are really stinky, but they'll be lying flat, so that you can't see them. I'll look out my window and—it only takes a few seconds—you'll see people start sniffing and making faces and rolling their windows up. They can't tell where it's coming from, but they know something smells really, really bad.

"And if they get stuck behind me on a two-lane road for a long time, look out. When they finally get a chance to pass me, they'll give me the finger or drive past holding their nose. I've had people actually turn around in their seats as they're driving, craning their necks around to look at me as they go by to see what I've got in here.

"One guy, who must have been following me for a while, even held up a sign as he went past that said, 'You stink!'

"I know people look at my truck with all of those smelly deer and figure there must be some kind of hillbilly in there, with no teeth and a hayseed hat on. They must figure I'm some kind of barbarian," Calandrella said, laughing. "I just smile and wave and let them go on by."

I caught up with Calandrella on an early October morning in the parking lot of a Gander Mountain store. He had told me during our phone conversation to look for him in a white Ford pickup truck, and his was the only F350 of that color in the lot when I arrived. But he wouldn't have been hard to spot even if there had been twenty such trucks there. Who else would have been parked at the edge of the lot, a half dozen or so once graceful but now stiff deer legs sticking above the sides of the truck bed?

It was 10:30 when we met, warm but not too hot—short-sleeve weather—and still it didn't take me long to appreciate Calandrella's warning about getting together in late summer. The pungent, almost palpable odor of decay hung around his truck like sticky goo. You couldn't smell it inside the truck, with the windows shut tight. Outside, though, each shift of the wind brought a sickly-sweet hint of what Calandrella must endure in summer. I was glad he had turned me away in August.

It had already been a busy day. Calandrella begins each morning by reviewing the list of dead deer faxed to him by the regional PennDOT office. It lists each deer, the road it's on, nearby landmarks he can use to locate it, and the agency that took the call. He takes a look at what he's got, plots out a route that will get him from deer to deer with the least amount of backtracking, then sets off.

Starting at about 8:00 that morning, Calandrella had picked up seven deer by the time we met. Over the next four hours we would collect ten more, and Calandrella would still have at least half a dozen to go when I left. One of our first stops together was along a stretch of two-lane road in farm country. I looked out the window at what was ideal deer habitat: small woodlots and fence lines separating rolling cornfields. It's just the kind of edge habitat deer love, and the hunter in me saw the possibilities. Before I could daydream too much, though, I spotted two legs

A buck that still has its antlers is a rare find for Lou Calandrella, since hunters often saw the antlers off road-killed deer.

sticking up in the air from the road's edge. It was Calandrella's deer, and we pulled over to get it.

It turned out to be a rare find: a buck, and the head and antlers—or in this case, antler, as it had a half-rack with three points on one side—were still attached. The collectors hadn't gotten to this one yet.

"Very seldom do I get a rack," Calandrella said when I told him I knew several people who carry a hacksaw in their vehicles at all times, just to be ready in case they see a dead buck still sporting antlers along the road. "A lot of times, guys have already got their racks cut off. Or the whole heads will be cut off.

"One time I went to pick up a deer, and as I was driving by two guys with a hacksaw were cutting like crazy to get the antlers off. I slowed down and waved as I drove looking for a place to turn around, and they started sawing faster. I didn't care," Calandrella said. "I have no use for the racks, and a lot of them are smashed and broken if I do find them, but some people really want them, I guess."

Calandrella loaded this buck the way he does so many other deer. He dragged it across the road to the vehicle, wrapped a cable around its neck, and winched it up across a piece of plywood and into the bed. Other than the little bit of blood that bubbled from its nose and the few drops of urine that ran from its bladder, the deer looked healthy enough to run off. But instead it was just a big-bodied deer gone to waste. The winch hummed, the cable drew the deer up, and it was over. Calandrella turned off the light atop his truck, logged the time and place he collected the deer, and moved on.

But not very far. Fewer than fifty yards down the road we spied another dead deer. It wasn't on Calandrella's list but it was on the state road, so he was allowed to pick it up, log it, and get paid for disposing of it. Unlike the big buck, this deer looked every bit the roadkill. "Oh, that's a nice one, huh," Calandrella said. I could tell the deer was a doe, but that was about it. Loading this deer required no winch. Calandrella tossed the front half of the animal into the truck, backed up fifty feet, and put the other half in. Gruesome as such a deer is, it's far from than the worst Calandrella has seen. His contract is written in such a way that he only needs to find a portion of a smashed deer to get paid for it, and sometimes he's lucky to get that.

"The very first day I went out on this job, I had a good location, with a good landmark, for a deer right in front of a golf course. I thought, 'Okay, here we go.' I went out and I drove by the golf course once and didn't see anything, turned around and came back, still nothing," Calandrella said. "I was on about my third pass when I saw this little patch of something in the middle of the road. I thought, man, that's so small, that can't be it, but it was. There was nothing left but a little patch of fur.

"It's like that a lot of times. I don't know where the meat goes, but it's gone. All you find is the fur. The rest is just ground into the road, I guess."

At other times he has to pick up the kind of carcasses that a wildlife conservation officer with his own share of experience in collecting road-killed deer referred to as a forty-footer. "I asked him what he meant, and he said, 'You know, a deer that's spread out over forty feet of road,'" Calandrella said. "I said, 'Oh yeah, I know what you mean.'"

Summer is the worst time for encountering gore. That's Calandrella's slowest season, but it's also the most challenging, weather-wise. He tries to get every deer he can within twenty-four hours of being notified, but even at that the sun and heat can do a number on them. And some don't necessarily get reported until they smell bad enough to catch someone's attention. "I might only get a hundred deer a month in June, July, and August, but they're a hundred stinky ones," Calandrella said. "If you can get through those months, you're all right, but man, they can be bad."

Calandrella recalled one particular situation when he had gone out to collect a deer that had been killed while trying to cross a road near a busy intersection. He's not sure how long it had been there, but it must have been at least a few days. The deer was obviously overripe. Calandrella pulled off the road and waited for the light to turn red. He then dashed across the road, grabbed the deer by a front leg, and started dragging it back to his truck. About halfway there he looked up to see the friend who was riding in his truck with him laughing hysterically.

"I looked back where he was pointing and realized I only had half a deer. It was so rotten that the whole front half had pulled off at the shoulder," Calandrella said. "There was an elderly couple sitting there at the light, right in front of me, watching and gagging inside their car. But what could I do? I threw the front half of the deer in the truck and got the second half right away, but when the light changed they tore off out of there pretty quick."

Calandrella's job is an odd one, to be sure. He's picked deer up from people's driveways and front yards. He's come across a teenager, slumped over the steering wheel of his father's mangled Audi, whom Calandrella feared was dead. The deer he had hit certainly was. Calandrella knocked on the window to see if the teen was okay, but the boy refused to lift his head. "He just kept saying, 'My dad's going to kill me' over and over," Calandrella said.

Calandrella has also found mirrors, plastic grillwork, and auto parts of all kinds embedded in deer that met their end courtesy of a vehicle. "You know what I find a lot that's really weird, though?" Calandrella asked, passing me one of several bottles of hand sanitizer he keeps at the ready at all times. I hadn't touched anything more than the side of the truck, but I washed up anyway, just to be safe. "Rubber gloves, like surgical gloves. I'm not sure if people use them to drag the deer off the road, or if they pet the deer as it's dying, I don't know. I just don't know. But when I get there, there they'll be, sitting right on top of the deer."

Calandrella's deer come in all shapes and sizes and from all kinds of terrain, though some areas are worse than others. Calandrella visits some stretches of road several times a week—regardless of whether he's taken a call about that area— because dead deer show up there so often that almost every trip turns out to be a moneymaker. There's even one two-mile stretch of Route 217 between Blairsville and Derry, marked by a mix of woodlots and fields around a quarry, that he calls "deer alley" because he gets seventy-five to a hundred deer there every year.

"Sometimes I'll come through and there will be four or five dead deer a day laying there. There will just be bodies lying everywhere," Calandrella said. "And while

I'm picking up the dead ones I'll see a bunch more in the fields feeding. The place must be loaded with deer."

Other roads can only be visited at particular times of day. Interstate 70, for example, is a very busy four-lane highway that runs from the Ohio line eastward. It's split by concrete Jersey barriers and gets its share of regular commuter traffic. Plenty of tractor-trailer trucks looking to link up with the Pennsylvania Turnpike and other main highways use it as well. Bordered by farms and fields, it also gets lots of deer. More than a few fail in their bid to cross it.

"I dread getting them on that road. There are certain roads you don't go on at rush hour and that's the worst of them," Calandrella said. "The deer just get absolutely crushed by those big trucks. And there's so much traffic and not a lot of room to get off the highway—it's dangerous. The truck drivers are pretty good. They'll move over. But the cars, sometimes I think they want to see how close they can get to hitting you. You've got to find a place to get off the road, wait for a break in the traffic, and run over and run back with the deer. Hopefully it's not a big one."

Certain times of year are worse than others, too. Early in May, pregnant deer, perhaps looking for a suitable birthing spot, will get hit, often hard enough that their fawns pop out of their bodies and lie dead alongside the road with their mothers. Later in the month and into June, more than a few of the fawns that survive coyotes, black bears, bobcats, and foxes fall prey to sedans, SUVs, and trucks. Calandrella and his fellow deer collectors refer to it as "fawn flipping" season.

"If mom gets hits, usually within a couple of days her babies will get hit, too," Calandrella said. "That's what mom taught them, where to cross. I remember one time I was picking up a dead doe and her two fawns were standing there, just off the road, looking at me. If someone had come around the corner it would have looked like I was waiting for them to get hit, but I waited until there was a break in the traffic and tried to shoo them away.

"They left, but the next day they got hit, too, and I had to pick them up from where they were laying on the side of the road in the grass, right where their mother got killed the day before."

October, November, and December are without doubt Calandrella's busiest months, though. The onset of the rut—the breeding season for whitetails—and the beginning of hunting season prompt deer to move more often during daylight hours, when traffic is generally heaviest. The result is that more end up dead along the road. Calandrella has collected as many as forty-four deer in a single day and averages four hundred to five hundred per month during that period. His all-time record, though, is the 620 deer he collected one November. "Pretty soon I'll go from daylight to dark and I still won't even be able to get them all," Calandrella said on that October morning we met.

He's not alone in this regard. Insurance companies find themselves extra busy in fall, too, courtesy of all those deer-vehicle accidents. I talked with Darrin Birtciel, then a rate analyst with Erie Insurance Group. A hunter as well as an insurance company employee, Birtciel compiled statistics on deer-vehicle collisions in Pennsylvania and when they're most likely to happen. What he found is that fall is prime accident time, with the first day of the firearms deer season particularly bad.

"We did a study of every day of the year in terms of the number of claims for each day. From January to August, we averaged a little less than twenty-five claims a day in Pennsylvania. From September through December, that jumps to about fifty or sixty claims a day," Birtciel said. "On the first day of [deer] season, though, that really spikes." On the first day of the 1998 firearms deer season, for example, Erie recorded more than 150 deer-vehicle collision claims. "That's more than six times what we had on any given day in the spring and summer," Birtciel said.

What's most disheartening, though, is the sheer volume of dead deer that can be found along Pennsylvania's roads at any one time. Each year tens of thousands of deer are killed on interstates, country roads, and everything in between. And the problem seems to be getting worse.

The Game Commission used to try to keep track of road-killed deer in the days when its officers, and not PennDOT, were primarily responsible for collecting road-kills. By the late 1990s it was estimating the number at more than forty thousand annually. No one really believed that, though. Even agency staff were convinced the number was too low, failing to account for deer that were killed but never reported or deer that were hit and died out of sight of the highway. But what everyone agreed on even then was that, with the deer population steadily growing and the number of vehicles on the road increasing at the same time, the number of deer-vehicle collisions was growing.

In Monroe County, for example, the Game Commission reported 306 deer killed on the highways in 1960. By 1994 the total was 1,125. In Erie County the kill jumped from 82 in 1960 to 1,233 in 1994. In Allegheny County—which surrounds the city of Pittsburgh—the roadkill tally climbed from 61 to 2,343 deer in the same time period. More recently, the Insurance Institute for Highway Safety has estimated that the number of deer-vehicle collisions in Pennsylvania increased by 54 percent between 1994 and 2000.

Today there's no agency that tries to tally all of the deer roadkills across the state, and so no one knows the exact number. Some have estimated it might be as high as a hundred thousand animals a year, though. A look at the figures that are collected—and a glimpse at the holes in the system—suggest there's reason to suspect that might be true.

PennDOT had fourteen contractors, including Calandrella, collecting deer in thirty-six counties in fiscal year 2002–3. Combined, they picked up about thirty-three thousand deer. The number of deer actually killed by vehicles in those counties, though, is undoubtedly higher. In Westmoreland County, Calandrella has been collecting about three thousand deer a year. That's significantly more than the twenty-five hundred his contract requires. Yet he only gets paid for—and so only collects—deer killed on certain designated state routes.

In Murrysville, a bedroom community on the western edge of Westmoreland County that's marked by housing developments, small farms, and several municipal parks, Calandrella can collect deer only from state Route 22. That wasn't addressing the problem, so Murrysville officials contracted with Steve Boeser to collect the dead deer Calandrella can't touch. Boeser picked up another 224 animals in fiscal 2002–3.

Add those deer to the ones Calandrella collected and you still probably don't have the total killed by vehicles in Murrysville, Boeser says. Oftentimes other people will beat him to a deer. He'll arrive at the location where a deer was to be, and all that remains is a bloody spot or a little bit of hair, or perhaps the deer's entrails. Anyone who wants to can take a road-killed deer home and keep the meat. They're supposed to get a free permit from the Game Commission first, but some don't. Either way, the deer disappears before it ever becomes an official statistic.

Boeser—like Calandrella and many others—also believes that many deer hit by vehicles live only long enough to get off the road, then die out of sight and out of mind.

"Their will to live is just outrageous. I've found some that had two broken hips that had still managed to get fifty yards off the road before I had to put them down. I've seen them run off with two broken front legs, running on their knees," Boeser said. "One time, when I was actually going out to collect a dead deer, I had an eight-point buck run right into the side of my truck, and I mean he hit it hard. But he bounced off and ran into a field. He was just standing there looking at me, so I stopped to see if he was okay or what he would do, and he just stood there for a few minutes before he walked into the woods like nothing happened. Their will to live is a lot stronger than people think it is," Boeser said.

The deer killed in the thirty-one counties without a PennDOT contractor don't show up on any list. Nor do the deer picked up or at least pulled off the road into a ditch or hidden behind a guardrail by wildlife conservation officers working for the Game Commission and regular PennDOT road crews.

Also unaccounted for are the deer killed along the roads operated by the Pennsylvania Turnpike Commission. The commission manages several toll roads around the state, including the 360-mile turnpike, which traverses the state from the New Jersey to the Ohio border. No statistics specific to deer-vehicle collisions are kept for the turnpike, but the commission does track what it terms "reportable" accidents, those where the vehicle can't be driven away. There are about twenty-two hundred such accidents on the turnpike each year.

"Right now, about 10 percent of those accidents involve a deer," said Commission spokesman Carl DeFebo. "And we've seen that number jump from the 1990s, when it was 5 or 6 percent, to now, where it's about 10 percent."

The problem of deer-vehicle collisions is bad enough that the commission maintains a pit in the median between the eastbound and westbound lanes of the Turnpike near the Allegheny Tunnel. There, at the top of a bank that's out of sight of motorists, commission employees dump deer carcasses they collect from alongside the highway.

Raymond F. Cecchetti, foreman of the Turnpike Commission's Harrison City maintenance facility, says it costs him about $60,000 a year to send crews out on overtime to collect the sixty or more deer that die every year on just the twenty-five-mile stretch of turnpike between the New Stanton interchange and the Oakmont plaza.

"That's a lot of deer for us to handle," Cecchetti said. "We shovel them up if they're real bad, or lime and bury them if they're in areas with no homes around. We had one go through a car's windshield once when it was hit, and it pierced the driver in the arm with its antler. We even had to cut one down that must have run across the turnpike and then got its hoof caught in the fence when it tried to get off the road. It hung from the fence by its hoof all night. Then, after my guys got it down, it tried to attack them before they could chase it into the woods. They're stupid animals. They're beautiful animals, but they just don't have any sense," Cecchetti said.

There's a cost to all of that carnage, aside from the $1.2 million PennDOT paid Calandrella and his fellow contractors to pick up dead deer. According to PennDOT figures, thirty people died as a result of hitting deer between 1998 and 2002, twelve of those fatalities occurring in 2002 alone. The number of deer-related human deaths may actually be greater, though, according to Gary Hoffman, PennDOT's deputy secretary for highway administration. Each year PennDOT sees a number of fatalities where a driver goes off the road for some unknown reason and ultimately hits a telephone pole, building, or some other object. Hoffman suspects that some of those people were swerving to avoid hitting a deer when they crashed.

Each of those fatalities—factoring in a lifetime's worth of lost wages, emergency expenses, and more—probably costs about $3 million, Hoffman says. The thirty-three "major" accidents—those that are very serious, but without a fatality involved—that PennDOT sees on average in a year's time probably cost another $1 million each, he adds.

What must be added to those figures are the costs associated with more minor deer-vehicle collisions. According to PennDOT, there were 2,532 reportable deer-vehicle accidents—defined as those where someone was injured or killed or their vehicle was rendered not drivable—in 2001. Even that figure, though, represents but a fraction of the deer-vehicle collisions that occur in a year's time. Erie Insurance is the second-largest auto insurer in Pennsylvania, providing comprehensive coverage for about 1,149,000 vehicles. In 2002, 16,700 drivers filed a claim for hitting a deer. That works out to be about fifteen accidents per thousand people insured, though the likelihood of being involved in a deer-vehicle collision varies, from about seven per thousand people in places like Allegheny County to seventy-six per thousand in Sullivan County. The average claim cost per accident is $1,930.

Add all of those things up, Hoffman says, and "I think it's fair to say the costs of deer-vehicle collisions in Pennsylvania are on the order of hundreds of millions of dollars. And that may be a conservative number."

The sight of dead deer lying along roadsides has an indirect cost, too. Kelly Ruddick, a public relations assistant at the Pocono Mountains Vacation Bureau at the time we spoke, said 8 million tourists visit the Poconos every year, spending more than $1 billion. Bureau staff draw some of those visitors to their corner of northeastern Pennsylvania by touting the area's natural attractions, including its wildlife. Having that wildlife lying smashed on the side of the road isn't the best advertisement.

"We have many tourists come up every month, and having them seeing dead animals all over the road, it's not very attractive. That does not display the image we want," Ruddick said. "When people from out of the area come here, and especially kids, they see that deer and think of Bambi. We don't want that."

There's a cost to the deer themselves, too, of course. When it becomes commonplace to see them dead along roads and highways—and even in the yards and driveways where they ran before falling—people can start to look at deer not as beautiful, graceful woodland creatures but as menaces. Deer become devalued.

Vince Smodic views whitetails as little more than "road hazards." He called me at work one day after reading a story I had written about the Game Commission's efforts to bring the deer population down. I found it interesting that, while Smodic was once a deer hunter who shot a few whitetails, though without any particular malice, he's now a nonhunter who hates deer and would like to see them all gone. Colliding with deer half a dozen times—totaling three vehicles in the process— has turned him against whitetails.

"The last time I hit one I was coming home at night on Route 51 and there were fifteen of them standing right in the middle of the road," Smodic said. "They totally destroyed my car. And none of them died. They just walked away, and I know I hit three of them."

"If I had been in a smaller car, I'd have been dead," added Smodic, who was driving a Pontiac Bonneville at the time of that collision. "To hit one at sixty-five miles per hour, it's amazing. It's traumatic. They definitely need to be trimmed way down as far as I'm concerned. I don't go out at night worried about getting a DUI or a speeding ticket. I worry about hitting a damn deer."

Smodic said he went to his insurance agent after his last accident to complain. He wanted to know what his insurance company was doing to lobby for a reduction in the size of Pennsylvania's deer herd. "He said they weren't doing anything, and that they'd just raise my rates if I kept hitting deer," an angry Smodic said.

That's hard for some hunters to believe. Whenever the subject of reducing the deer herd comes up, some are quick to point the finger at auto insurance companies and suggest that they are paying off biologists within the Game Commission or influencing deer management decisions in some other way.

John Dowbman laughed when I told him this. Dowbman is secretary and counsel for the Insurance Federation of Pennsylvania, a trade organization that represents about two hundred companies and half of all the insurance premiums in the state. It's his job to lobby legislators in Harrisburg, the state capital, on issues that affect his organization's members. He said he's never been asked to address the size of the deer herd or the deer herd's impact on insurance claims and rates.

"I don't think anybody here has ever even called the Game Commission," Dowbman said. "I can't imagine it's a significant part of any company's loss costs. That doesn't mean we wouldn't support reasonable controls on populations. Nor does it mean that some of our members haven't talked to someone on an individual basis. Anything they can do to reduce the carnage on the roads, we're in favor of that. But any cry to reduce the deer herd is certainly not a unilateral industry position."

Deer-vehicle collisions are nothing more than "part of the cost of our doing business," agreed Mark Dombrowski of Erie Insurance. "We provide educational materials to our policyholders to try to warn them of the dangers of hitting deer and to alert them to when they might be most likely to see deer on the roads. But that's all an attempt to try to reduce accidents and keep drivers safe. We don't get involved in saying how big or small the deer herd should be." A spokesman at the Pennsylvania Department of Insurance told me that this agency doesn't bother to track deer-vehicle collisions, either.

When it comes to deer-vehicle collisions, another issue is what to do with all of those dead deer. If the average deer weighs a hundred pounds, and Calandrella collects three thousand deer a year, that's three hundred thousand pounds of meat and bone that end up in a landfill or at a rendering plant. Contractors pay disposal fees up front but pass the costs on to PennDOT and ultimately to taxpayers. If a hundred thousand hundred-pound deer are killed on the roads statewide each year, that's a staggering 10 million pounds of deer.

There are ongoing discussions about how to save some money and make better use of all that organic material. The Lehigh County Office of Solid Waste is developing a program that would turn dead deer into compost. According to Cary Oshins, the county's composting specialist, the idea is to take dead deer—"the more mangled the better as far as composting"—and bury them in mounds six feet tall, twelve feet wide at the base, and two hundred feet long, spread over two to three acres. In time, the deer would become compost that could be used to grow plants along roadsides and elsewhere.

If Lehigh County moves forward with this plan, it will be the first such effort ever in Pennsylvania. The idea of composting dead animals has been around for a while, however. Farmers, particularly in the southern United States, started composting dead chickens in the early 1990s. By the close of the decade, as disposal costs kept increasing, the practice had spread to piglets, then full-sized pigs, and finally cattle. There's no reason deer can't be composted just as successfully. "The deer are already

Most deer killed along the highway end up in landfills. There is some talk of turning the deer into compost, but that's a long way off for most areas.

dead," says Oshins. "They're already a problem. And there is a certain 'yuck' factor associated with these deer. People just don't want to deal with them.

"The whole idea with this is to get the deer into piles as soon as possible, maybe even by the end of the day after they were hit. That would eliminate some of the disposal problem. As long as you don't disturb the mounds after the deer are in there, no odors escape. And six months later all that's left are the large bones."

The compost facility would have to charge some kind of fee—perhaps $4 or $5 per deer—to cover its costs, says Oshins. But it could conceivably handle four thousand each year. The deer compost should be totally safe, too, though it will all be tested just to make sure.

Deer are already being composted in a few states. The West Virginia Division of Highways began composting road-killed deer from seven counties in the eastern panhandle in 1997, after landfills started rejecting the animals and incinerating them proved too costly. It's composted thirty-five hundred deer a year ever since without any problems, says Bob Ampower, maintenance engineer for the eastern panhandle region of the West Virginia Department of Transportation.

The West Virginia Division of Highways has seven composting units, each with five bays that are twelve feet square and four feet tall. They're built on concrete pads and feature walls with vents. A layer of horse manure is spread across the bottom of the unit. Alternating layers of dead deer and manure are piled on top of that until the bay is full. A layer of sawdust may be spread across the top if any odors are detected, though that hasn't been a problem. Ampower says the state has three composting units located adjacent to residential housing developments and has yet to receive any complaints from neighbors.

The contents of each bay are stirred and re-covered on occasion, usually at least once within the first week after a bin is filled. After that, nature takes over. So long as temperatures within each bay stay at about 140 degrees—and they're monitored daily to make sure that's the case—bacteria develops that decomposes the animals. The result is that the deer "cook down" within five or six weeks, Ampower says. What's left is a fertilizer that gets used on highway medians and in wildflower plots in the Shenendoah Valley.

"The deer just disappear. Occasionally there will be a chunk of bone or some hair, but mostly it's just good black dirt," Ampower says. "And all of our tests show that the material we produce is environmentally safe. For growing grasses and flowers and what not, it makes a very good dirt. It really makes nice wildflowers."

It cost only about $15,000 to build five bins, and much of that money came in the form of grants from the Soil Conservation Society. It takes one person only fifteen to twenty minutes a day to check and stir them when necessary, too. That's a bargain, considering what the highway division was paying to collect and dispose of dead deer previously. "We think, in the long term, that the savings in disposal costs will more than make up for our composting costs," says Ampower. "And we're actually improving soil conditions at the same time. It's been very effective for us."

Of course, the best solution would be to eliminate deer-vehicle collisions altogether, but that seems unlikely, at least in Pennsylvania, where a recent report showed that the state is losing about three hundred acres of wildlife habitat every day to home and road development. The answer, then, is to find ways to minimize the number of collisions.

Researchers have been studying the issue, with a case in point being the study done in 2003 for the Insurance Institute for Highway Safety. That study—which blamed deer-vehicle collisions for $1.1 billion in economic damage and 150 deaths annually nationwide—looked at three strategies for reducing deer-vehicle collisions:

modifying driver behavior, modifying deer behavior, and reducing the number of deer. What it revealed is that there are no easy—or inexpensive—ways to cut back on the number of deer-related collisions. In fact, it's easier to say what doesn't work than what does.

Virtually no method of modifying driver behavior has ever proved successful, for example. About half of the fifty states—including Pennsylvania—try to alert drivers to the dangers of deer-vehicle collisions at peak times of year. In Pennsylvania, the Game Commission and Penn State University issue press releases each fall warning drivers to watch for deer. Various insurance companies and insurance associations do the same. None of those efforts has ever been evaluated, according to the Insurance Institute study. But there's little reason to think they do much, given that general education campaigns for other traffic safety topics, like seatbelt use, have never worked unless police backed them up by ticketing drivers who fail to participate.

Roadway lighting is costly, especially in relation to any small benefit it might provide, as is purchasing extra-wide rights-of-way to clear vegetation from the road. Lowering speed limits isn't the answer, as it rarely leads to a decrease in actual driving speeds, the study said.

Putting up deer crossing signs doesn't do much good, either. Passive signs— like the yellow diamond-shaped ones PennDOT uses, with the silhouette of a jumping buck—are routinely ignored by drivers, PennDOT officials admit, and lighted signs aren't much better. Even temporary signs aren't much good outside of the American West, where mule deer migrate according to specific routes at certain times of year.

The one type of sign that may hold some promise is an active sign that lights up only when a deer or some other animal is detected near the road. Pennsylvania, in cooperation with fifteen other states and the Federal Highway Administration, is experimenting with just such a system. A pilot project, kicked off in the spring of 2004, uses a beam-break system that operates much like a burglar alarm to check for deer crossing the highway. Installed on a half-mile of road at the Thompson Town interchange of Routes 322 and 22 in Juniata County, the system flashes a warning on a lighted deer sign whenever a deer or other large animal breaks the invisible beam.

"It's just an additional warning to motorists that, hey, there's a deer or bear or something in the road," said PennDOT's Steve Chizmar. "You know, with deer, not only is there the issue of potential loss of human lives, but there's also the enormous cleanup costs for the state every year. We're hoping this system might help with both problems."

A similar system used in Nugget Canyon, Wyoming, did cause drivers to slow down by about four miles per hour on average, but that research was too limited to suggest whether the active signs might be a real solution, according to the Insurance Institute study.

It's a little easier to control deer than it is to control people, but it's just as costly, if not more so, according to the study. Highway crossings—known as "critter crossings"—that allow deer and other animals to pass over or under a highway work to some extent in the West, but not so much with whitetails in the eastern United States. Repellents that can be sprayed on roadside vegetation and flagging and reflectors meant to scare deer away from highways are useless.

"Deer know what are and are not natural predators, and reflectors aren't a predator," says Paul Curtis, a Cornell University researcher and one of the authors of the Insurance Institute study. "We see that a lot in agricultural areas, where deer pretty soon learn what's a real danger and what isn't. They learn to ignore those things that are not a real danger to them."

For similar reasons, deer tend to ignore those deer whistles that drivers can put on their bumpers. If anything, they might exacerbate the problem of deer-vehicle collisions by giving drivers a false sense of security, Curtis says. The only effective way to keep deer away from roadways is to fence them out, the study concluded said.

"Every review of [deer-vehicle collision] control methods during the past 20 years has concluded that properly designed and maintained fencing, used together with appropriate underpasses, overpasses and one-way deer gates, is the most effective method for reducing deer-vehicle collisions" in the United States, the report reads.

There are two problems, however. First, fencing deer away from roads is very costly. To keep deer from leaping over it, fencing must be nearly eight feet tall. Fenced sections must also be 6.7 to 7.8 miles long or deer simply go around their ends and wind up on the road. Fences require regular maintenance, too; research has shown that deer regularly test fences for weak spots and can scoot under openings less than ten inches high. Add all these factors together and it costs about $42,000 to fence a one-mile section of roadway—and that's just one side of the road.

Improperly designed fencing, or fencing not meant to keep deer out, can't be substituted. Carl DeFebo, the Pennsylvania Turnpike Commission spokesman, recalled an evening when he and his children were returning home from a visit to a shopping mall. They traveled a three-mile stretch of the turnpike near Valley Forge, infamous for its outrageously large deer population. The turnpike there is lined with right-of-way fencing. It was never intended to keep deer off the roadway. A good thing, apparently, as it certainly wasn't doing the trick.

"We were coming through at about 6:30 P.M. and my children and I counted forty-two deer within that three-mile stretch. They were inside the fence, just grazing right off the edge of the highway," DeFebo said. "And that was just on the westbound side of the road. We didn't even have time to look on the eastbound side. It was crazy."

The second problem with fencing is that the areas most likely to have a high rate of deer-vehicle collisions are typically the routes least likely to be fenced, says Paul Curtis. That, together with cost, makes fencing impractical on a large scale. "Fencing is not realistic at all," Curtis says. "I think what we will tend to see might be fencing put up in some specific areas where the incidence of accidents is the highest and the conditions are just right. But national statistics show that high-speed, two-lane rural roads are where most of the deer-vehicle collisions occur, and I think we're unlikely to see any fencing in those places."

Given these obstacles, the only practical way to reduce deer-vehicle collisions on a large scale seems to be to reduce the size of the deer herd, the study concluded. "Although herd reduction can be controversial, common sense and expert opinion agree that substantial and continued herd reductions will reduce deer-vehicle collisions," according to the study. In most cases, that means turning to hunters to get the job done.

Curtis is doing research in New York on the use of contraceptives — or fertility controls, as they are known among academics — to control deer numbers. The day may come, he thinks, when a contraceptive vaccine will be found that can be used to control deer numbers in small, specific urban or suburban areas where hunting isn't permitted, whether because of regulation or social values. But that day has not yet arrived.

"In the last twenty years there have been literally millions of dollars spent on research into wildlife fertility controls, and we have seen no success in terms of coming up with something that's applicable on a large scale," Curtis says. "I think we're years away from that. If and when we do find such a vaccine, it's never going to be something that could be applied on a landscape scale. There is no oral vaccine, so every single deer in an area has to be injected by darting, which is expensive and time-consuming, and all of the vaccines are experimental, so you have to tag every deer to tell people you can't eat this animal. There are a number of logistical hurdles that we've never been able to overcome. Given all of that, I think hunting is still going to be the primary tool for managing deer in rural areas and across large landscapes in the Northeast," he concludes.

The Deer-Vehicle Crash Information Clearinghouse (DVCIC) at the University of Wisconsin–Madison—which maintains the website www.deercrash.com—seems to agree. The DVCIC examined numerous studies focusing on deer-vehicle collisions and concluded that more research of the cause-and-effect relationship between herd reductions and deer-vehicle collisions is needed. "There is a need for a focused study of the causal connections between hunting or herd reduction management policies and their potential impact on deer-vehicle collisions," reads the DVCIC report. "The small area studies described in this summary suggest promising results, but the deer-vehicle collision data from these studies (and future studies) should be more properly evaluated," it concludes.

But how much do deer herds need to be reduced before the number of deer-vehicle collisions is considered acceptable? How far from problem roads should herd reduction plans be carried out? Will hunters accept such plans? These questions need to be answered, though the answers aren't likely to come easily, according to Curtis. "As we see sprawl and development continue to encroach into the fringe areas separating urban and rural areas, and as we end up with higher deer densities in areas that have a growing human population but still some good deer habitat, much of which may be posted and off limits to hunting, the problem is going to get worse," he says. "But I think that as states start to look at the economic cost of these collisions, they start to consider lower deer densities. That will be controversial—deer management is controversial everywhere—but it's probably the only realistic solution. We certainly don't want to see deer devalued."

Smodic plans to push the issue if the Game Commission doesn't act first. He said that if he hits another deer, he will sue the Commission—which is responsible for managing Pennsylvania's whitetails—for allowing the herd to grow out of control. "I don't know if it will fly," he says, "but I'll definitely pursue it. The Game Commission is responsible for us having this many deer. They're promoting deer and making money off of them. They have to do something about it."

Gary Toward, a wildlife conservation officer for the Game Commission in northern Westmoreland County, would like to see the number of deer-vehicle collisions reduced, too, for reasons of his own. Toward and his deputies once collected 976 dead deer from along the roads in his district, which makes up just one-third of the county, in a year's time. With Calandrella on the job, they don't have to handle nearly as many dead deer anymore. Still, that's a terrible loss, no matter who is responsible for doing the dirty work. "Dead deer are not a manageable resource," Toward says. "It can be a drain on your resources. Something needs to be done."

Calandrella is quick to agree. At midday we stop at a Subway shop to grab lunch. He's careful to park at the far end of the lot, away from the doors of the restaurant and any other customers. He figures no one will walk past his truck and its load of mayhem so long as it's off to the side. This lunch is a rare treat, he tells me, as we wash our hands yet again, using another of those bottles of soap floating around the cab of his Ford. "Usually my wife packs me a lunch and I eat it wherever I can find a spot to park," Calandrella said. "I don't think people would really appreciate me pulling up to their door too often with all of these deer."

I have no doubt that Calandrella is right. While the search for a solution to the problem of deer-vehicle collisions goes on, though, men like Calandrella must go about the business of collecting dead deer from along our roadways. He told me the work has been an eye-opener for him. Forty-one years old when we met, he'd been hunting deer since he was fourteen and never realized how many deer were roaming Pennsylvania's woods. He's learned quickly, though.

After twice blowing the transmission on his first truck by trying to pull a trailer with as many as sixty-five dead deer in it, he realized this was a job requiring a bigger, hardier vehicle. "They've learned to adapt," Calandrella said of the state's deer. "They can live in the smallest patch of woods you can imagine. It doesn't take long to fill up the truck," he added as he loaded up the last deer collected during our time together. It was another badly mangled doe, lying atop a small bank that separated two roads, one of which fronted a woodlot while the other was marked by houses with small lawns set amid the trees. The deer left a trail of blood and gore as Calandrella dragged it to his truck through the gravel and grass.

"I know about every deer crossing in the county, I think. But it's such a waste. Such a waste. I'd rather people pick them up if they can use them, instead of them going to waste like this. But I guess if we're going to keep hitting them someone's got to pick them up. And I guess that's me. If people ask me how I do it, I tell them I can hold my breath a long time. And that I'm good under water, too. Then they either laugh or roll their window up and drive away."

7

HEROES OR GOATS?

We were in the car, my father and I, going I don't remember where. I do know that it was spring and that I had fishing on the brain. My dad did not. Fish that have yet to be fooled, whether by fly, lure, or worm, hold little appeal for him. He prefers his caught by someone else and delivered breaded and on a bun.

I asked why. He had tried fishing, he said, but just once. When he was a child, his parents took him and his four brothers to a state park for a picnic and some angling. Not only didn't they catch anything, it poured rain the entire time. The whole experience was so miserable for everyone involved that the fishing poles got put away in the walk-in attic.

It fell to my mother, Marg, to tell me later that my dad had actually tried fishing a second time. It occurred sometime after that family picnic, when he found himself roaming around the third-story attic with a bit too much time on his hands. Picking up one of the rods, he opened the window and let fly with a cast.

There was no lake in the yard below and no fish. But when my dad felt a tug, he set the hook and started reeling anyway. He had his younger brother, Norman, on the line, foul-hooked in the ear. Now, Norman was no Alaskan salmon surging through a swift current, but he put up a respectable fight by all accounts, with a few strong runs around the yard and a jump or two thrown in.

Unfortunately for my dad, Norman was as loud as he was frantic, which brought my grandmother on the run. Less than impressed with the scene she found—she didn't even weigh Norman to see if he might be some kind of front-lawn, line-class record—she put an immediate and painful end to my dad's fishing career.

My dad never hunted, either—much to Norman's relief, I'm sure. When I wanted to give it a try, it fell to my grandfather on my mother's side, Hugh Pry, to take me into the woods. We were an odd couple. I was fourteen, quiet but full of energy. He was seventy-two, a talker, and prone to charley horses and muscle cramps if he tried to walk too far. We were kindred spirits, though. When the hunting bug bit me, it sank its fangs deep, just as it had done to him sixty years or so earlier, and we became a team.

With Pap's skill and my enthusiasm, we roamed fields and forests. He knew where to go and what to do when we got there. I was the muscle—all 133 pounds of it—scrambling up banks, reaching back to bring the unloaded guns up next, then offering a hand to help pull Pap up behind me. It was wonderful. I couldn't get enough of the woods, and the end of our first hunting season came much too soon.

I spent every day of the following winter roaming Bushy Run Battlefield and the small farm that was next to our house with Patches, our beagle-spaniel mix, and my BB gun. Patches would follow her nose through the snow while I'd look for deer tracks, practice aiming at the squirrels that scampered up and through the trees, and shoot at stumps.

It was at about this time that my uncle Norman, long since unhooked and working for a nearby school district, married my love of reading and the outdoors. He brought me half a dozen copies of *Outdoor Life* that the librarian was going to throw away. I can't say I read them cover to cover, since most of them didn't have any covers left. But I read every page of each magazine. When I got some money I ordered a subscription, then got one to *Field and Stream,* too. A year or so later I subscribed to *Pennsylvania Game News* and *Pennsylvania Angler,* the magazines of the state's game and fish management agencies.

I knew almost to the day when my magazines would come. On those mornings I would wait for the sound of the mailman's Jeep, then hustle to the mailbox as soon as he pulled up. I read every article in every magazine, including the ones about fishing for flounder in places like Massachusetts, even though my dreams of outdoor adventure were always set in places like the wilds of Alaska rather than the outskirts of Boston.

Never once do I recall reading on any of those pages a single story suggesting that there might be such a thing as too many deer. In fact, quite the opposite was true. Writers pointed to the nation's huge populations of white-tailed deer—and elk, wild turkeys, pronghorn antelope, and other wildlife species across America—as evidence of a great conservation success story. It was hunters who paid to reintroduce those species across the nation, the writers said. It followed that the more deer we had, the greater was our triumph and the better our hunting.

Outdoor writers weren't the only ones spreading the "more is better" gospel. I still have in my wallet a card printed in 1994 by the National Shooting Sports Foundation. According to a blurb on its cover, it "contains current facts and statistics on the hunter's vital role in wildlife conservation—ready whenever needed to debate the merits of hunting." The card notes that hunters contribute billions of dollars to conservation every year. The proof that it's money well spent is easy to see, it suggests. In 1900, the card reads, there were fewer than five hundred thousand white-tailed deer in the entire nation. By 1990 there were more than 18 million.

Even the Game Commission, for the most part, saw the abundance of deer as a good thing. I can recall reading a story in the *Game News* prior to the start of deer season sometime in the early 1980s, when deer populations were booming. The article broke down the estimated number of deer by county. It was with excitement that I read that Greene County—where Pap, Uncle Larry, cousins Butch, Jeff, and Brett, and I all hunted—was among the top ten for number of deer per square mile.

I wasn't surprised, really. We hunted a mix of woods and fields near Jollytown every fall, and it was nothing to see thirty, forty, even fifty deer a day each and every time we were there. Just before dark, when we'd gather at the truck, we could routinely look forward to seeing a dozen or more deer—almost always all does—feeding in the pastures that separated the grassy spot where we parked from the woods.

I forget now just how many deer the Game Commission estimated there were in Greene County. What I am sure of is that there was no hint that there might be too many for the good of the deer themselves, or the habitat they lived in, or the hunters like us who pursued them.

That's not surprising, said Commission deer biologist Bret Wallingford. It's true, he said, that hunters and anglers deserve credit for being America's first conservationists. Without them, there would have been no one to raise the money or do the legwork required to reestablish populations of deer and other wildlife across the continent. That's especially true in Pennsylvania, where the Game Commission still today relies almost solely on hunting license revenues—it gets no state tax money—to pay for wildlife management for all citizens of the commonwealth.

There came a time, though, when the growth of the deer population began to outpace the forest's ability to sustain it. If hunters did not notice or understand what was happening, that wasn't really their fault, according to Wallingford. Deer hunters look for deer. They are not trained to go into the woods and see what plants and animals are missing because of overbrowsed conditions. Biologists and foresters and other scientists are, but they weren't reporting the facts, at least not long enough or loud enough or to enough people.

"The Game Commission staff has plenty of blame for the situation we're in. We failed at public education. We failed to bring hunters into the equation," Wallingford said. "Deer are beautiful creatures, they're fun to hunt, but there are limits to how many you can have. We never did a good enough job communicating that before."

Gary Alt, former head of the Commission's deer management section, and his team have tried to solve that problem in Pennsylvania. Lectures at hundreds of sites across the state, blow-by-blow accounts of deer research posted on the Game Commission's website, articles in popular magazines and newspapers, TV interviews—Alt and his deer team have used every tool in their toolbox to teach hunters and others about deer dynamics.

The hope is that hunters, given information about how forests work and the role they have to play in conserving those forests for deer and other wildlife, will lead the charge for healthier ecosystems. "The goal is to have that great majority of people out there, those who don't hunt, who say they have no interest in hunting, say they want to have hunters control the problem, to fix the forest. I want them to see hunters as performing a free ecological service," says Alt. "I think that's the greatest hope that I can offer, that hunting will become seen as not just something we do for recreation, but as something valued by society at large."

If you love to hunt, that sounds great. Going into the twenty-first century, however, two questions remain to be answered. Can hunters really handle the job of managing deer, and are they really willing to?

"Sport hunting and deer management were both built around a scarcity of deer and that made perfect sense when the goal was to help build up herds," says Jan Dizard, a professor of sociology and American studies at Amherst College and author of a book on Massachusetts deer hunters and deer hunting. "It was win-win. Hunters were seeing more deer and managers were succeeding in building up the deer herd."

It's less clear whether that marriage of hunters and deer managers will work in the twenty-first century, when the goal of deer managers is to lower deer numbers through doe hunting in many places. "That raises the question, can sport hunters, who proceed with the ethos of wanting to take buck deer so that you have plenty of does available to grow herds, do that? Does that sporting ethic still work? I argue it isn't working very well," says Dizard

There's no doubt sport hunting faces several challenges in the years ahead. For starters, the number of hunters is shrinking nationwide, and has been for at least two decades. Pennsylvania, for example, sold 744,856 general resident adult hunting licenses—available to those between the ages of seventeen and sixty-four—in 2003. That's down from 831,369 in 1996 and from a record 1,019,645 in 1992. Sales of senior licenses, available to those sixty-five and older, have declined, too, from 62,527 in 1995 to 46,121 in 2002.

"If you are a wildlife management agency, you should be very scared," says Jody Enck, a research associate in the College of Natural Resources at Cornell University who has studied the issue. "There are many challenges to getting enough hunters, and also to getting hunters who are able and willing to take enough deer to meet your goals. If you're looking for answers, I'm not sure we can see them right now."

Efforts to recruit new hunters are ongoing. A coalition of sportsmen led by Westmoreland County resident Ron Fretts, a member of the National Wild Turkey Federation's national board of directors, in late 2004 began an effort to change the law to allow children as young as six to go hunting (the minimum age now is twelve), provided they are accompanied by a mentor. Twenty-six states have no minimum hunting age. Pennsylvania has to join that list if it hopes to see any real increases in its hunter numbers, Fretts says.

"I know for a fact that if I go ask my eight-year-old grandson, 'Do you want to go hunting tomorrow?' the answer is yes. I absolutely know the answer is going to be yes," Fretts says. "If I go ask a twelve- or thirteen-year-old, 'Do you want to go hunting tomorrow?' I'm not sure what the answer is going to be." By that age, Fretts says, children are often too deeply involved in organized sports, school activities, computer games, and the like to have any time left for hunting. "We're waiting too late to mentor our children," he says. "We're waiting too late to introduce them to the fraternity of hunting."

The Game Commission, through special youth-only seasons, mentored hunts, and other activities, has already sparked an increase in the number of junior license buyers—those sixteen and younger—taking up hunting. Junior license sales increased for four straight years in Pennsylvania beginning in 2000–2001.

With the number of hunters having declined consistently over the past twenty years, there has been a renewed emphasis on attracting youngsters to the sport. The effort has seen some success, as Pennsylvania's junior hunter ranks increased between 2000 and 2004.

No other state in the country can say that. Still, the number of junior hunters was 168,546 in 1976. In 2002 it was 105,099.

"In 1976 I started teaching school up in Elk County. I was a shop teacher and I had all boys in my classes," recalled Surra, the state legislator. "We got the first day of deer season off to hunt. If I came back and went to school on the second day of buck season, I was the only one there. All the kids were out hunting. If you jump forward to 1990, my last year teaching, half of my students weren't even hunters at all. And it's worse today. If you look into the future, there's a light at the end of the tunnel, all right. But it's from a train and it's coming right at us."

If agencies like the Game Commission are going to turn this situation around, they're going to have to do it soon. Only 11 percent of the state's hunters are sixteen or younger, and even with those kids factored in the average hunter is nearly fifty years old. With research showing that most hunters start dropping out of the ranks in their mid-sixties, the day when Pennsylvania's baby boomers begin leaving the sport in big numbers is not far off.

Figuring out how to pay for wildlife management with the few remaining license buyers will be tough. Figuring out who will carry out that management on the ground could be tougher. "We've got some modeling that shows within twenty or thirty years we might only have five hundred thousand hunters in this state," says Marrett Grund, the former Commission biologist. "Pennsylvania has traditionally struggled to manage its deer population with a million or more hunters. Doing it with five hundred thousand would be very challenging, to say the least."

If hunter numbers do drop that low, it's going to be more critical than ever that those who remain be effective in killing deer. Certainly, Pennsylvania has a lot of excellent, woods-wise hunters, says Natural Resource Consultants' Bryon Shissler. But it has some who aren't so good. Up until now, those less skilled hunters have been able to get by because of the sheer number of deer and the high number of hunters pursuing them.

"The tradition in Pennsylvania has been that you have this high density of deer and a high density of hunters and you stir them all up and wait for a deer to run past you," says Shissler. That worked well enough for hunters to kill more than half a million deer in three of the four years between 2000 and 2004. That formula is not going to work—at least not to the degree needed—if there are going to be significantly fewer hunters and a smaller deer herd in the future.

"The future of deer management depends on skilled hunters," Shissler says. "We have to take the perception that hunting is a form of recreation that's based on luck and change it so people see it as a craft that's based on skill and woodsmanship."

Alt thinks it may fall to the Game Commission to help bring that change about. The Commission, perhaps working with sportsmen, may need to raise hunter skill levels by hosting hunting seminars, deer workshops, or similar educational events. "We've got what you might call alpha, beta, and omega hunters. Alpha hunters are the best we've got. They have the skill and the willingness and the desire to kill multiple deer year after year," Alt says.

"Next are what we call beta hunters. They are interested in shooting deer and have some skill and some time, and take deer occasionally, but not every time. At the bottom are our omega hunters. You could put them in a ten-by-ten-foot room with ten bullets and ten deer and nothing between them and the deer but a small tree. They would come out two hours later having shot all of their bullets without ever killing a deer.

"We've got to find ways to turn more of our omega hunters into beta hunters and more of our beta hunters into alpha hunters," Alt says.

"Our hunters may have to learn some new skills, or relearn some skills they haven't had to use in a while. But there's nothing wrong with that. That's a large part of the experience," agrees DuBrock, head of the Commission's Bureau of Wildlife Management. "That's why it's a hunting sport, not a shooting sport."

Some research has been done recently to see just how woods-wise hunters really are, or at least how willing they are to use their skills to get to where the deer are. In 2001 and 2002, crews from Penn State University conducted a study in the southern portion of Sproul State Forest. The Sproul contains about 280,000 acres in western Clinton and northern Centre Counties, in what's known as the Allegheny Plateau region. It is some of the most rugged and remote forest land in the state.

During the study, conducted on peak activity days during the two-week firearms deer season for two consecutive years, researchers surveyed fifteen hundred hunters. Some of them hunted from camps in the area, while others were commuters who drove in to hunt and then went home at night. All were asked things like how they hunted, where they hunted, and how far they traveled.

Researchers did more detailed follow-up surveys after each season with eight hundred hunters each year. They also flew over the study area during the hunting season, using geographic information systems technology to plot the sites where they saw hunters and document their density and distribution.

The study found that certain characteristics play a role in determining how and where hunters hunt. For example, the study showed that camp hunters start hunting later in the morning but stay in the woods later into the day. Hunters who drive in on a daily basis tend to arrive earlier, but they also leave earlier.

Most interesting, though, was what was revealed when researchers asked three hundred hunters each year to carry Global Positioning Sattelite (GPS) units while hunting. The units recorded a hunter's location every four minutes to determine where he hunted, when he moved, and how often he moved.

"We've been putting radio collars on deer for decades and tracking their movements, seeing what habitats they use, studying when they move and their density on various landscapes. We've never done that with hunters before," says Duane Diefenbach, assistant unit leader for the Pennsylvania Cooperative Fish and Wildlife Research Unit at Penn State University. "I think this is truly revolutionary in terms of how we manage deer."

What all of that surveying and flying and GPS tracking showed is that hunters don't walk as far as they think they do, and that very few venture too far from a road. "We've always done a lot of surveying work, asking hunters to mark on a map where they were hunting. And we always assumed that people knew where they were," says Gary San Julian, a professor of wildlife resources at Penn State. "What we found was that that's not always true."

"Most hunters thought that they had walked one and three-quarter miles from the road, when in reality they had walked a half mile or less," adds Craig Swope, now an employee of the USDA's Wildlife Services Division but at the time the graduate student heading up the hunter movement study. "There may have been a variety of reasons for that, like they were walking uphill or through the snow or just because they were walking slow. But the bottom line is, hunters are not always walking as far as they thought they had."

Some aren't walking at all. When one hunter turned in his GPS unit at the end of the day, it showed that he had traveled about fifty miles since morning. When asked, he admitted that he'd gotten cold early and spent the rest of the day driving around in his truck, looking for deer that way.

While that's an extreme exception, the fact remains that some areas of the Sproul—and as a result some of its deer—saw hardly any hunters. The flyovers showed that 45 percent of the study area saw just 25 percent of the hunters, even on the busiest days of the season. Overall, the average density was less than four hunters per square mile of forest. "If you assume that the deer density in that area is in the low twenties per square mile, then even if every hunter got a deer, you're only harvesting 20 percent of the population at most," Diefenbach says. "That brings up the question, what impact is recreational hunting having on deer populations in areas like the Sproul? Maybe not much."

Lest anyone think hunters are inept, Swope points out that similar research done on hikers and others has shown that they haven't always traveled as far as they think they have. And the interior forest areas avoided by most hunters are often especially rugged—swamps, rocky outcroppings, steep hillsides, thick blowdowns resulting from tornadoes. Black bears will often walk around such places, following the path of least resistance, so it should be no surprise that hunters do too, Swope said, especially if the average hunter is older now than ever before.

It's also important to remember that getting into an interior forest area is only half the battle, at most. Getting back out, dragging a deer behind, is the really hard part of the job. The mere prospect of that might be keeping otherwise woods-savvy hunters from getting too far from roads, Swope says, adding, "But in terms of deer management, if you are looking to remove deer from the landscape, that could be a problem. If people don't have to go in there to shoot a deer, they aren't going to do it. There are some. I'm not saying there aren't any. But they are few and far between."

Another problem is that, sometimes at least, hunters don't want to walk or run or even drive to where the deer are. They want the deer to come to them—not out of laziness, but out of tradition. Hunters with long ties to hunting camps that have been in their families for generations like to go to those places with friends and family for the camaraderie they experience.

Dr. Grace Wang, then an assistant professor of natural resource policy and administration at Penn State University, surveyed a thousand adult Pennsylvania hunters. Among the questions she asked was what they consider prime hunting habitat and how they determine where to hunt. Her research found that hunters pick their hunting spots based on two things: evidence of deer, including buck rubs, deer trails, droppings, and sightings of live deer, but also according to personal history. Hunters just like to hunt on property they own or on property that they and their fathers and grandfathers have been hunting year after year. The problem, the conundrum for deer managers, is that those hunters also want to see and shoot deer in those special places. And if the deer aren't there in the numbers they want or remember or expect, they get upset.

There is some anecdotal evidence of this in a few phone calls that came into the newspaper where I work, the *Tribune-Review,* in 2003. The paper publishes the names of hunters who bag a deer, along with details like the hunter's hometown, how big their deer was, and where they got it. When I took off the first four days of the 2003 firearms deer season to hunt, the job of fielding those calls fell to my nonhunting colleagues. Most of those who called in while I was gone had gotten a deer and were satisfied with their deer season. A few others, though, checked in to complain that they couldn't find any deer, at least not where they wanted them. Typical of those cases was the conversation our sports editor, Mike Dudurich, had with one unhappy hunter.

"This guy called just as mad as could be. He was going on and on about how there are no deer and the Game Commission was ruining the sport and what not. When I could get a word in I told him that I didn't know about any of that, but that we had received a lot of calls and e-mails and faxes from hunters reporting deer. I told him there must be deer somewhere," Dudurich said.

"He asked where they were coming from and I said all over. He asked, well, where specifically, so I started going through the list and naming some counties. Westmoreland, Fayette, Butler, Crawford, Somerset, and on and on. He was quiet for a second, and then he said, 'Well, those aren't the places I hunt. My cabin's in Jefferson County.' I thought to myself, I'm no hunter, but if it was me, I'd go where the deer are," Dudurich said. "That seems pretty obvious."

Obvious, yes. Easy to accept, no, according to Lowell Graybill, a past president of the Pennsylvania Federation of Sportsmen's Clubs. Hunting—as traditional an activity as there has ever been—is, for many people, equal parts shooting deer and bonding. For decades hunters have been able to experience both at the same time in the same place. Being told they perhaps now have to choose—hunt where there are lots of deer or go away to camp—is not something they want to do.

"It's true that a lot of us have motivation to continue hunting where our fathers and grandfathers did. That's true even though those are typically the areas where we should be easing up," Graybill said. "But the feeling you get when you go into a developed area to hunt, getting used to that takes a mind shift. You can hear all the traffic. You can hear dogs barking. You can see all that's going on in the neighborhood. You can shoot a deer to within fifty yards of someone's house. There are deer there, yes, but that's not all some guys are looking for."

"Why do people go hunting? They go hunting to get into the woods," Dizard adds. "They don't go hunting to lurk behind a jungle gym or the basketball hoop in the drive. Some hunters can make that change, but others can't. They feel more like exterminators than hunters."

Hunters can adapt to new conditions, however. Walter Poole is a sixty-four-year-old hunter from Westmoreland County, which has seen more and more of its farms and woodlots gobbled up by Wal-Marts, housing developments, and highways over the past twenty years. Poole still does most of his hunting close to home, but the spots he frequents now are not the same ones he has always hunted. The fields where he used to chase pheasants as a kid, for example, are now part of an airport.

But Poole has adjusted, changing his deer-hunting habits to concentrate a large portion of his time on hunting "red tag" farms. He likes to see and shoot deer, and these farms typically have lots of them. "I went to one and the farmer told me it was a bad year for deer. I asked why and he said because he hadn't seen more than fifty-seven deer in his fields at any one time. That was less than he was used to," Poole said.

What the farms generally don't have is an equal number of hunters. Poole—who shot seven deer, including six does, in Pennsylvania in 2003–4—can attest to this, based on what he sees in the field. That same fall, for example, hunters flocked to a new piece of public property near Conemaugh Dam in Indiana County. Relatively few chose to do what Poole did, which was to hunt the red tag farms around it.

"We came past one of those farms during the regular rifle season and there must have been fifty deer feeding in a meadow, and it was still legal shooting time. But there were no hunters," Poole said. "We went to another farm just like it to hunt does—the farmer won't let you hunt bucks, but he'll let you hunt does—and I got a deer in ten minutes. It took longer to walk from the farmhouse to my stand than it did to get a deer.

"You've just got to be willing to adapt," Poole said. "You know, I go to Erie to fish for steelhead a lot. If I see a guy catching fish and I'm not, I pay attention to what he's doing and how he's doing it. And I pay attention to what kind of water he's fishing because I go there to catch fish. If I fish one way today in one hole and I don't catch anything, and I go there again tomorrow and don't catch anything, I'd better be willing to go somewhere else. It's the same way with hunting. Guys have got to be willing to change. They've got to be willing to move. But some guys won't."

There's a perception, too, that hunters don't always have the option of going where the deer are. About 75 percent of Pennsylvania's open space is privately owned and, increasingly, it's posted against trespassing and/or public hunting. That trend is not likely to change any time soon, either, according to San Julian. A Penn State survey of landowners found that most believe posting will only increase in their lifetimes.

The salvation for hunters is that the same survey revealed that posted property is not always nonhuntable property. Landowners said they post for a variety of reasons, but not necessarily the ones some might suspect. The survey showed that landowners do not, by and large, post to keep all of the game to themselves or because they fear for their safety. Most just want to know who's going to be roaming their woods and fields. Provided with that information, three of every four landowners who post allow some hunting.

"Oftentimes, it was some form of poor behavior that led to the landowner posting his property," San Julian says. "It may have been littering, it may have been someone hunting within a safety zone, it may have been someone driving through a field. Landowners don't want that, obviously, and said posting gave them control over who was on their property."

Hunters can get around such worries, but they have to work a little harder and be a little more polite, says Jim Finley, another Penn State researcher who worked on the posting study. "You don't walk onto a farm and say, 'How's the hunting?' You say, 'That's a nice bunch of cows you've got there,' or 'That's a nice field of alfalfa.' You've got to build relationships," Finley says. "I've gained access to a lot of nice hunting properties by going and unloading a load of hay once in a while."

"I don't pay to hunt any of the places I go to," added Poole. "But I stop by all of those farms before Christmas with a fruit basket or something. It's just a little token of my appreciation, but I think it goes a long way."

The issues of decreasing hunter numbers and how to get them to the deer, however, might be the least troublesome aspect of deer management for the Game Commission. What do you do if hunters flat out refuse to shoot deer?

Biologists will tell you that the key to controlling the size of a herd lies in shooting enough female deer, or does. If deer are few and far between, as they were in the early twentieth century, you want to protect as many does as possible. When deer reach or exceed acceptable levels, though, the doe kill must of necessity climb to maintain healthy deer and healthy forests.

"If you try to save all of the does, you eventually end up with deer that are smaller, less healthy, and that produce one fawn or maybe none because they've destroyed their own habitat," says Kip Adams, the Quality Deer Management Association's biologist for Pennsylvania and several other northeastern states. "Then, no matter how few does you shoot, the population never really gets any bigger because the habitat is too far gone to support more deer. If you shoot a few more does, though, the overwintering population of deer might be smaller, but the deer are bigger, they're healthier, and the does that come out in the spring produce more fawns, usually twins and sometimes even triplets. It's what we call the reproductive maximum.

"There are more bucks because fawns are born in a fifty-fifty ratio of males to females. The age structure of the herd is better. And the number of deer peaks in time for the fall seasons, so hunters have just as many deer to shoot as ever. It's good for hunters as well as the deer herd."

The Game Commission has never done a very good job of selling that idea to the general hunting public, though, and it has caused problems for decades, says retired Commission deer biologist George Kelly.

"One of my uncle's favorite sayings was 'they play the way they're coached.' He was talking about seventh-grade basketball, but I think it applies to deer hunters, too. We've never really sold our sportsmen on the idea of balancing deer with their habitat. We have not helped them to make the connection between deer numbers, their habitat, and the quality of deer," Kelly says. "As an agency we sold them on the idea of protecting does very strongly, and when there were only about fifteen hundred deer in the state, that was a good idea. It's not such a good idea when there are a million five."

The Game Commission has made several attempts to teach hunters about the importance of shooting does. It has always been a struggle. In 1916, Kalbfus, the first director of the Game Commission, wrote, "In many sections of the state female deer have increased exceedingly, and because of the law giving them absolute protection, have apparently come to believe they belong in a privileged class that can do as they please, and they are so acting that in my opinion, it will be necessary in the near future, perhaps at the next session of our legislature, to declare an open season for does for a fixed period, during which some may be killed and others taught their place."

No one was ready to take such a step, though. Pennsylvania didn't have a statewide doe season until 1928, and it was about as popular as the plaque. Sportsmen, acting out of a sincere desire to do what they thought was best for deer, raged

Some believe Pennsylvania's best deer hunting is yet to come. If the changes meant to balance deer with their habitat succeed, hunters should be able to pursue bigger and healthier deer.

against it. Newspapers chastised the Game Commission for sponsoring the shooting of does rather than importing more bucks. It wasn't until 1957 that the state had a permanent annual doe season. Even then, some hunters opposed it very vocally.

Roger Cowburn, the Potter County deer guide, knows all about that. He started hunting in 1940, when he was twelve years old. He grew to accept shooting does and even took other hunters out—acting as an outfitter, charging $10 per hunter per day—to help them shoot does as well as bucks. This made him unpopular with his own family.

"My dad was deathly against the doe season. He hated it," Cowburn recalled. "His theory was that you were shooting all of the button bucks and spikes. Guys like my dad and my uncle used to go around to sportsmen's clubs and buy all of the doe tags and then not hunt. They'd buy them up and burn them up. They wanted to make sure nobody killed the doe."

Cowburn, who succeeded his dad and uncle as president of the Ulysses Conservation Club, tried to convince them they were wrong. The overabundance of deer was killing farmers, he told them, and destroying the deer's own habitat. He couldn't reach them, though. "My dad used to fight me something awful over the doe," Cowburn said.

What made things worse was that, for most of the twentieth century, hunters were limited to shooting one deer per year, with doe season traditionally falling after the conclusion of buck season. The best hunters had killed a deer and put their guns away before doe season ever arrived. Those who went through buck season without filling their tag still had a chance to put meat in the freezer, sure. But missing out on getting something with antlers and having to settle for a doe was like missing out on a romantic evening with the homecoming queen for a blind date with the girl with thick glasses, bad skin, and a figure that only Rubens could appreciate.

"Who shot does? People who failed at shooting a buck. By design, if you were a lousy hunter, you were going to hunt does," says Gary Alt. "And who are those does? Are they deer? No, they're second-class citizens. Too many hunters treat does as if they're not a game animal. It's a consolation prize, really. It's amazing. You talk to some hunters and ask them if they got a deer. If they got a buck, they're all smiles and have a story to tell. But if they had to shoot a doe, they all but stuff their hands in their pockets and look at the ground and dig their toe into the dirt while they tell you about it, like they got caught with their hand in the cookie jar."

That may be an attitude tied somewhat to age. Wang's survey, at least, found that opposition to doe hunting was strongest among older hunters. Even they can change, however. Ed Grasavage, president of the Pennsylvania chapter of the Quality Deer Management Association, is in his fifties now. He grew up hearing his father tell him never to hunt does. He did, but only intermittently, and even then he didn't want too many people shooting them where he hunted.

As recently as a few years ago Grasavage used to patrol his two-hundred-acre farm to make sure no one snuck in to shoot any does without permission. He, like many, believed that taking too many females out of the population would hurt the deer herd. He believes that no more. "We've started seeing a better buck-to-doe ratio, bigger deer, nicer bucks, fatter does since we started hunting does more aggressively," Grasavage said. "The weights of our deer are up 15 percent. I think it's made all the difference in the world."

Dave Kerner, a fifty-something-year-old hunter who lives in St. Mary's, Elk County, agrees completely. While he's always been a doe hunter, he and his family and friends used to avoid hunting does in the same places they hunted bucks. "We didn't want to shoot does because we didn't want to kill our deer population. That's what everybody thought," says Kerner.

He changed his mind after his group of hunters voluntarily began shooting more does on the private and public property they hunt. It was only then that they saw the habitat, which had been destroyed over the years from too many deer, bounce back. Woods that once had virtually no understory for a hundred yards at a stretch again have shrubs like blackberry bushes. With that have come better deer. While there aren't as many as there were two decades ago, they are healthier and bigger.

"We can see it just in the bucks we're taking out there," Kerner told me one day a few seasons ago. "Just myself, in the last four years I've gotten two seven-point bucks and an eight and a friend's gotten an eight and a nine. We'd been used to shooting spikes, threes, fours. The biggest buck we ever took out of there before was a six-point." Such concrete proof of the benefits of a healthier deer herd may be what sways more hunters to hunting does, he added.

The Game Commission is trying what it can to break down the resistance to shooting does. An October muzzleloader doe season for hunters armed with flint-locks and inline percussion rifles, an October season in which junior and senior hunters can shoot does with a rifle, increased doe license allocations, a deer management assistance program that allows hunters to get extra doe tags for sites with too many deer, have all proved popular with hunters.

All of these programs are new, too, so participation in each is likely to grow in time. Shissler is among those who already like the new seasons. "I know hunters who say, 'I've never shot a doe because I never had to.' They'd always gotten a buck. I think, given the opportunity to hunt does in another fashion, a lot of them, myself included, enjoy it," he says. "It's a way to enjoy a nice, leisurely hunt and still have time to process that deer before buck season rolls around. I've snuck up and shot does that were lying in their beds, completely unaware of my presence, and I'm just as proud, if not more so, of getting those deer as I am of any buck I've gotten."

Former game commissioner George Miller of Brockway, who says he always voted to promote doe hunting, believes Alt's ideas on promoting doe hunting are not only "the smart thing to do" but the one thing that must be done. He hopes hunters take advantage of the new opportunities before them. "Pennsylvania has tolerated too many deer for over fifty years," Miller says. "It's sad, because there are a lot of other wildlife resources out there that would like to share that habitat. And they can't do it because of the white-tailed deer."

Cowburn believes the hunters of the twenty-first century might be more willing to shoot does than his father and uncles were. "That generation is gone. They were good hunters and good sportsmen, but they missed the boat on doe. I think at least some people today are starting to realize that, and it has to be. It has to be," Cowburn said.

Not all hunters have made the switch to doe hunting, however. There are others who are convinced the Game Commission is kowtowing to special interest groups in knocking the deer herd lower than it needs to be, largely through unnecessarily large doe harvests. Unified Sportsmen's Greg Levengood, for one, says most everyone will admit that Pennsylvania had too many deer in the 1970s. He believes the population reached a sort of equilibrium by the late 1990s, though. Since then, it's been trimmed too much.

Already this belief is causing some people to quit hunting in Pennsylvania, he says. Needlessly driving the deer population down further will only exacerbate that problem, convincing youngsters to try other activities in place of hunting and bringing the Game Commission's fears about a smaller license-buying base to fruition that much quicker. "I just think it's gone too far the other way," Levengood says. "I think deer sightings, going into the woods in hunting season and just seeing deer, are very important to people. My guess is that there are more hunters in Pennsylvania interested in seeing good numbers of deer than there are interested in seeing fewer quality deer.

"I mean, you can be standing out there freezing and you warm up instantly every time you see a herd of deer go by. They don't all have to be eight pointers. I think you have more people subscribing to that line of thinking than any of that quality deer stuff."

Levengood has shot a few does in his lifetime, but none in the past fifteen years or so. He admits that he gets no thrill from it. If others do, that's okay, but they should probably limit themselves to taking one per person per year. To take more, he says, is shortsighted.

The Unified Sportsmen tried to take that message to hunters in the spring of 2004, right after the Game Commission issued a record 1.039 million doe licenses. Unified put out a paper calling on hunters to boycott doe licenses. It didn't work, by any measure. Though Levengood said later that it was never meant to keep hunters from buying licenses at all—but rather to persuade them to buy no more than one—more than a million of the licenses sold.

That's too many, in Levengood's opinion. "It's almost like catch-and-release fishing. If you want to have trout to catch, throw a few back. If you want to see more does, don't shoot so many. You can still go out there and see some deer and have fun," he says. "The hunter has the final say in what deer management is going to be. You can either pull the trigger or not pull the trigger."

"I believe guys will get unhappy with going out there and not seeing deer," adds fellow Unified Sportsmen director Wayne Haas, who hunts from a camp where none of the hunters take does. "I think we're going to lose hunters. I don't think the Game Commission will admit it's because we're shooting too many does already. And the decline will be such a gradual loss that people won't see the blame of it. But I already know guys who are saying they're not going to go out and carry a rifle and not be able to shoot."

Certainly, research suggests that seeing lots of deer is important to hunters. A study by Jody Enck and Daniel Decker in New York State in the early 1990s found that, when asked to list the "single greatest satisfactions" they get from deer hunting, sportsmen listed not only relaxation and spending time with family but also visual evidence of deer. The "single greatest dissatisfactions" experienced by deer hunters were related to poor hunter behavior, posted land, and not seeing evidence of deer.

It's just those kinds of expectations that make managing deer so problematic, though, Shissler says. The deer management debate is not about knowing how many deer we can have, not really. Biologists can study the forest and tell hunters how many deer an acre of ground can support. But hunters don't have to like the answer. And as long as they let those desires motivate them to ask for more deer, the deer wars of the twentieth century will rage on.

"The challenge we face is that this is not an issue about data and science. It's an issue about values," says Shissler. "And the bottom line is, if your value is about seeing lots of deer when hunting as opposed to healthy forests, you're not going to want to hear the message. That's the problem. That's why I guess I don't know if hunters can or will solve this problem. If you look at history, you see that if you're not adaptable, you usually go extinct. As hunters, we must be willing to adapt and to change to meet the reality in front of us. We can want it to be the 1950s again, but it's not. It's just not.

"My hope," Shissler says, "is that hunters will start to look at the ground and start to make the relationship between what's on the ground and the deer they see or don't see. Will they? I would like to see hunters leading the charge, but I haven't seen enough yet to know whether they are willing to do it."

Hunters shouldn't be faulted for liking to see deer, or for having grown used to seeing lots of them, says Pennsylvania Audubon's retired deer expert Ron Freed. Most if not all Pennsylvania deer hunters grew up expecting to see lots of deer every time they went into the woods, and more often than not those expectations were fulfilled. A hunter himself, Freed recalls plenty of days when he saw as many as fifty deer in an afternoon. But that doesn't change the fact that hunters need to embrace changes that will be good for deer and the forest habitats they live in.

"Just because some of the plants that were once there aren't there now doesn't mean they can't come back," Freed believes. "The seed source is there, so we could see our ecosystems come alive again. But hunters have to help make it happen. I think the majority of hunters will be okay with that once people like Gary explain to them what needs to be done and why. But there will always be others who are simply going to want to see deer and they aren't going to care if there are trilliums or ovenbirds out there, or any understory for them to live in. And I don't think you're ever going to change their minds."

If biologists hope to change the attitudes of additional hunters, they need to study them—to see what they believe, what they know, what they don't know—and then reach out to them in an attempt to share their knowledge, much as Gary Alt has tried to do since early in 2000. Wang, in her study, found that many hunters say they don't really understand how biologists come up with things like deer harvest goals and deer populations. As a result, they don't always trust what they're told.

"We understand deer pretty well. We understand our forests pretty well. What we don't understand is the people," Wang says. "We've kind of left off the people, the human dimensions aspect, which is of course the most important part."

Game Commission biologists and board members seem to agree. The agency has been doing a survey of hunter opinions and attitudes, asking them about things like whether they hunt does, what they think of antler restrictions, and where they hunt.

The hope is that, armed with information, they can head off some problems, like those they encountered just a few days into the 2003 firearms deer season. Terrible weather early on got the season off to a slow start, and there was a hue and cry from some hunters who feared that the lack of deer kills after a few days was proof the herd had already been trimmed back too much. Ultimately the numbers showed that there were still lots of deer to be found. The season produced the second-highest doe kill of all time and the fourth-highest deer harvest overall.

If hunters didn't understand what was happening, or why they were being asked to kill so many deer when it seemed there just weren't that many, it's because biologists had repeated their mistake of the past and not done enough to educate them, according to Graybill. Biologists need to help hunters see how things really are if they want them to do the legwork of managing deer and perpetuating hunting. Hunters, Graybill said, want to be included in the decision-making process, rather than be led blindly down the path.

"A lot of what I hear is, 'Okay, if we're going to have to shoot more deer or lower deer numbers, we really want to know we're doing this for the right reasons in the right places,'" said Graybill. "I know I'm not interested in being appeased. I'm interested in seeing good data and hearing good explanations for why you're doing what you're doing. Let's get all the cards on the table and see what we're dealing with.

"Obviously, the biologists need to do some more work. They need to do something to get hunters to buy into their program. The Game Commission and its biologists can't just say, 'Like it or not, this is what's best.' They can't afford to take that position. I think they need to continue to work with sportsmen and bring them along."

Former game commissioner Bob Gilford agrees. The challenge before the Game Commission lies not in finding a way to put a smile on the faces of those people who want more deer all the time. The challenge, he says, is finding a way to manage deer based on the amount of available habitat while still keeping hunters happy enough that they remain interested in hunting. It's those hunters, after all, that the Commission has to rely on to serve as its foot soldiers, carrying out management policies designed to conserve the state's wildlife. If they disappear, no deer management plan can work, no matter how well designed.

"Our job is not to put a deer in everyone's bag. Our job is to manage deer in some proper fashion," Gilford says. "No question, hunters are going to see fewer deer than they used to see. The question is, how many deer will the habitat support, and how many deer will hunters be willing to accept and still keep hunting? That's going to be the secret to the thing."

Larry Schweiger, a lifelong hunter, longtime friend of Gary Alt, and president of the National Wildlife Federation, issued a warning, though. There will always be deer hunters who are complainers, he said, some well meaning, others not. What the Game Commission must remember is that while it needs to work with those people and consider their opinions, it also has to respect the advice of its professional biologists who are paid to manage deer. "When I was younger I worked in an auto repair shop and we had what we used to call 'sidewalk mechanics.' They were people who brought their car in and then told you how to fix it," Schweiger said. "Well, if they really knew how to fix it, they wouldn't have been bringing it to us.

"You have the same thing in wildlife management. People will sit around and give you wives' tales. And they're well intentioned. But they don't know what they don't know. You have to trust science and the people who know the science, and Gary Alt knows the science. If deer management is set by public opinion or campfire conversation, we're in trouble," Schweiger added. "We desperately need hunters in America today to keep deer herds under control. Fortunately, I think the hunters who know what needs to be done, who have been paying attention, will get behind Gary and help him to move this thing forward for the benefit of the deer and the forest and the hunters and all wildlife."

It's possible that the "proper fashion" Gilford mentioned and the "science" Schweiger discussed will, as Levengood fears, drive some people to leave the hunting ranks, game commissioner Roxane Palone admits. But that may be the price the agency has to pay for keeping deer at acceptable levels for all 12 or 13 million of Pennsylvania's residents.

"I enjoy hunting, and I hope everyone loves it as much as I do," Palone says. "But I don't worry too much about losing a few hunters. I would rather do the right thing and have a good, sound deer management program and lose 10 percent of the hunters who aren't dedicated or interested in hunting for the right reasons than do the wrong thing in an attempt to keep everybody. I don't think that's the way to go."

"We work for all the people of the commonwealth," agrees former game commissioner Sam Dunkle. "Some sportsmen are not going to like hearing that.

They've always been our primary concern, and they still are important, without question. But they are not our only concern."

If hunters fail to manage deer for a society that cares little about who controls the deer herd so long as someone gets the job done, the consequences could be serious. John McDonald is a wildlife research specialist with the U.S. Fish and Wildlife Service. A Pennsylvania native, he is worried that hunters have a narrowing window in which to show that they can manage deer properly. That's why he and several others organized a symposium on deer management at the annual conference of the Wildlife Society, an organization of wildlife professionals from about sixty countries, in September 2004.

At that gathering, held in Calgary, McDonald talked a bit about his days working as a deer biologist with the Massachusetts Department of Fish and Game. One of his responsibilities was to go into urban and suburban areas and try to convince people suffering from too many deer that hunting was the best option for removing those animals. It was often a hard sell, partly because many of those residents had no idea what hunting was like. "They would ask, 'Okay, if we have hunting, how many people can we expect to see killed?' Well, the answer was none, of course, but they didn't know that," McDonald said.

An equally big problem, though, was that while hunters can take credit for growing deer herds everywhere, there are fewer examples of places where they have controlled deer. "If I had a good set of antihunters, and I mean good from their perspective, I could point to hunters and say, boy, we've given you guys a century to get things right and you haven't done it," McDonald said. "That's why I was always afraid, when I went to these places, in the back of my mind, what if someone does come up with a technological breakthrough where we can have a single dose of some kind of contraceptive that works? Then how do you justify hunting?

"I think the way to do it is to show the role of hunting. What kind of wildlife do we want to have on the landscape? If you're going to manipulate something as fundamental as the internal working of a deer's breeding, you might as well put plastic animals out there so people can drive by and see them," McDonald said. "But for hunters to make that argument, they have to show they're willing to manage deer, which in many cases means managing at lower densities. When we say hunting is the best tool for managing deer, we've got to have some success stories to point to on a large scale."

DeNicola, the wildlife biologist and sharpshooter, agrees, saying that commercial shooting of deer could replace hunting, even outside urban areas, if hunters don't start managing herds better. It might not look exactly like the work he does, but it could succeed. Market hunting, he noted, was very effective along the entire East Coast earlier this century—it almost totally wiped out deer populations in states like Pennsylvania, remember—and could work again.

"If hunters are not willing to do what it takes to control deer, there might have to be some sort of profit-type mechanism to do it. Just to kill the sheer number of deer that are going to have to be killed, people could get desperate enough to create some type of bounty situation," DeNicola says. "I can't say for sure it's going to happen, but it's possible. And it will be a sad day if it does."

The good news for hunters is that there's evidence that nonhunters—even those who might lean toward being antihunters—can accept deer hunting if it's presented in the right way and shown to be an effective tool for promoting healthy deer, healthy landscapes, and healthy people. Fox Chapel Borough is a case in point. Given the chance to make a difference there, hunters proved themselves.

"I'm not a hunter, so when we started this I asked my wife what she thought of when she heard the word 'hunter,'" said Fox Chapel police chief David Laux. "She pictured some guy in a pickup truck with a rifle in the back, driving through the borough shooting anything that moved." More than a decade into Fox Chapel's hunt, that image has changed. "Now, when you say 'hunter,' the perception is of someone who's professional, who acts professionally and who is ethical. And they're helping the borough," Laux said.

"Hunting is not justified unless it's science-based," added Schweiger. "It's not justified unless it's working to conserve forests and wildlife in perpetuity. I think Gary Alt and his program will be very careful to keep hunting in a positive light. I think Gary Alt and Gary Alt's ilk will keep hunting where it needs to be. If anything, I think proper deer management is definitely going to be a factor in inspiring people to hunt and to come back to hunting. Hunting needs to continue and to prosper and one way to do that is to show people how it can protect nature for tomorrow."

Shissler, too, is optimistic that deer hunting's best days are in the future, provided hunters can transform the image of their sport with the general public, much as they did for Laux's wife. That doesn't mean the hunters of tomorrow will necessarily hunt out of a sense of duty or obligation. Hunting is a personal way to connect to nature, a way to get meat, and just plain fun, says Shissler. Those will always be the main reasons people are drawn to the sport. But there's no reason hunters can't enjoy what they do and do right by their neighbors and the state's forests at the same time.

"Hunting is not a right. It's a privilege. You can't go into a public forest and cut down a tree and take it home. Yet we want to go into that same forest and harvest a deer and take it home," Shissler says. "We have a unique relationship and we have to work with landowners, the people who spend the money to maintain that land that supports those deer, if we want it to continue."

"We've got to somehow show them [the public] that we can solve their problem," Dunkle says of sportsmen and the Game Commission. "If we don't do something, our people will be working for someone else."

Alt is hopeful that if hunters can overcome the challenges before them—by adapting to changing seasons, by improving their skills, by recruiting more youngsters into the sport, by building relationships with landowners to access new properties, by accepting doe hunting—hunting itself stands to benefit greatly. The suburbanites who want to plant and grow shrubs without having to fence them in, the farmers who want to be able to make a living, the birders and hikers who want a healthy forest will rise up and find someone to tackle the deer issue. The only question is who that will be.

Alt hopes it's hunters. "Society will decide this issue," he says. "That's what ties hunters, nonhunters, and antihunters together, the fact that this is something that impacts everyone. It's not about seasons and bag limits and whether you're going to shoot an eight-point buck this fall. It's about managing wildlife so that it's in balance with its habitat. Eight-five to 90 percent of all hunters in the eastern United States are deer hunters, so what happens to deer hunting is what happens to hunting overall. If hunters don't allow us to manage wildlife properly, they're liable for that. And I don't want that to happen."

The majority of Pennsylvania's hunters have, so far, shown themselves to be pretty adaptable, according to Russ Schleiden, the game commissioner from Centre County. As recently as 1999, deer hunting in Pennsylvania meant a few weeks of archery hunting followed by a two-week buck season and then three days of doe hunting. Since then, they've adjusted to having concurrent buck and doe seasons, October doe seasons, antler restrictions, DMAP, and sharing the woods with hunters using inline rifles and crossbows.

Hunters themselves didn't even know if they could live with all those changes, he says. "If it's brown, it's down" was how some hunters expressed their fear that concurrent seasons would lead people to shoot at anything brown first and make sure it was a deer later. Others worried that letting hunters use rifles in October,

Since antler restrictions were put into place, taxidermists have noticed an increase in the quality of bucks coming through their shops.

when the leaves are still on the trees, would lead to an inordinate number of hunting accidents. Neither of those things has happened.

"In my opinion, sportsmen have done a pretty good job," says Schleiden. "We knew we were asking hunters to change a lot of traditions. And being creatures of habit like we are, change is difficult. But I think hunters have done a wonderful job of cooperating with us."

Palone, too, thinks the educational efforts that have accompanied all of those changes—efforts like Alt's lecture tours—have made a difference. She's optimistic that hunters are returning to their roots as environmental stewards. "The market hunter and consumer of centuries past was responsible for the exploitation of both wild game and the forests of Pennsylvania. It was a different kind of hunter who was responsible for the reemergence of wildlife and forests," she says. "That hunter was called a conservationist. They were partly responsible for the origins of the state forest system, the national forest system, and of course the Game Commission and its extensive game lands.

"Somewhere during the last fifty or sixty years, some hunters again began to be perceived as part of the deer management problem because they demanded more deer than the system could support. The good news is that I believe we are seeing a change for the good in the hunter of the twenty-first century. I firmly believe the direction of our new programs and their related research will change the image of the hunter in the eyes of the nonhunting public. The image of the hunter will go from zealous consumer and return to its rightful place as steward of our state's outdoor heritage," Palone says.

"Hunters are at the point now where they can be the heroes or be the goats," says Kelly. "If we continue to manage the forest for a single species, the white-tailed deer, we may get to where the other 11 or 12 million people who live here say you guys are ruining it for everyone. We're at a pretty critical turning point here. There isn't a lot of antihunting feeling in Pennsylvania right now. Most of the non-hunting public in Pennsylvania is not antihunting. But we don't want to push them that way. And we could."

Interestingly, Alt uses an analogy similar to Levengood's catch-and-release fishing story to explain why hunters, if they can shrink the size of the deer herd in many places, can have healthy forests and put themselves in a defensible position in relation to society. "It's okay to like to catch fish," Alt says. "But if you like fish you had damn sure better be pretty interested in clean water, too. If the water is polluted, you can throw all the fish in the world back but they're not going to survive. The habitat is just not there.

"It's the same with deer. You can pass on shooting does all day long, but if there's no habitat for them, if there's nothing for them to eat, if you aren't getting regeneration of oaks and other seedlings, you can never grow more deer. They won't be there when you want to hunt them because there's nothing for them to survive on.

"We've got to cross the line separating hunters and nonhunters and get the rest of society on board," Alt says. "We have to make them realize the services hunters can provide, show them what hunters can do. People are looking down their noses at hunters, more so than they did twenty or thirty years ago, because fewer of them hunt or have any connection to the land.

"What I'm hoping is that we can put hunters in a positive light. I'd like to get to the point where, instead of sportsmen having to visit landowners to get a place to hunt, the landowners are calling sportsmen, saying, 'I've got a problem here, can you help me out?' To get there, though, hunters in the twenty-first century are going to have to be more knowledgeable about their role in society, their role in wildlife management. Management shouldn't be, and can't be, based on what hunters want. It has to be about what's best for wildlife management for all of society. Ironically, in most cases, that's what's in the best interests of hunters anyway.

"I've always said we have almost no chance of solving this problem unless we get the hunters on board. We absolutely must have the hunters supporting us or we're dead," Alt says. "But we've got to take a first step."

8

QUESTIONS AND ANSWERS

Standing at the edge of the road, looking up at the hill that started on the opposite side of the ditch at our feet, I felt a little nervous. Man, it looked steep. I had worn my leather boots to keep my feet dry from the dew and a sweatshirt over my T-shirt to keep the early morning chill at bay. Now, though, I was secretly wishing I had gone with lighter gear.

We were in the Penns Valley area of eastern Centre County. Greg and I had gotten up before daylight and driven almost three hours to get here so that we could tag along with a bunch of twenty-something college students as they captured white-tailed fawns. The crew was one of two in the state gathering data for a fawn mortality study.

In this spot, where the habitat is a mix of hayfields, pastures, and cropland interspersed with woodlots and small towns, finding fawns involves a lot of walking. These students had already been at it for a few weeks, climbing over logs, negotiating their way through thickets, and breezing through meadows. If they weren't in shape when they started, they were by now. I hoped we wouldn't look too pathetic by comparison.

We were here because about ten days earlier we had visited with Gary Alt when he had held a press conference in State College. Alt had announced that the Game Commission planned to spend much of the next decade studying Pennsylvania's deer. He promised they were "launching one of the most major studies of white-tailed deer in the wild" ever done. "We want to be able to manage deer based on what's happening with our deer in our state right now. We don't want to rely on what happened in an enclosure in Texas in 1952," Alt had said while holding a fawn outside the deer pens at Penn State University. This study was the first part of that effort.

The same technology that makes possible things like hand-held video games, electronic pocket-sized day planners, and CD players was behind this fawn study. A decade ago, radio transmitters—like older computers—had to be big and bulky to also be powerful. Now, in an age when even the first Walkmans seem quaint and old-fashioned, transmitters can be both strong enough to be practical and small enough to fit on a fawn.

"Ten years ago we couldn't have done this study," Duane Diefenbach, of the fish and wildlife research unit at Penn State, had said on that warm afternoon at the deer pens. "Because of technological advances, we have what we need to make this kind of study a reality."

Now here we were, tagging along as students did the legwork that put this technology to work. We started climbing, single file, headed for the meadow atop the hill. Wendy Vreeland, the field crew supervisor, led the way, her eight-member crew and Greg and I strung out behind her. There were no Sherpa guides among us, although halfway to the top, already hot and sweaty and sucking air, I expected to see one at any minute. Don't look up, I told myself. Just keep walking, one foot in front of the other.

It was a struggle. There was no path to follow, really, so we were making do as we went along. Sometimes the going was pretty clear. At other times, greenbriars clutched at our sleeves and rocks rolled under our feet. Up ahead, most of the crew members who were setting the pace were also carrying some kind of gear. Several had backpacks stuffed with transmitters, antiseptic, surgical gloves, and charts for recording field data.

The ones who really stood out, though, were the students carrying oversized fishing nets. The wide-mouthed nets were more than big enough, I thought as I looked at them, to catch my beagle, Hunter, at home. Each net was at the end of a handle that was about three feet long. Awkward to carry through the woods, the nets were nonetheless needed on occasion to scoop up tiny fawns that were thinking of running away.

We kept climbing. When we finally made it to the top, we stopped to allow everyone to gather and catch their breath. Greg and I were a bit off to one side.

"Some hill, huh?" I said to him, taking my ball cap off to wipe the sweat from my forehead with a sleeve. I saw that Greg was as out of breath as I was, which may have had something to do with the fact that he was carrying a heavy digital camera rather than the notebook and pen that I was, but I didn't care. At least I wasn't the only one whose heart was pounding.

"I kept hoping they were going to take a break."

"Me too," Greg said. "I wasn't going to ask, though. I know this sounds macho, but there was no way I was going to say anything and let one of these girls know they were kicking my ass. I figured if I died you could just scoop me up in one of those nets and carry me to the car."

That was funny, but no funnier than the thought that we were somehow going to catch fawns this way. Yet chances were that we would. This crew had already caught close to three dozen in the weeks before we arrived.

The goal of this research project was to capture at least forty fawns each year for two years at this site and at a second in Quehanna Wild Area. The area we were in now was a mix of woodlots, cultivated fields, and homes. The Quehanna is a forest of oak, hickory, and maple in Elk, Clearfield, and Cameron Counties and is, with the exception of a few hunting camps, gas wells, and a single business, a large unbroken woods. By choosing two such contrasting areas, biologists were hoping to determine whether there were differences in survival among big woods deer and farm country deer.

Each fawn that was captured would be outfitted with ear tags and a radio collar that would transmit a unique signal. So long as the fawn was alive and moving periodically, the transmitter would give off one type of beep. If the collar did not move for four hours—signaling that the fawn was dead—a mortality sensor triggered it to give off a different beep. By checking on each deer at least once and sometimes as often as three times a day, crews could monitor their activity. When they suspected that a fawn had died, they could move in and find what was left of it and determine what had killed it.

That information was important, Justin Vreeland, the graduate student coordinating the study, told me, especially in Pennsylvania. There's been a long-standing, commonly held belief among many hunters that coyotes prey heavily on deer and are in fact the main factor in suppressing deer populations. Studying fawn survival rates from birth through their first winter, and determining the cause of death of fawns that die, could reveal whether that was true, he said.

"We're gathering the pieces to the puzzle that we need to put together to see what is happening to fawns at these two study sites," added Bret Wallingford, the Game Commission deer biologist assisting on the study.

First, though, came the business of actually catching deer. Standing at the edge of the meadow at the top of that killer hill, Wendy Vreeland explained what we would be doing. Female deer generally give birth to and hide their fawns in dense tangles in the woods, in hayfields, or along stream banks, because that's where the cover is typically thickest, she said. We were going to check those kinds of places by stretching out in a skirmish line, with each person five yards or so from the next. We would then walk from field to forest to meadow.

The Penns Valley crew had access to about eight thousand acres of ground, most of it privately owned, so they had been walking just that way for eleven hours a day, six days a week, she said. At the dawn of this day's search, she told us to keep our eyes open. "You have to expect the unexpected with fawns," Vreeland said. "It's wherever mom thinks is best. We found one fawn a few days ago under a pine tree. That was probably the perfect place for it. With the dappled sunlight and the red pine needles under it, you could hardly tell it was there. But we find them all over."

I knew from talking to Vreeland and her crew earlier in the morning that they had caught many of their fawns in the few days immediately before we got there, so they seemed optimistic we would catch one or more for Greg to photograph. Still, I couldn't help but wonder. This seemed like a pretty daunting task, walking through the woods looking for fawns the size of small poodles.

Passes through two fields that turned up nothing but a groundhog didn't do much to bolster my confidence. Walking through a brushy woodlot that separated two other fields, though, something jumped up in front of us and took off, nothing but the swaying grass giving it away until it broke into an opening.

As one, everyone in the line stopped, tensed, and held their breath. Then I heard someone from the end of the line mutter, "stupid housecat," and our hearts sank a little lower. We kept walking. The sun rose high in the sky, sweatshirts came off and were wrapped around waists, water bottles came out. And then it happened—we were trudging along a hillside woodlot when one of the crew, Brooke Connell, gave the signal to stop. She had found a fawn.

A whisper passed along the line and swiftly and silently we closed in, encircling the little deer, which lay motionless, hoping it would go unnoticed. Crew member Gino D'Angelo dropped one of those salmon nets over the deer to keep it there, just in case, though it never moved more than to blink an eye. Others started emptying their backpacks, putting on gloves. Connell then picked up the tiny deer while Ryan Reed slipped a blindfold, made from a sock with the toes cut out, over its eyes.

"Somebody get a neck circumference," Vreeland said, as they took the fawn out from under the net.

"Twelve point seven [centimeters]," answered D'Angelo. "That's just under five inches. That's tiny."

"That collar's really loose," Vreeland said, watching as Reed slipped it around the deer's neck. A dusty tan color to match the deer's hide and built to expand with the deer as it grows, it has to be tight enough to stay on, yet not so tight as to harm the deer. "I'll bet that fawn's not very old, maybe a day or so."

"This is the smallest one yet," Reed said as he read the fawn's radio collar frequency to someone else holding a clipboard used to record all that data. He then attached numbered tags to each of the deer's ears.

Next it was time to weigh the deer. Crew members stuffed a pillow case full of grass, leaves and other vegetation collected at the site, then weighed it. They then put the deer in the case—confident the vegetation would mask any human scent that might get on the fawn—and weighed everything again, subtracting the weight of the bag and grass to get the weight of the fawn.

This little fawn weighed 1.7 kilograms, or about three and three-quarters pounds. That's only a little over a pound more than the state record bluegill.

Throughout the whole process, the fawn made a sound only once, giving a tiny bleat when one of the ear tags was applied. The crew had worked fast—it had only been about four minutes and they were ready to release the fawn again. Connell put it back in nearly the same spot where it was found and we moved on.

"The deer doesn't know exactly where she left her fawn. She'll come back and snort and they'll find one another," Vreeland said.

Finding that little fawn was exciting. Roxane Palone, who accompanied the Penns Valley crew on a day in which they found twelve fawns, described it as "almost a spiritual experience for me, all these little miracles of God." That's a pretty good description, I think.

But if catching fawns early in the birthing season is a gentle, tender game—much like reaching into a crib to pick up a newborn child that's beautiful, yet delicate and helpless—capturing fawns later in the summer is like chasing an energetic toddler with a nonstop motor and a giggle to match. Crews worked from early May through June capturing fawns, until they ran out of collars. They found that getting their hands on fawns later in the season—when they were older, bigger, and more likely to flee—required being ready to move, and fast.

"We call them runners," said Randall Males, another member of the Penns Valley crew. "You'll see them jump up and take off and then it's a race to see if we can catch one in the net or turn it back into the rest of the line. It's tough, though. They can fly."

Greg and I learned just what he meant later. Walking through a hay field, a fawn jumped up in front of our line. The cry "we've got a runner!" went up, and like sprinters off at the crack of the starter's pistol, the same students who had been moseying through the field a second before took off in hot pursuit.

The deer gave a few leaps, pivoted ninety degrees to the right, and headed for a tractor lane on the edge of the field. Vreeland, who was on that end of the line, saw it, took two quick steps to put herself in its way, squared her hips like a linebacker getting ready to make a tackle, and was promptly bowled over by the deer. She managed to hang on, but it wasn't graceful. When the rest of us caught up, she was lying on her side in the dirt, her hat on the ground behind her, her long hair in her face, her glasses cockeyed on her face. But she still had the deer.

Things were just as exciting for the crews working in the Quehanna Wild Area, though it took a little longer for them to get their fawns, at least that first year. That's because the skirmish-line technique did not work there, where the vast expanses of forest and lower deer densities made it difficult to determine where to even start looking for fawns. Ultimately, they settled on a different method of finding newborn deer.

"The teams drive the roads looking for nervous does that, by their nervousness, might indicate a fawn is nearby," Wallingford told me. "Then the students jump out and search the immediate area for a fawn. There's a little bit of an art to it, but once they got started they did a pretty good job finding fawns."

I couldn't help but wonder what a nervous doe looked like, so I asked Steve Repasky for a description when I got the chance a year later. Repasky was project leader for the Quehanna half of the fawn study. We had gone to that area of forest to see how he and his crew found deer. Bouncing along in his Bronco over an unimproved road, kicking up dust, the sound of gravel under tire rubber coming in through the open windows, Repasky laughed.

"You almost have to see a couple to know what you're looking at," he said. He described a couple of telltale signs that might indicate a doe with the jitters. Does that are reluctant to leave an area, that stare in one direction, perhaps toward where a fawn is bedded, or that are still sporting their winter gray coats instead of their red spring ones because they're devoting their energy to nursing a fawn, are all likely suspects.

Twice, as we were riding through the Wild Area, we came upon does that fit that description. Repasky rolled down his window each time and imitated a fawn's bleat. Hearing that, one of the does acted suspiciously enough that we jumped out of the truck and sprinted toward her. You have to chase does away fast, Repasky said, in case there's a fawn in hiding. You want it to react by hugging the forest floor instead of running after mom. That doe took off and we made a few circles around the spot where she had been standing, but if there was a fawn there, we didn't find it.

That was okay. It would have been neat to see another fawn, but on this trip we were really searching for death rather than life. Capturing live fawns is fun. A study like this one only works, though, if you invest just as much time in finding dead ones. That's what we were trying to do on this day. Greg and I were following Repasky, Wallingford, Alt, and a few others as they investigated fawn deaths.

We meandered along the maze of roads that bisect the Wild Area, Repasky stopping every so often to listen to the "beep-beep-beep" sounds coming through his telemetry equipment. Finally he heard the unique note he was listening for, a mortality signal. Repasky pulled to the edge of the road and shut off the truck. We piled out of the vehicle and followed him into the woods, across a seep of moss-covered rocks and beyond, where the forest floor was an appaloosa pattern of light and shadow under the late morning sun. We had gone only a little ways when he drew up.

"Here," Repasky said. "This is where it ended."

He pointed to a small depression at the base of a giant tree, shaded by the new life of some young saplings. Their fresh, whiplike limbs parted under his hand to reveal the scene, within sight and sound of the road.

The tiny body was tucked under a blanket of last year's leaves, its limbs neatly folded. The fawn's wounds were almost surgical in their precision: the body had been disemboweled, the midsection cleaned down to the smooth skin. Only the puncture wounds at the base of the skull told the story of just how violent death was.

"You can see hemorrhaging there," Wallingford said, pointing to the area where the head and neck meet. "That's how you know that was the fatal wound. There may be a variety of wounds on the body, scrapes and cuts and bites, but there can only be hemorrhaging when it was still alive because after that the blood stops flowing.

"Now it's dead. Now we need to try to figure out what killed it. That's what we're doing all of this work for."

Predators kill in different ways, leaving different clues behind. Coyotes most often kill with a bite to the head, near the ears, that suffocates the fawn. Their eating patterns are unique, too. In many cases, coyotes concentrate on eating a fawn's viscera—the heart, lungs, diaphragm, and liver—because they contain more fat than any other organs or meat. In many cases in Penns Valley and Quehanna, that's all the coyotes ate. Coyotes will occasionally eat a fawn's stomach, but only if it is still surviving solely on milk. Once the fawn starts eating solid food, coyotes avoid the stomach.

Interestingly, coyote kills are often identifiable because the predator will chew the ends of a fawn's ribs. No one is sure whether that's to give them to better access to the internal organs, because they like the taste of the ribs, or because they use them as chew toys. "But the behavior seems similar to that of domestic dogs chewing on bones or rawhide chew toys," Justin Vreeland had said.

Coyotes will also sometimes eat just a portion of the fawn at one sitting, then cache the rest to eat later. They don't always do it; biologists suspect the activity is more common when they have pups or food is scarce. But when they do, they'll often scrape out a shallow depression, then place the fawn in it and cover it with leaves and soil.

On his knees, examining this case, Repasky decided it was a coyote that had killed this fawn, our first death of the day. While the fawn's nose was intact—coyotes usually eat that, too, he said—all of the other clues were there. The skull was crushed, the vital organs were gone, the rest of the body was lightly buried beneath leaves.

"It's almost a perfect cache," Repasky said with a scientific admiration. "You wouldn't have even been able to see it if it weren't for the collar, and even then only because of that one tiny hoof sticking out."

Bobcats take fawns on occasion, too, and also cache their kills, though in a much more haphazard way. They kill by suffocating their prey with bites to the neck. Because bobcats can be smaller than the deer they attack, though, and because they are armed with sharp claws, their kills usually also show evidence of deep scratches on the back, neck, and sides. They avoid eating organs, too. "They're more finicky," Repasky said. "They usually go for the meatier parts of the fawn first, like the hams and shoulders."

Black bears will knock fawns down with a blow from a paw, sometimes killing them outright by crushing their backbones, necks, or skulls. Those fawns that don't die this way are done in when the bear bites them on the head and neck, suffocating the small deer.

When it comes time to eat a fawn, black bears generally eat everything from nose to tail, including the skull, skin, and bones. In most cases in the Quehanna, all that

Steve Repasky examines a fawn that was collared as part of the Game Commission's fawn mortality study. The clues at this scene indicate that this fawn was probably killed by a coyote.

remained of the fawns killed by bears were a few radio collars, parts of a leg or jaw, or some hide. Bears also have a tendency to roll around when eating, creating wallows where grasses, fens, shrubs, and saplings get bent and broken.

That's what we found at the scene of another fawn's death, this one in the midst of a thick tangle of saplings and briars that grew up after a tornado hit the area a few years earlier. The scene reeked of an eerie, raw power. A circular area in the leaves, some bare earth, and snapped sticks popping up at odd angles marked the spot where a fawn had spent the last few violent seconds of its life. A trail had been created when the lifeless body was dragged for a bit, with blood smeared on a fallen log the bear must have crossed with its prize. There was, though, no fur, no meat, no bones—even the ear tags must have been eaten or carried away. All that remained was the fawn's collar, more blood on its battery pack.

"This has to have been a bear. The fact that we found all of this disturbance, the drag marks, the scuff marks," Repasky said, holding two strands of black fur pulled from the bark of a tree near the drag marks. "This is a piece of evidence, a piece of the puzzle."

"The whole investigation is like a crime scene," Wallingford added. "You're doing forensics. The main thing you look for is a carcass, just like looking for a body at a murder scene. After that, they have to put all the pieces of evidence together," said Wallingford of Repasky and his crew members. "It might be four or five things, and it might be all circumstantial, but that's all they have."

"The only thing we don't have is fingerprints," Repasky said.

They didn't need them, either. In the end, the Penns Valley and Quehanna crews caught 218 fawns in 2000 and 2001, 108 in the Quehanna and 110 in Penns Valley. Combined, that was more than had ever been caught in any single study in North America.

What they found is that fawns die from a variety of causes. Predation was the leading cause of death, with nearly one in four fawns being eaten by something else. What surprised many people, though, was that bears are as big a predator of fawns as are coyotes. Of the thirty-seven fawn deaths where the identity of the predator could be determined, coyotes killed eighteen and bears sixteen. Bobcats took three.

It is interesting to note, too, that 84 percent of the predation deaths occurred in the Quehanna Wild Area. In Penns Valley, fawns were much more likely to die of other natural causes, like pneumonia. Nine fawns died after being struck by vehicles, three after being struck by farm machinery used to cut hay. Three fawns were poached, two were shot for crop damage, and eighteen were taken by hunters.

Gary Alt says he's pleased with how the study went, and not only because it gives the Game Commission the data needed to justify and defend its deer management program. Interest in the study—gauged by the number of people visiting a fawn study journal updated periodically on the Game Commission's website—was high among the public, too. Even other professionals have paid attention to the study.

"I remember when we decided we wanted to do this study," Alt said. "We knew what we wanted to accomplish and we came up with the idea of sending kids into the field with nets to catch fawns, but we didn't know if it would work. We called around to biologists in other states and told them what we wanted to do, hoping they would say, without us asking, how they did something similar.

"Well, they all said they thought the study was a good idea. But then they said, 'Okay, how are you going to do it?' I thought, uh-oh. But it worked, and it worked very well. We couldn't have asked for it to be any better, in fact. Those other biologists are going to be looking to Pennsylvania in the future because we're going to be the leader in deer management in this country."

If the fawn mortality study had its moments of fun, the Game Commission's fawn conception study most assuredly did not. I didn't ask to tag along on that one, and for good reason. The study, which is still in progress, involves examining fawn embryos. By weighing and measuring the embryos, biologists can determine when they were conceived. Armed with that information, they can determine when the breeding season—known as the rut—begins and ends, and when it peaks.

It's important that most does be bred within a few weeks of one another. In that kind of situation, a year's worth of fawns are born at about the same time, flooding the ecosystem. Some will fall to predators, but with so many born at once they overwhelm the bears and coyotes and bobcats and so sustain the population. It's like throwing ten quarters into the air. Throw them one at a time and someone might catch them all, one after another. Throw them all into the air simultaneously, though, and while a person might get a few, he probably won't get all of them. Does that are bred on time also give birth to fawns early enough in the spring to allow them to grow fat and healthy before the onset of fall and winter.

Collecting embryos is no job for the faint of heart, however. To get them, Alt and his fellow biologists asked the Game Commission's wildlife conservation officers to remove embryos from does that had been hit and killed by vehicles. "Let me tell you, removing an embryo from a dead deer along the edge of the highway is nothing like gutting a deer when you're out hunting," Alt said. "They might be mangled or rotting or covered in maggots. It's no picnic, believe me. It's a dirty, smelly, stinky job. But our officers did it and they're to be commended for it."

Conservation officers collected 3,180 embryos in the first four years of the study. This yielded some interesting information. While out with Repasky that day, for example, we had pulled over at a wide spot in the road to take a break from looking for deer and drink some water. As we leaned against the truck, lounging in the afternoon sun, Alt got a call on his radio from Dick Bodenhorn, a wildlife conservation officer in Elk County. Bodenhorn said he had something he wanted Alt to see.

We waited, and a short while later Bodenhorn arrived, his truck visible at first as little more than a grille and a windshield through the cloud of dust billowing up from the road. He parked, got out, put on a pair of surgical gloves, and pulled a tiny blood-red embryo, with delicate cloven hooves, from a bag. It was clearly deer shaped, though with still-developing buds where its ears would be. And it was small, about the size of a newborn puppy.

Bodenhorn had collected embryos from twenty-three does, but none matched this one. Though it was already June, this embryo was just 102 days old, meaning it had not been conceived until February 26, nearly three months after the peak of the breeding season. Whereas most fawns are born in late May or early June, this one would have been born around September 14, or about two weeks before opening day of the state's archery deer hunting season.

At one point, Alt and other biologists worried that such late breeding was evidence of a wide gap in the number of bucks and does in the state. Pennsylvania hunters had traditionally harvested 75 percent or more of the state's bucks each hunting season prior to the implementation of antler restrictions. The fear was that such a harvest was keeping does from being bred in a timely manner. That's bad not only for the herd's adult deer—if there are too many does and not enough bucks, the males would have to burn a significant portion of their winter fat

Pennsylvania Game Commission officers pulled fawn embryos from road-killed deer to determine the peak of the breeding season. This fawn, collected in Elk County, where the habitat is poor, would not have been born until mid-September, just two weeks before the start of archery deer season.

reserves chasing does for months on end—but also for the fawns that will be born late and have less time to get ready for winter.

The fawn conception study showed that the majority of the rut takes place within an acceptable time frame, however. Pennsylvania's whitetail rut runs from September into February, it's true. Fawn does are typically bred between November 5 and January 16, meaning that bucks are still actively chasing does through and beyond the state's traditional rifle deer season. But nine of ten adult does are bred between October 27 and December 10, with the peak of the rut falling in mid-November.

"From these results, we can conclude that Pennsylvania's deer population contains enough bucks to breed does in a relatively short time period," wrote Chris Rosenberry, the new head of the Game Commission's deer management section, and Wallingford in a report on the fawn conception study.

"It's not an ecological disaster, like we were afraid it might be," Alt admitted. "We think we can tighten it up a bit and improve the health of the deer herd even more. That's what we're trying to do. But it's not a disaster."

By the same token, though, the fawn conception study did provide evidence of another problem that many believe has reached crisis proportions. Far too many of the state's female deer are breeding later in life than they should be, and giving birth to fewer fawns than they should, simply because the habitat they're relying on to survive is damaged—the damage, ironically enough, having been wrought at least in part by the deer themselves.

Sexual maturity in fawns is related to body size, which is affected by quality and quantity of food as well as birth date. Does can breed at age six months in places where they have plenty to eat, or as late as age eighteen months in areas where they don't. In Pennsylvania, the study showed, nine of ten adult does get pregnant each year. Among fawn does, those about six months of age, only about 26 percent get pregnant.

Take a closer look at things, though, and you see that those are averages, with some areas of the state exhibiting higher conception rates than others. Fifty percent of the fawn does in the most productive areas of Pennsylvania, like the southeastern and western counties and along the lower Susquehanna River, are breeding during their first fall, Alt says. Less than 10 percent of the fawn does in the north-central region where Bodenhorn works—and where the habitat is most severely overbrowsed—are breeding their first fall.

"That's quite a difference," Wallingford said. "But when you consider the vastly different environments these deer inhabit, it quickly becomes apparent just how important habitat is in defining a whitetail's life. Our highest reproduction came from agricultural settings, the worst from our overbrowsed big woods counties. This isn't about overharvesting deer, but rather soil fertility, agricultural crop availability, climate, overbrowsing, and deer health."

The study showed that habitat plays a big role in determining how many fawns individual does have, too. In Pennsylvania, the deer that breed in areas of good habitat are having more fawns than are those living in poorer habitats.

Fawn does most often give birth to single fawns, but among adult does—those two and a half years old and older—twin fawns should be the norm, with triplets rare but not unheard of. You couldn't prove that by Bodenhorn's experience, though. He's spent about two decades working in the state's big woods country and says he's never seen that kind of evidence of a healthy deer herd there. Of the does he examined in one year of collecting embryos, 37 percent had not been bred. Of those that were pregnant, 42 percent would have had only one fawn and just 21 percent would have had twins.

"I've seen one set of triplets in my district, ever. And that came from a deer that lived in Ridgway Borough. It had probably been eating the neighborhood shrubs for years," Bodenhorn said.

Looking at the little embryo Bodenhorn had collected, Alt said that this is the message hunters and the rest of society need to understand: it all comes back to habitat. "If you've got a deer herd where the does don't even breed until eighteen months of age, and where the does are bred late, and the fawns are born late, they've got a lot of strikes against them, and that all goes back to habitat," Alt said. "If you don't have good habitat, you can't raise a healthy deer herd. Or a healthy black bear population, or a healthy turkey population, or anything else. And there's no doubt there has been enormous environmental damage caused by deer.

"That damage must be repaired. This is not an optional thing. But once we do that, we can grow more deer, more birds, more wildflowers, all while maintaining a healthy forest. We just need to stop looking at the deer and look at what's behind them," Alt said. "We need to stop looking at deer numbers and look at their impact on the land. What can that land support?"

Interestingly enough, another Game Commission study—this one decades old—helps to illustrate the relationship between deer and habitat. Each April since the mid-1970s, the Game Commission has sent its wildlife conservation officers out walking. They trek along one-mile sections of three streams in their districts, looking for deer and turkeys that might have died as a result of the winter weather. They check the same stream sections year after year after year.

The idea is not to count or even estimate the number of deer killed in any one particular winter, Wallingford said. "You're not necessarily looking for the area where you will find the most dead deer," he explained. Rather, the goal is to compare winter mortality from year to year. By having conservation officers take those walks, biologists know that the worst year for winter kills was 1978, when the statewide average was 1.94 dead deer per mile of stream. By comparison, the winter of 2002 revealed only 0.2 dead deer per mile.

Such numbers can speak not only to the severity of a particular winter but to how well the state's deer were prepared to meet it, Wallingford said. If the deer herd is healthy and there is enough habitat to support them, officers should expect to find few carcasses. If the winter is particularly bad, however, and deer go into it in less than optimal shape, the young and the weak don't always make it.

I had heard plenty of stories about such winter kills. Game Commission records indicated there had been bad winter kills periodically from the 1930s through the late 1970s. Bob Gilford, the former game commissioner who spent decades working as a deputy conservation officer and is the son of a conservation officer, saw firsthand what a hard winter can do to deer. Talk to him and he can recall what was a spring ritual in the 1950s and 1960s—going out each year to collect the carcasses of deer that had not made it through the winter.

"The deer herd was much larger than it is today, and it went into the winter in poorer conditions," Gilford said. "It was nothing to see a dozen or two dozen deer within three or four hundred yards that had starved to death. We'd pick up truckloads of dead and dying deer every spring anywhere there was a seep with some hemlock, or down along the creek bottoms, anywhere there was some cover. You'd fill pickup trucks with dead deer, then take those and fill up bigger trucks. You talk about a smell? It was bad."

The winter of 2002–3 was the state's worst in at least a decade, so when the opportunity came along I spent a day in May with wildlife conservation officer

Brian Witherite. He's the officer for southern Somerset County, which borders the Maryland state line. Some late snows in the mountains had lingered into spring, and he was just then getting ready to do his winter mortality walks. I met up with him where McClintock Run crosses under a two-lane country road, and we set out to look for dead deer.

A short way downstream from two trout fishermen casting into a rocky pool surrounded by some freshly green vegetation, we found our first deer. An empty rib cage, tufts of hair, a battered rack still attached to the skull—all that remained of a six-point buck, legal to hunt in that part of the state—were crumpled near the water. It was impossible to pinpoint what had killed the deer. "It's hard to say," Witherite said, circling the deer to look for any clues. "With all of the hair scattered, the cartilage gone, you just don't know."

The mere fact that the buck was there was disturbing, however. In his first two years in the district, Witherite found no dead deer during his walks. In this, his third year, following the worst winter in at least a decade, he would find two along this stream alone, the buck and a small doe.

That increase in dead deer proved to be fairly typical. The southwest region of the state does not get the worst of the winter weather—at least in comparison to the northern tier—and there have been plenty of years when few if any dead deer were found on these mortality walks. Following the winter of 2002–3, however, officers and others reported finding dead deer in places where they'd never seen any before.

"We got hammered by the weather," Witherite said. "You couldn't turn on Channel 6 without hearing about snow in the Laurel Highlands. I was afraid we'd find some dead deer, and we did."

"We even had some winter mortality in Greene County, and we never get any winter mortality here," added Palone, a lifelong resident of the county. "I guess they just couldn't find enough to eat."

Charlie May, the retired conservation officer from Fayette County, found five dead deer while doing his stream walks. One or two may have been deer that were shot by hunters but not recovered. At least two, though—both small deer—were probably done in by the weather. "I think that if we lost any to the weather, it was probably a lot of small ones like those, maybe late-born fawns. That's typically what happens," May said. "The younger ones aren't as strong to start with, and they have a tougher time competing for food if things get rough."

Not every area of the state saw winter-killed deer. In southern Butler County, conservation officer Randy Pilarcik said he didn't find any dead deer while on his walks. He attributed this, though, to alternative sources of food available to deer—sources that are not typical deer fare. "Around here, what food the deer couldn't find in the woods, they found around people's homes," Pilarcik said. "They move closer to town to survive."

There's no way to entirely eliminate winter mortality, Wallingford said. Deer that enter winter injured or unhealthy—whether from a wound suffered in hunting season, or a fracture from a collision with a car, or weakened by age or disease—will always struggled to survive. Even healthy deer can be taxed by winters in which snow and ice and cold temperatures persist late in the season. "That's one of the problems with being a mammal. You have to burn calories to stay warm," Wallingford said. But it makes more sense to keep deer numbers under control, to let hunters shoot and make use of deer in the fall, and have the herd enter the following spring healthy, than to let deer suffer and go to waste by trying to carry more than the habitat can support, he said.

But can hunters, given the opportunity, find and harvest enough antlerless deer to improve forest habitat and thereby limit things like winter mortality? The Game Commission's newest deer study may answer this question. Beginning in February 2005, biologists were planning to kick off a two- or three-year study tracking doe dispersal patterns, survival rates, and their vulnerability to harvest, especially in relation to varying levels of hunting pressure. The last variable—vulnerability to harvest—is especially intriguing, as it could settle some long-standing questions about things like the "overharvesting" of does that some hunters fear.

Can or do hunters really shoot that great a percentage of the state's does? If not, how do the does escape? Do they hide among the hunters, not moving? Do they travel far to get away? Are there certain types of cover they use to remain undetected? The study could answer those kinds of questions. Similar studies have been done elsewhere in the country, but this will be a first for Pennsylvania, says Rosenberry. "This will give us a better sense of how our deer management program is working on the ground with individual deer," he says.

As was done in a study of antlered deer, antlerless deer are being captured using drop nets, clover traps, and rocket nets. The objective is to collar 140 deer per year, half that number from each of two study sites. One study site is located largely on state forest in the "big woods" areas of north-central Pennsylvania. The other is located on state forest land in Pennsylvania's southern tier ridge and valley country, though in years two and three of the study it will expand to include some nearby private property.

Hunters will be allowed to shoot collared deer at each of the sites beginning with the 2005 seasons, just as they would any legal antlerless deer. In fact, it's critical that they not avoid collared deer if the study is to reflect how things really are in Penn's Woods, says Rosenberry. "Our preference would be that hunters treat them the same as they would any other legal deer. We would hope they wouldn't give them any preferential treatment either way," he says.

Whether hunters took that advice is open to debate. When Game Commission crews went looking for their collared deer after the 2005–6 hunting seasons, they found that hunters had killed only about eight percent of the available deer in the Sproul and only about 20 percent in the Tuscarora. Some, like the Unified's Wayne Haas, said that was a reflection of the fact that hunters were choosing to pass on shooting does because they feel the herd has already been reduced too much.

Others, however, wonder about that. Penn State's Diefenbach said fly-overs of the study areas found relatively few hunters in the woods, even on the weekends. That raises the question of whether hunters, in those limited numbers, could control deer even if they wanted to. The study also suggests that fears hunters are killing too many deer are unfounded, said Shissler. "This data, while preliminary, suggests that deer numbers are as low as they are in those places not because we're overharvesting them, but because the habitat is so poor. It's the habitat, or lack of it, that's managing deer, not hunters," Shissler said.

The study, preliminary as it is, also points out that hunters perhaps need to give deer a little more credit, said Greg Isabella, a Game Commissioner from Philadelphia. Just because hunters can't always find deer doesn't mean they aren't there. "Deer adapt to hunters. They're not sticking around to get a .30-06 slug in the shoulder."

The biggest study the Game Commission might yet undertake, though—and the one that might really showcase the wisdom of using hunters to control deer— would be what Alt has called a forest restoration area study. Preliminarily designed as a multiyear study, it would examine the impact of varying levels of deer on the landscape.

The goal will be twofold: to monitor the impact of changing deer populations on forest health, and to monitor the impact of various seasons and bag limits on deer numbers, using tools like infrared sensors mounted on planes to count deer at night.

To get this kind of information, Alt had hoped to have crews put radio collars on adult does on several twenty-five-thousand-acre sites on state forest land. The sites—which would again be split between northern and southern Pennsylvania—

would be comparable to forests statewide, based on factors like road densities and vegetation. Each site would be representative of a specific habitat type, too, like an oak forest versus a cherry-dominated forest.

While collaring deer, researchers would also inventory the variety and abundance of mature and immature tree and plant species at each site to get some baseline data. They could then tinker with seasons, bag limits, and the like to see how many deer hunters could remove from the landscape—a goal might be to reduce the herd by 30 percent each year of the study—and monitor what happens to the forest as they do.

It's extremely important that biologists collect that data, says Marrett Grund, the former Game Commission biologist. Right now, biologists don't really have sufficient data to say just how many deer Pennsylvania can realistically have, while still allowing for forest regeneration, songbirds, and other game and nongame wildlife. A study like this one could provide that number.

"That's something that's still being worked on," Grund says. "Our whole deer management plan is based on ecosystem management, looking at deer as part of the whole landscape, so it's a tough thing to say, whether it's ten deer per square mile or fifteen deer per square mile or twenty deer per square mile or whatever." Biologists know they need three things to control deer, says Grund: adequate numbers of hunters, access to the deer habitat, and time for those hunters to get the job done. The study would attempt to get all three of those tools and put them to use.

Each forest restoration site could be a test site for various deer management strategies before they go statewide. On study sites, for example, hunters might be able to get an unlimited number of doe tags. There might be unlimited seasonal and daily bag limits. There might be extended seasons, controlled hunts, doe tags that feature expiration dates, or party hunting, where one hunter could shoot a deer for every member of his group, provided they had licenses with which to tag them.

Some of these tools might fail. Others might be promising enough to expand their use statewide; still others might prove to be viable only for specific wildlife management units, Grund says. No matter what, though, biologists would be getting answers to questions that have too long been the subject of myth and guesswork.

In addition to looking at deer impacts, the study could also determine what role things like acid rain and exotic, invasive species play in forest regeneration. "Deer are clearly one factor that impact regeneration, but we realize there are others, too," says Grund. "I don't know, no one knows, not a scientist in the country knows, how the forest is going to respond. But rather than focus just our deer management program on numbers, we want to focus it on a habitat-based program. In the United States, at least, this will be the most comprehensive deer habitat study ever done to look at that. We'll be taking a look at deer and their impacts on a forest on a landscape scale."

How soon the study might get under way, or whether it would ever begin, are questions still being debated. Representatives of the Game Commission and the DCNR have met to talk about coordinating their efforts. Some at the DCNR had suggested they study the forest restoration-type issues—monitoring things like tree and plant regeneration and small game and songbird habitat using its own biologists and those from various universities—at the same time and at the same sites where the Game Commission is doing its doe study. DCNR wildlife biologist Merlin Benner said such cooperation could prove fruitful without requiring either agency to bear the cost alone. "It won't be one study or the other. We'll be funding our part of it and they'll be funding their part of it and we'll sort of do it in a coordinated manner," Benner said.

Biologists remain hopeful that the study will get done, because, among all of the research done to date and all that's planned for the future, the forest restoration study has the greatest potential to show that hunters, given the chance, can fix the forests, according to Gary Alt. It could show that hunting—by regulating deer numbers at no cost to society at large—can shape the deer herd not only to sportsmen's satisfaction but to the benefit of those who want to maintain a sustainable hardwood forest, see birds, or hike through a forest that has a variety of plants, from delicate trillium to mighty oaks.

"It's all meant to determine how to manage the habitat today so that we preserve hunting and our hunting heritage for the future," says Grund. "It's exciting to have science explore these kinds of issues so that we can put conservation programs in place to meet our challenges."

"I believe this could be the greatest testament to the value of hunting we'll ever have," adds Alt. "We'll prove that not only can hunters fix the forest, but that they will fix the forest for the benefit of all Pennsylvanians. We'll be out front leading the charge. I believe that's the greatest legacy we can leave for our children and grandchildren."

9

GETTING TO THE POINT OF MANAGING DEER CORRECTLY

Josh Schrecengost's words—"From this point on, we're pretty much silent"—belied the chaos that was to come.

Schrecengost and three other members of a deer capture team were walking up a forest road, Greg, Marrett Grund, and me in tow, headed for a clover box trap that held a whitetail. Their task was to put radio transmitters and ear tags on antlered deer, and they were hoping this deer was a button buck.

Their work was the backbone of a study, carried out by the Pennsylvania Game Commission, U.S. Geological Survey, and Cooperative Fish and Wildlife Research Unit at Penn State University, that began in the winter of 2002. The buck study, as the project was called, was meant to do four things: determine the survival of bucks between the ages of six and thirty months; see when bucks disperse and how far they go when they do; see how antler restrictions—scheduled to go into effect for the first time the following fall—would change the male age structure of the deer herd; and measure hunter satisfaction with antler restrictions.

The study, it was obvious even then, was critical if the Game Commission hoped to earn public acceptance of antler restrictions, the most radical change to Pennsylvania deer management proposed in half a century. For about fifty years, any buck with one spike at least three inches long or one antler with two points had been considered legal game in Pennsylvania. Gary Alt had proposed that hunters be limited to shooting only those bucks with at least three, and in some places four, points to one side of their rack. Adopting this strategy, Alt said, would have two benefits. It would let more bucks survive to breed when they're older, healthier, and stronger; and it would give hunters the chance to harvest higher-quality bucks. Prior to antler restrictions, many of the state's hunters had never had the opportunity to shoot a really big buck, he said, because Pennsylvania's deer program didn't allow that to happen.

White-tailed deer experience their greatest antler growth between the ages of two and three. In Pennsylvania, though, hunters had typically killed 90 percent of the state's bucks each fall. With more than 80 percent of them yearlings, fewer than one in a hundred bucks ever lived to reach four years old. Statistics for 1999 showed that a little more than 13 percent of all the bucks harvested statewide were spikes.

Things weren't too bad in areas of prime habitat, where even young bucks could grow decent antlers quickly. Just 1 percent of the bucks harvested in Lawrence County in 1999 were spikes. In Butler County, the percentage of spikes was 6, in Lancaster 5, and in Westmoreland 8. In the state's northern-tier counties, though—the site of the big woods but also the worst deer habitat in the state—spikes were much more common. In Tioga County, 17 percent of all the bucks killed in 1999 were spikes. In Clearfield, the percentage was 18. In Clinton and Susquehanna counties it was 20, in Cameron it was 21, and in Potter and Centre Counties it was 22 percent. In Elk and McKean Counties, 26 percent of all the bucks shot were spikes. In Forest County, the figure was a whopping 32 percent.

The fact that Pennsylvania hunters grew up accustomed to shooting small deer made them popular around the country, said Brian Murphy of the Quality Deer Management Association (QDMA). Their expectations were so low that outfitters in other states found them easy to please. "It's sort of a joke, but it's true," says Murphy. "They can take a Pennsylvania hunter out and let him shoot a two-and-a-half-year-old buck with a thirteen- to fourteen-inch spread and eight points, and he thinks he's shot Old Mossy Horns because he's never seen anything like that. They can give Pennsylvania hunters an average deer and save the bigger bucks for other hunters."

Things don't have to be that way, Alt says. And they shouldn't be. "We kill a greater percentage of our bucks each year than any other state in the country. Why? Because our grandfathers taught our fathers, who taught us, that if you see a buck, you killed it," says Alt. "You just flattened it. I don't think that's anything we should be proud of. We can grow massive bucks in this state, but we can never grow them if we shoot them as soon as they grow antlers. We have the potential to grow massive deer here. Much bigger deer. The question is, can we make it happen?"

Growing bigger bucks for hunters is not the only reason—or even the main reason—for antler restrictions. Antler restrictions are good for the state's deer, Alt says. Carrying more mature bucks into the fall—coupled with shooting more does before the breeding season, something that's being accomplished courtesy of the October doe season—has increased breeding competition and ensured that only the biggest, healthiest bucks are breeding does. That's comparable to what's been going on for decades with the state's elk.

"We've got some world-class trophy bulls out there and you can bet they're doing all of the breeding. Those spike bulls don't have a chance, and that's what you want. We need to do the same thing with white-tailed deer," says Alt. "Older, stronger bucks. That's what we want. That's what's served whitetails well for 3 million years."

When Alt first proposed antler restrictions, though, there were questions. How many of those seventy-thousand-plus bucks that hunters would be required to pass up would survive till the following hunting season? How many would get hit by cars? How many might be shot illegally? How many others would die as a result of predation, accidents, or other natural causes? What would older bucks look like if they did survive another year? These are the mysteries the buck study was meant to solve.

"We'll answer the question, 'What does the average Pennsylvania buck have on his head as a yearling? As a two-year-old. As a three-year-old. We'll be able to say that if you pass up the average yearling buck, this is what he should come back looking like a year later," Alt says.

It fell to Schrecengost, leader of one of the buck study teams, and his crew to get those details. They were working in Armstrong County, trapping deer exclusively on private property, in an area where a mix of woodlots and agriculture provided pretty good habitat. A part of wildlife management unit 2D, Armstrong County was also one of those places where bucks had to have four points to a side to be legal.

A second crew was working in Centre County. That county—split between two wildlife management units, 4D and 2G—offered a mixed habitat. The eastern portion of the county was largely private ground, with wooded ridges separated by agricultural valleys. The western half included large tracts of public land, namely, state game lands, typical of the big woods country of the northern tier. It was all a three-point area.

The goal, between the two sites, was to put transmitters on two hundred bucks each year for three years. This would be enough to rank the study as "one of the most extensive radio-telemetry studies of male deer dispersal and survival and antler development ever attempted in the United States," Grund had said.

Former Game Commission deer biologist Marrett Grund releases a yearling buck after it has been given ear transmitters so that crews can monitor its movements and home range.

On this day, we stopped talking as we approached the trap, the only sound the squishing of our boots in the road, muddy from melted snow. Schrecengost, a football player during his high school days, was flanked on one side by the equally burly Jason Kougher. To his left were Susan Cooper, stopwatch and clipboard in hand, and Khara Strum.

At a bend in the road, four minutes of carefully orchestrated mayhem began. Like crazed linebackers breaking in on a defenseless quarterback, the four rushed the deer, penned five yards off the trail. Schrecengost and Kougher each went to one side of the trap, spreading a net across the door. Strum ran to the back, pulled the cord that raised the door, and tried to scare the deer out in their direction.

"Go, go, go!" she yelled. "Get out, get out, get out! Other way! Other way!"

The deer, which had been contentedly bedded, was now a pinball, bouncing off the trap and bowing its wire mesh sides with each desperate leap. Seeing Schrecengost and Kougher at its rear, the deer tried to bull its way out the closed end of the trap, past Strum.

Five wild seconds went by. Eight. Ten. Finally, out of options and panicked, the deer dashed out the door and into the purse net. Kougher tackled it by its legs, Schrecengost by its head. The deer went down and Schrecengost pulled a blindfold—made from a cutoff shirt sleeve—from his forearm. That went over the deer's face.

Only then were they able to tell that the deer, pinned to the ground by the weight of its captors and bawling all the while, was a doe—a "non-target animal." It received ear tags anyway, for the parenthetical evidence they might provide should the deer be taken by a hunter later.

Then it was time to let the deer go, no easy task in itself.

"Fawns—well I guess you can't really call them fawns anymore, since they're nine months old—they're more scared," Schrecengost said later. "Some of those older does, they seem to want to kill you." That's why crew members decide who is going to do what before they rush a deer. "Everybody has a purpose," Kougher said. "We're not just hog-tying the animal."

This one just wanted to put distance between itself and the capture crew. Schrecengost counted to three, yanked on the blindfold, and rolled off the deer at the same time Kougher did. The deer jumped up, leaped past Strum no more than arm's length away, noisily scrambled up a near-vertical hillside, and was gone.

Cooper clicked the stopwatch. "Three minutes twenty seconds," she said. Another capture successfully completed.

While this deer was not a buck, several others we caught a week later were. On that night, though, Schrecengost and his crew used a seventy-foot-square drop net to catch deer. Four poles sunk into the ground hold the corners of the net up. An eight-foot center pole supports the middle, above corn spread out as bait. Crew members hide some distance away—how far depends on the terrain and cover—and drop the net using a remote-control device that looks like a small transistor radio with its antennae and buttons. When a crew member trips the remote, the four corners of the net fall to the ground, taking down the center pole with them and trapping deer underneath.

Crew members made a habit of checking the net's trigger before every session, but experience had taught them that it was especially important to do so on cold days. "We sat out here one night when it was freezing, and when the deer finally came in and we tried to drop the net, it wouldn't work," said crew member Matt Silicki. "The cold had completely drained the battery."

The real advantage of drop nets is that they have the potential to catch multiple deer at a time, a fact demonstrated by Schrecengost that night. He was to be the triggerman who would watch the net, then call for Silicki, Cooper, and crew member John Rohm if and when he caught some deer. They would wait in their truck below the crest of the hill, out of sight.

In the cabin where we met before going into the field, Schrecengost asked if Greg and I wanted to sit in the blind with him so that we could see the whole operation for ourselves. We hadn't expected to be given that chance—the last blind we'd seen was too small to squeeze us in and we didn't know this one was going to be bigger—so we were dressed pretty lightly. We had coats and gloves, but that was about it. Schrecengost didn't look any more prepared there in the cabin, though, wearing jeans and a sweatshirt, so we said we'd tag along.

We should have known we were in for trouble when, just before we left, Schrecengost started layering up—overalls, additional shirts, a heavy hat, mittens. We soon understood why. The blind turned out to be a partially open-sided tree-house-like stand thirty feet above the ground. A blind for hunters during deer season, it sits on the ridge of a sloped, then-barren cornfield, about a hundred yards away from the net that was tucked into a corner at the tree line.

We climbed the homemade ladder into the blind and hunkered down. "Can you believe two weeks ago I was out here wearing just a flannel shirt with a windbreaker? And that was February," Schrecengost said.

No such luck this time. When the wind was calm, you could see through the bare trees to the snow-covered ground of a hillside five hundred yards distant.

When the wind blew and the snow flew, our eyes watered and the faraway hillside became little more than a shadow in the sky.

"Seven-thirty is generally quitting time," Schrecengost said between gusts. "If you haven't seen anything by then, you're generally pretty ready to pack it up."

I was pretty close to being ready then, and it was only 4:30. I put up the hood on my sweatshirt and pulled the strings until it closed over almost my entire face, leaving just a slit for my eyes. I pulled my fingers inside the palms of my gloves, then buried my hands inside my sleeves. I had long underwear on under my jeans, which was more than Greg had, and I was still shivering.

"We were sitting in the truck with the heater on, listening to the wind howl, wondering how you were doing," Rohm said later. "But Susan said you were outdoor writers and did this all the time, so you must know what you were doing."

Uh, right. Fortunately, about an hour after we had climbed into the blind, when I was seriously wondering how I was going to climb down the ladder and out of the blind if my muscles were too frozen to work, Schrecengost said the words we'd been waiting to hear—"we've got deer approaching the net."

He had been optimistic that we would get deer that afternoon. This was the first time this net site had been used, and that's generally when the nets are most productive. Still, the sight of deer had seemed a long time in coming.

We peeked over the edge of the blind and saw four deer working their way toward the net. They hesitated, seemed to play in the field, then slowly, one at a time, began to make their way to the bait. Before Schrecengost could drop the net, however, four others appeared. Then four more, then three more after that.

Five moved under the net. Schrecengost hesitated, tempted by the thought of setting a new record. Crews had captured as many as seven deer in a single drop, and Schrecengost saw the potential to beat that. He was also worried about "educating" the deer that were not under the net, as the crew planned to use this site again. Those that come close to getting trapped but escape are leery of returning to bait sites again.

"But we'd gain one, lose one. Gain one, lose one. I decided I better just drop the net," Schrecengost said. He did, and five very surprised whitetails were caught. Four became so tangled almost immediately that they couldn't even stand. One made a few frustrated jumps, then went down, too. Schrecengost called the crew on his radio and we scrambled out of the blind to go charging down the hill, stumbling in the ruts of the plowed field. When they got to the deer, each crew member lay down on an animal, using their body weight to keep the deer pinned to the ground so it couldn't hurt itself. Schrecengost went from animal to animal, blindfolding each.

Game commissioner Roxane Palone, at right, helps to capture a yearling buck as part of the Game Commission's buck study.

He felt for antlers as he went. Four of the five deer were button bucks.

"I couldn't believe it," he said later. "I just kept feeling buttons."

"That's our best ratio yet," Silicki said. "Five deer and four bucks."

Cooper gave each deer a shot of sedative—"it sort of relaxes their muscles, but leaves them aware"—before going back around, this time putting a tag in one ear and, in the case of the bucks, a radio transmitter in the other. When she finished, each deer got a shot of a second medication, a "reverser" that neutralizes the effect of the sedative. The crew then had to untangle the deer and set them free.

"It's easier if they don't flop around so much under the net and get even more tangled. That's one of the reasons it's important to lay on them," said Rohm.

Crew members cradled the deer or lifted them by their legs to get them out of the net. The dazed deer stood, wobbly, for a few seconds. Then with a pat on the back they wandered off, slowly at first, then with more speed as their senses returned.

The whole process of blindfolding, tagging, and releasing those five deer took thirty-five minutes, not a bad time in Silicki's estimation. That's a lot better than the first time the crew worked with a drop net, Schrecengost said. On that occasion, the crew caught seven deer in one drop, after dark. "It was like stepping into a hurricane," Schrecengost said. "When you don't know what to expect, it was overwhelming. The deer were so tangled and it was so dark, it was a mess. You have to keep your head about you because no two deer are the same. But, boy, is it a rush."

It was a rush crew members would get to experience many times. Over the course of three winters, crews caught 2,023 deer, 551 of them bucks. Armstrong County gave up 331 bucks, all from private land, while Centre County gave up 220, 66 of them caught on state game lands. As of March 20, 2004, 239 bucks—68 button bucks and 76 adults in Armstrong County, 48 button bucks and 47 adults in Centre—were still on the air. The result is that biologists have learned a lot about catching deer in general and about Pennsylvania's bucks in particular.

Clover traps and drop nets were the two most successful means of catching deer, far outpacing dart guns and rocket nets. Cold weather was the best time to catch deer. Perhaps drawn by the food used as bait—"enticer corn," the crew calls it—deer responded best when the temperature dropped below freezing or snow covered the ground.

You would think that being captured once would be enough for any deer, but that was not always the case. Schrecengost's crew caught thirteen different deer at least twice each, and some more often, in the first year of the study alone. "People say, 'I bet those deer wise up fast' when we talk about trapping them," Grund said. "Well, they do, but in the wrong way. Sometimes they keep coming back to the traps because they know that corn is an easy meal."

Researchers also learned a lot about where Pennsylvania's bucks travel, how far they go, and when they go. That information came from people like Sarah Frantz and Heather Halbritter, two deer crew members working in Armstrong County. Their job was to spend spring, summer, and early fall searching for bucks that had been radio tagged the previous two winters and plotting their locations on a map.

I tagged along with them one day hoping to get a look at a tagged buck, but this wasn't to be. We bounced along a few country roads—some paved, some not, but all of them narrow and windy—in their hand-me-down Game Commission Bronco looking for bucks. Using a radio transmitter—big antennas linked to earphones that pick up the telltale "beep, beep, beep" of tagged bucks, each of which has its own unique frequency—and a laptop computer, they located several deer, some of them seemingly fairly close by. But following a buck by the beeps from his tag and actually getting to see him are two different things.

"It's pretty tough to get a visual," said Halbritter as she plotted a deer's coordinates on a computerized map. "People are always asking us, 'Where are the bucks?' and we always tell them that we know they're out there. But we don't get to see them much."

"Sometimes you'll know that a buck is really close because he'll be busting your ears out over the transmitter," said Frantz. "But getting to see him is hard."

I did learn a little bit about just how much Pennsylvania's bucks move when they are young, however. Though the study wasn't then finished—crews were tracking deer through the 2005 hunting season—early returns have shown that 71 percent of the study bucks in Armstrong County and 44 percent of the Centre County bucks dispersed from the home range they occupied as fawns. Armstrong County bucks traveled greater distances on average, moving about seven miles, compared to four miles for Centre County bucks. The farthest an Armstrong County buck moved was an amazing twenty-six miles, a trip that included a swim across the Allegheny River. The farthest a Centre County buck traveled was sixteen miles.

"Some of the individual movements have just been shocking," says Eric Long, the Penn State University graduate student who's coordinating the study. Biologists aren't sure why Armstrong County's bucks are more likely to move or move farther, says Gary Alt, although it might be a reflection of the fact that Armstrong County's habitat is more fragmented.

One thing that's been pretty consistent at both study sites is just when bucks start to move. Bucks tend to stay in much the same spot through spring and summer, according to Grund. But by late September or early October their home range may double or triple, depending on the available food and habitat. In mid-November, when the rut starts to peak, bucks really move.

Bucks that leave an area don't tend to come back, either. As a result, hunters who shoot a button buck needn't worry that they killed a buck that they might have been able to get later, after it had grown. "I hear guys all the time saying they don't want to shoot that button buck they've seen on their property before it has a chance to grow up. Based on what we've already learned, I don't think that's going to be a problem," Grund said. "It probably wasn't going to be around anyway. Chances are that buck's going to be long gone by the time hunting season rolls around."

Of all the things the buck study revealed, however, two are most important to hunters and deer managers. First, antler restrictions do allow more deer to reach older age, and second, those older deer do survive from year to year, meaning they get the chance to do more breeding.

In 2002, the year before antler restrictions went into place, fewer than 10 percent of the bucks captured by the crews were adults (eighteen months old or older). Crews caught one adult for every seventeen button bucks. "Those kids felt like celebrating every time they caught a mature buck because it was just so rare," Alt said.

By 2003 crews were capturing one adult for every nine button bucks. By 2004, the ratio was one adult for every two button bucks. For hunters, this meant that there were more adult bucks to choose from when hunting. In wildlife management units 2A and 2B, in the southwestern corner of the state, for example, yearling bucks accounted for 83 percent of the buck harvest in 1999–2000 and 84 percent in 2000–2001. In 2002–3, the first year after antler restrictions went into effect, only 66 percent of the buck harvest was made up of yearlings. "That's a remarkable change," Grund said. "Antler restrictions are clearly working in western Pennsylvania."

Bucks are living longer across the rest of the state, too. Game Commission crews visit butcher shops across Pennsylvania each fall during the two-week firearms deer season, collecting jawbones to age the deer taken by hunters. They have found that the percentage of yearling bucks in the harvest is going down everywhere.

As for what happens to those bucks that hunters pass up, the study has shown that nearly 90 percent of the adult bucks that survived the 2002 hunting seasons were still alive and available to hunters in 2003. Eighty-eight percent of bucks surviving the 2002–3 seasons were still available to hunters in 2003–4.

This is important because some hunters had worried that the bucks they passed up would be shot by poachers, killed by vehicles, taken by archery hunters, or lost in some other way before the next firearms deer season. Some worried, too, that hunters would shoot bucks first and count their points later, leaving the too-small ones in the woods to rot. All indications are that none of those things have happened.

Archers—who have six weeks to hunt, from the beginning of October through mid-November—aren't killing an inordinate number of bucks. In Centre County, for example, just one of the marked bucks fell to an archer during the study's first two years. In Armstrong County, only ten of ninety-one marked bucks harvested were taken by archers. "The archery season is not decimating the buck population," Grund said. "It's clearly a recreational opportunity, and that's in line with what we intended the season to be."

As for poachers, only nine of 161 bucks that were marked over the course of the study had fallen to poachers by the spring of 2004. Vehicles had accounted for a similar number of buck deaths. While even one deer lost to those two causes is too many, Grund said, the numbers are not too alarming. If anything, they point to the fact that Pennsylvania probably has more deer than anyone realizes.

"We don't account for deer killed on the road. We don't account for deer that are poached," Grund said. "If a farmer doesn't allow hunting on his property, and a deer never leaves it until someone shoots it illegally or it gets hit by a car or just dies, it never shows up in our population estimates. We don't know what we have, other than the bare minimum. This information should help us develop a better estimate."

That said, the Game Commission hopes to further investigate the issue of poaching on a landscape that should feature older and bigger bucks by doing a "robo-buck" study sometime over the next few years. The Commission has used robotic deer—life-sized mounts, covered with real deer hides and featuring heads that turn or tails that twitch—to nab poachers for close to a decade, says Mel Schake, information and education supervisor in the agency's southwest regional office. Conservation officers follow strict guidelines when using the robotic deer, setting them out only in areas with reported poaching problems and putting them out only on the slowest days of hunting season and in somewhat hard-to-spot places, rather than in the middle of a field.

"That's all done so that we don't take the occasional guy who might be out driving and just sees a deer in a field and can't resist such an obvious temptation," says John Smith, law enforcement supervisor in the Game Commission's southwest region office. "It's the individual who's really serious, who's really hunting for these things, that we're after with these deer."

The wildlife conservation officers who already use the robo-deer offer anecdotal evidence of where and when most poaching occurs. The study would be designed to quantify that while also examining whether the bigger bucks resulting from antler restrictions spark an increase in poaching. "Is poaching worse in the four-point [antler restriction] areas, in remote areas, along roads? Is it a bigger issue right after hunting season, or before, maybe as early as August? That's what we'll find out," Grund said. "I think hunters and the general public will be interested in those answers, too."

As for mistake kills—cases in which a hunter shot a deer only to learn it didn't have enough points to be legal—relatively few are occurring. Vern Ross, then executive director of the Game Commission, said the agency had expected to see between five and ten thousand mistake kills the first year of antler restrictions, based on what had happened in other states. There were just 2,096 mistake kills in 2002–3, however, and just 1,471 in 2003–4.

It's important to note, too, that not all of those mistakes are related to antlers and antler restrictions. Warren Stump, law enforcement supervisor in the Commission's north-central region office, said the agency has always had to deal with cases of hunters shooting a buck mistaken for a doe, or of shooting at one deer and killing two. That remains true now. In 2003–4, for example, only about 60 percent of the 274 mistakes recorded during the first week of the firearms deer season in the north-central region were related to antler restrictions.

"We've always had mistakes. We always have, and we always will," Stump says. What's encouraging, he says, is that the number of mistakes isn't higher, which he attributes to hunters' doing a good job of dealing with the sometimes tricky business of counting antler points before shooting. If that were not the case—if hunters were shooting bucks that were too small and then either leaving them in the woods or sneaking them home—there would probably be signs of that, Stump says.

The Game Commission has traditionally received tips about people who have shot deer out of season or shot too many deer or deer that were too small. There's been no increase in the number of such reports since antler restrictions were put in place, as might have been expected if there was a significant jump in unreported mistakes. "If that was happening, I think we would have seen an increase in some of those other indicators, and we did not have that," says Stump. "I think that reflects what's happening out there."

What is happening is that hunters are killing bigger deer. Fred Frederick, owner of Fred's Taxidermy in Westmoreland County, usually mounts about thirty bucks during archery season. In 2002, the first year after antler restrictions had been put in place, he got sixty-two. He also got a hundred bucks—almost all of them truly fine specimens—the first three days of rifle season alone. "I always get a lot of nice deer, but I get a lot of mediocre ones, too. This was the best year so far," he said then. "The racks had a lot more mass and there were a lot of nice ten points and eights."

Dan Snyder, owner of Otter Creek Taxidermy in Greenville and president of the Pennsylvania Taxidermy Association, has experienced much the same thing. In the years since antler restrictions have been in place, the deer coming into his shop have definitely improved, both in terms of antler development and body size, he says. While the number of bucks being brought in is down—something other taxidermists across the state have told him they've noticed, too—the deer coming in are definitely bigger.

"I'm seeing a lot of deer that are two and a half or three and a half years old, whereas before a lot were yearlings," Snyder said. "I think we're going to see as big deer here as anywhere. I think it's going to be really interesting to see what happens over the next few years."

"I saw more big bucks [in 2003] than I had in past years," added Kip Padgelek, owner of Kip's Deer Processing in Carnegie, in Allegheny County. "I saw more 150- and 160-class bucks than I ever did in a season. I had a lot more people looking for those."

Hunters are even changing as a result of antler restrictions, according to Snyder. Whereas rifle hunters in particular used to be quick to pull the trigger on the first buck they saw, now they have to wait, and many seem to like it. "The rifle guys are getting more like the archers. They're getting time to look over an animal and decide if it's big enough, if they've got a good shot, if they want to take that animal," he said.

"It used to be that if you didn't get your buck on the first day you were disappointed, because they were tough to find," said Ed Grasavage of the Pennsylvania chapter of the Quality Deer Management Association. "Most were shot that first day. Now people have found out that the sky doesn't fall in if you don't shoot that first buck that wanders by."

Ron Freed, the deer expert formerly of Audubon Pennsylvania, certainly appreciates what antler restrictions have done. He quit hunting bucks in 2000 to focus on does, the better to back up his own call for a reduction in the deer herd. He was looking for a doe in the 2003 rifle deer season when he went hunting on some property he owns in Cumberland County. When one of the biggest deer he's ever encountered while hunting—a big-bodied eight-point with an eighteen-inch spread—wandered in front of him, though, he gave in to temptation and took it.

"I've shot a ton of spikes over the years, just like everybody else. If you didn't shoot it, somebody else did," Freed said. "But I'll tell you, the first thing I said when I walked up to that big buck was 'God bless Gary Alt.'"

Merlin Benner, a lifelong hunter who's been at it since he was twelve, has also shot some very big bucks in the past two years, a change from the early days of his hunting career. He can't even remember how many does he saw in his first seven years of hunting before he saw his first legal buck. "I remember as a kid reading books and magazines about some kid getting his 30/30 and shooting his first buck and it being a ten-point. I thought, yeah, right," Benner said. "I found out it does happen in the real world, just not in Pennsylvania before now."

Alt believes more hunters can enjoy similar experiences if they are patient and give antler restrictions a chance. The 2003–4 deer harvest produced more two-and-a-half-year-old deer than at any time in decades and he was predicting that the 2004–5 season would give up a few three-and-a-half-year-olds, which few hunters living in the state today have ever seen. "There's no doubt in my mind that in the long term this is going to lead to more eight-points in the herd than we've ever had," Alt says. "Most hunters have never killed a buck that's three years old. If we can push the envelope, we can have bucks that are bigger than most people have shot in their life."

Some hunters, though, don't like antler restrictions because they make it too hard to shoot a deer. Ed Mans is an Allegheny County hunter who, along with family, owns property in Armstrong County, near where the buck study was carried out. They have shot does in the past but are strictly buck hunters now. The problem, Mans said, is that it's difficult to count points while hunting deer by driving through the woods, as they tend to pass shooters on the run. He'd like a return to the days when hunters could shoot smaller bucks.

On opening day of the 2003 firearms deer season, he said he had to pass up four bucks, while his son passed up five, all because they didn't have time to count points. "When you're pushing deer through a wooded area, it's pretty hard to tell," said Mans, who estimated that fewer than 20 percent of the bucks they've taken from their property in the past thirty years would have met the new minimum standard of four points to a side. "Buck hunting is deer hunting to us. That's why, to me, a six-point is as good as a seven-point."

Others dislike antler restrictions because they fear they will hurt the deer herd by forcing hunters to take all of the superior bucks, leaving the inferior ones to do the breeding. They refer to it as the threat of "high grading," a timber term referring to the practice of harvesting the highest-quality trees from an area and leaving the poorer quality ones behind to serve as the seed source.

Ralph Saggiomo, a past president of the Unified Sportsmen of Pennsylvania, is one of those who worry what antler restrictions will do to the genetics of the state's deer herd. "I'm five-foot-seven and a half. I'm never going to play in the NBA. Neither are my children. I didn't pass on the genes," Saggiomo said. "The same thing goes with wildlife. You've got to have the genes."

The Unified's Woody Shields agreed, saying biologists should already know that antler restrictions don't work. The Game Commission's own policy, which prohibited hunters from shooting spike bucks between 1928 and 1953, didn't lead to bigger bucks then. This latest plan won't either, he said, and instead is likely to "turn the clock back seventy-five years to the flawed deer management policy of 1925."

"As I understand the proposal," Shields said when antler restrictions were first proposed, "they want to prohibit the harvest of small yearling bucks [spikes and Ys], while at the same time encouraging the unlimited harvest of large yearling bucks [five points or more]. Thereby, the small bucks would survive to breed and pass on their inferior genetics and through this strange process, the antler genetics of the deer herd would mysteriously improve. This is not a natural situation."

As evidence supporting that theory, Saggiomo pointed to a study done largely by Steve Demarais, a professor in the department of wildlife and fisheries at Mississippi State University. Demarais and several colleagues studied antler records from 220 captive bucks whose ages were known. The goal was to see whether selectively removing a portion of those bucks with larger or smaller antlers would affect the antler size of the remaining deer in subsequent years.

In several reports resulting from that work, Demarais said that antler restrictions can potentially lead to high grading. "If yearling bucks are able to express their genetic potential for antler development and if the harvest rate of eligible bucks is high, there may be some potential for negative impacts over an extended period of time," Demarais wrote. "Potential antler size and configuration is genetically inherited. Differential removal of yearlings with greater antler potential and protection of yearlings with lesser antler potential could ultimately impact inheritance of genetic potential for antler development."

Many of those who have latched on to such statements as proof that Pennsylvania should do away with antler restrictions ignore the rest of what Demarais wrote, however. He noted, for example, that the Mississippi State study was conducted using captive deer raised under optimum conditions. Whether the study results might apply to a free-ranging deer herd—one where late birth dates, poor habitat conditions, and scarce food supplies could affect whether even a genetically superior deer could grow legal antlers—is "speculative."

What's more, in another paper he wrote, Demarais said that antler restrictions, or selective harvest criteria, as he called them, can even protect yearling bucks and increase average antler size under some conditions. Most important, perhaps, Demarais did not suggest that antler restrictions be done away with so that hunters could go back to shooting smaller bucks. Instead, he said that if protecting yearling bucks is the goal, biologists should make things even harder on hunters and limit them to shooting mature bucks, as determined by various body characteristics.

This is similar to what Larry Castle would like to ask of hunters in Mississippi. Castle is director of the division of wildlife for the Mississippi Department of Wildlife, Fisheries, and Parks. Mississippi—along with Pennsylvania and Arkansas—is one of just three states nationwide with a statewide point restriction. Mississippi's restriction is four points, though that means four points total, not four points to a side as in Pennsylvania. The regulation was instituted not by biologists but by an act of the legislature. Castle makes no bones about saying that the point restriction "is not what we need biologically." "It was a positive for us at first. However, biologically, it is not the thing to do across all of Mississippi," Castle said.

Mississippi, like Pennsylvania, has long had too many deer, Castle said. Hunter expectations were set at a time when the state's deer population was two to three times as large as it should have been. That's created unrealistic expectations about how many deer the state should have and how many deer its habitat can support.

To correct this, Mississippi wildlife officials have been trying to ramp up the doe harvest while protecting yearling bucks at the same time. The problem is that Mississippi, again like Pennsylvania, is a diverse state. Some areas, like the Mississippi Delta, have rich soil and good habitat. Other areas are much worse. Instead of protecting the state's best bucks, a four-point antler restriction that doesn't account for those differences in habitat has allowed hunters to take some of the best one-and-a-half-year-old bucks out there. "We need to produce a system that protects all of the bucks in the one-and-a-half-year-old age class. In Mississippi, points do not work in any region," Castle said.

Castle believes the ultimate answer is to make Mississippi hunters look long and hard at any buck before pulling the trigger. "Beam length is a good criterion for aging deer. Antler spread is good. Beam circumference is good. You knock the ball out of the park if you combine all three with body characteristics, but that's a big learning curve," he said.

Some sportsmen have "grown" as hunters and are willing to hunt under those conditions, Castle continued. Others have not and argue that having to judge a deer too closely before shooting is too much to ask. Castle doesn't buy that. "I hear that argument every day. My answer to that is, if you aren't sure it's legal, don't shoot," he said. "My golly, I hear guys say they might miss an opportunity to shoot a legal deer if they have to stop and think that much. That's the same as saying that if I hear something in the brush that might be a legal buck, I should shoot. Well, it might also be a twelve-year-old junior hunter out for the first time. If you're not sure it's a legal animal, just don't shoot."

Arkansas, meanwhile, was the first state to adopt a statewide antler restriction. Its program began in 1998, when hunters were limited to shooting bucks with three points to a side. It, too, was accompanied by an increase in doe hunting. Prior to 1998, hunters shot an average of 55,000 does and 105,000 bucks every year. In the first year with antler restrictions, the kill flip-flopped, with 62,000 bucks taken and 100,000 does.

Donny Harris, chief of the wildlife management division with the Arkansas Game and Fish Commission at the time the point restriction was adopted, said most Arkansas bucks harvested prior to the point restriction were one and a half years old and sported spikes or four-point racks. He was optimistic early on—we spoke in mid-2000—that the point restriction would lead to bigger bucks. What he knew even then, though, was that antler restrictions had changed the way hunters hunted.

"The three-point rule has been valuable in that, for the first time ever, it forced hunters to pass up bucks," said Harris. "Before, they just weren't willing to do that. It put them in a new mindset. We're seeing that if you don't shoot that buck at one and a half, you can shoot him at two and a half and he'll be a bigger buck. It's not such a bitter pill to swallow at that point because they're seeing bigger bucks. They're seeing the rewards of exercising restraint."

A year or two into the program—and despite concerns that hunters might shoot a few more "nubbin' bucks," or what Pennsylvanians call button bucks—there was anecdotal evidence that antler restrictions were having a positive impact on Arkansas's deer herd. Whereas the average buck harvested in Arkansas in the 1990s was one and a half years old, by 2000 the average buck was two and a half. "It's still just a little early to tell, but in some areas we think we might be seeing bigger body weights and better antler configuration," Harris said at the time.

I called Arkansas again in 2004 to see if things were still going as well a few years deeper into the program. I spoke to Cory Gray, the new deer program coordinator for the Game and Fish Commission. He told me that Arkansas has had "fairly good success" with antler restrictions. Statewide, the antler size of harvested bucks had increased and a larger segment of the harvest had been moved into the two-and-a-half- and three-and-a-half-year-old age classes.

It was also true, though, that in a few areas of the state, inferior deer—those that were several years old and still sporting tall spikes—were showing up. Going into the 2004 hunting seasons, the plan was to allow hunters with special permits to take a few of those bucks to get them off the landscape.

Whether those deer are evidence of grading-point restrictions hurting the deer population through high grading is not clear. Antler development is tied closely to the quality of the soil in Arkansas, Gray said. It could be that the three-point rule is not restrictive enough to protect the best young deer from being taken in areas of good habitat. A three- to four-year study, being carried out with the help of the University of Arkansas, may answer that question.

"Our data is biased. It's only showing what we're harvesting. It's not showing us what's remaining on the ground," Gray said. "This study should tell us that."

Like Castle, Gray would prefer to limit hunters to shooting mature bucks based on something like main beam length or inside antler spread. Some who hunt from private clubs already do that. He's afraid this might be too much to ask of most hunters, though. "When you're talking about the hunter who only gets out for two or three days a year, that's pretty difficult for them. We want to make it as easy as possible for the general hunting public," he said.

Alt—who considered recommending an antler-spread requirement rather than a point restriction but rejected it because it would be too hard for hunters to judge—promised that if the buck study showed that antler restrictions aren't working, he would suggest trying something else to protect yearling bucks. He remains pretty confident that point restrictions will work in Pennsylvania, though, for several reasons. First, Pennsylvania's point restriction, unlike Mississippi's and Arkansas's, is designed in such a way as to account for variables in habitat. Biologists examined seventy-one thousand deer, pulled from every county in the state, before determining that some areas—five wildlife management units marked by good habitat—should have a four-point restriction, while the rest—marked by lesser habitat—should have a three-point rule. Such restrictions should protect more than half of all the bucks in any unit each year, he said, and keep any threat of high grading at bay.

Things worked out that way after the 2002–3 and 2003–4 deer seasons, anyway. In both years, 51 percent of the bucks marked in the buck study had survived.

Second, Alt also says that hunters have to remember that genetics is just one part of the equation when it comes to antler growth. Food and age are just as important. It's possible, he says, for a four-point buck in one area to be genetically equal to or even superior to an eight-point elsewhere. If the four-point was born later in the year, or suffered through a harsher winter, or had less food to pick from in the fall, it would have less energy to devote to antler growth and so would look smaller despite being a "better" deer. That's why it's not true to say that all spikes and small-racked bucks stay small forever.

Third, it also appears true, according to a review of scientific literature on the subject, that the unselective nature of doe harvests plays a role in limiting high grading. The female deer accounts for half of a buck's genetics and no one is shooting only the biggest and best does, Rosenberry said, so there are lots of them out there to breed.

There's ample evidence—directly from Pennsylvania—that letting deer live even one more year yields dramatic results, too, according to Alt. Biologists have studied dead deer taken by hunters in every county of the state. What they found in Pike County has been pretty typical. There, prior to antler restrictions, 31 percent of the bucks harvested were spikes, almost all of them yearlings. Of those that did manage to survive to two and a half, though, 54 percent had at least eight points.

"I think there are two things you learn," Alt said. "One, you can never grow big bucks unless you let them grow up. Two, the quality of the habitat has a lot to do with the antlers a buck will grow on its head. If the food is poor, you're going to have antlers that are spindly, a pencil-racked buck. If the food is good, the antlers are going to be much thicker. It's based on nutrition. Deer with better food grow bigger antlers."

Some other hunters, meanwhile, have opposed antler restrictions because they fear it will dramatically depress buck harvests and their chances of getting a buck every year. But Grund says that shouldn't be the case.

Pennsylvania hunters harvested an average of 192,000 bucks each year in the five years preceding antler restrictions, topping out at 203,247 in 2001. The kill dropped to about 165,000 in 2002, when there was a slim mast crop following a mild winter, and to about 142,000 in 2003, when there was a second straight weak mast crop following a tough winter.

Those conditions made it tough for many bucks to grow antlers that could meet the minimum standard to make them legal, says Grund, which is why the kill declined. This won't always be the case, though. It's true that buck harvests will probably never approach 200,000 animals again, but hunters can expect to shoot somewhere around 140,000 bucks a year.

"The harvest is always going to be slightly smaller than it used to, and it's going to be slightly variable, depending on environmental conditions," according to Grund. "It's going to be trickier predicting buck harvests in the future based on all those factors. But that doesn't alarm me at all or surprise me at all. And we'll be taking bigger bucks than we have in previous years."

Beyond genetics, though, deer hunters in the Keystone State have still expressed some trepidation with regard to antler restrictions. One segment of the hunting population worries that all this focus on antlers—for whatever reason, biologically right or wrong—promotes trophy hunting at the expense of true sportsmanship. Ray Martin, an officer with the Pennsylvania Federation of Sportsmen's Clubs, says he does not oppose antler restrictions in general. He worries, though, about the direction in which hunting is going, with its single-minded emphasis on racks. "I'm a little concerned that the focus is maybe shifting to things other than where it should be," Martin said. "There's nothing wrong with big deer or wanting to shoot one, but I'm a little bit worried we're forgetting why we are out there, or why we should be out there."

Those most dedicated to practicing what has come to be known as "quality deer management," though, say bigger antlers are a benefit to proper management, but not the only goal. Murphy, executive director of the Quality Deer Management Association, says quality deer management is also about managing habitat so that it can support a healthier deer herd—marked by a better age and sex ratio—as well as other species. "We certainly don't whack the heads off our deer and throw the rest away alongside the road," Murphy said.

"It's not trophies. It's not about antlers or anything else," agreed Kip Adams, QDMA's biologist for Pennsylvania. "First, it's about putting the right number of deer on the landscape. Second, it's about putting deer in all age classes. Do you get bigger antlers? Sure, but that's a by-product of properly managing deer."

Meanwhile, interest in the tenets of the QDMA is growing, especially in Pennsylvania. The concept of managing deer according to quality deer management standards first arose in the 1970s. The Quality Deer Management Association itself wasn't born until 1988, however, and Pennsylvania didn't get its first chapters until the late 1990s. It has eleven local chapters and a state chapter today—second only to Michigan among the twenty-four states with a QDMA presence—and has been growing faster in Pennsylvania than in any other state.

Hunters who worry that quality deer management means fewer opportunities to shoot a deer are mistaken, Murphy said. It actually promotes the harvest of antlerless deer as a way to bring deer densities into line with the available habitat, balance buck and doe ratios, and let hunters harvest a deer for its meat without shooting "every little bitty buck they can."

Indeed, Castle and Gray both say that protecting bucks and shooting more does must go hand in hand. If you're going to try and carry additional bucks over through the winter, you have to make room for them by removing additional does from the landscape. "You must consider deer mouths," Castle said. "Forget about antlers. It's going to be deer mouths eating those groceries. The habitat can only support so many mouths, and it doesn't care if it's doe mouths or buck mouths. If you're going to save more bucks, you have to harvest more does at the same time.

"The question you have to ask yourself is, what is best for the deer and what is best for the resource and what is best for the habitat. Hunters do not know the answer to that question," Castle said. "They're not supposed to know how to manage deer populations, no more than you or I are supposed to be able to look at an EKG and say what's wrong with a micro cordial valve. Just because I spend a lot of time chasing women doesn't make me a gynecologist. You must reduce deer populations if you're going to manage habitat and keep it from being destroyed, not only for deer, but for that whole suite of species that live in that six feet of forest from the dirt on up."

Scot Williamson of the Wildlife Management Institute says that wildlife professionals all across the Northeast are waiting to see whether antler restrictions can have an effect on the deer resource in Pennsylvania. "I think a lot of people are looking at Pennsylvania to see if antler restrictions can do something with the buck population. But I think more importantly, they're watching Pennsylvania to see if it can achieve overall deer densities that are in line with its goals using antler restrictions. That's what everybody, at least among biologists, is looking at."

The chance to shoot—or at least hunt for—a big buck is very important, too, though. And many hunters want something other than what Pennsylvania deer hunting has traditionally given them, Murphy said. That's why he thinks antler restrictions will become popular. "People are sick of going to public land and seeing more hunters than bucks. They want a new experience," he says. "They want at least the chance to match wits with a mature whitetail."

That's been the draw for members of a group known as the Nippanose Valley Alliance. The alliance is composed of hunting clubs from the area around Williamsport, Lycoming County—namely, the Sunnyside, Nygart Gap, North Face, Waldman Old Farm, and Lincoln Springs hunting clubs. They have been practicing quality deer management on their eleven hundred acres for close to a decade. Already they're seeing the results, says alliance member Schuyler Frey. Members are starting to see—and shoot—bucks with racks that would make most hunters drool. "When you start to see bucks like maybe an eight point with a sixteen-inch spread and that deer starts to look average to you, or even small, that's going to ensure that you're only harvesting mature bucks that are at least three and a half years old," Frey said. "That's when you'll be shooting big bucks instead of younger, smaller ones."

Greg and I had traveled to Lycoming County to talk to Frey and several other members of the alliance. The friendly banter around the table was of deer shot and deer that got away. But everyone agreed on one thing: once hunters get accustomed to chasing older, more mature bucks, they don't want to go back to hunting small ones. "That's what makes a sportsman out of you," said alliance member Steve Waldman. "If you let a buck go for four years, he's considerably more intelligent than ever, more difficult to hunt, more challenging to hunt.

"Then you're going into his house, where he lives, where he knows how to hide. You might walk past him many times and never even know it. But when you shoot something like that, that's hunting. That's the sport of it."

"Guys who pay, $3,000, $4,000, $5,000 to go out west to shoot deer like this can do it right here. That's what we're striving to do," added alliance member Dave Winter. "They can hunt big bucks in this state, in their own back yard."

If and when that day comes, antler restrictions and bigger doe harvests will be here to stay, Adams said. The generations of hunters coming up right now won't want to go back to the days of shooting spikes. "Do you think any of those kids out there are going to shoot that yearling? No way, because they know that big eight- or ten- or twelve-point is out there," Adams said. "They know first of all that shooting that yearling is not the best thing to do, but they know those bigger bucks are out there. It's a slow change, it's a slow course, but I think we'll see it."

Quality deer management is sometimes pursued on private property controlled by a select group of hunters who limit access to members. This has led to a sort of haves vs. have-nots attitude among some hunters, who, I suspect, dislike the approach as much for that reason as for how it operates. A few people—including some within the Game Commission—worry that the push toward quality deer management might prompt more clubs to join together and buy and post land that might otherwise have been open to public hunting.

Murphy says quality deer management can and does work on public ground, though, provided hunters are willing to harvest does to keep populations in line and let some bucks grow up. Pennsylvania was the worst state in the nation for a long time with respect to the age and sex ratio of its deer herd. That can change if hunters will let it, he says. And if they do, the need for hunters to buy their own land to manage deer in a way that's different from the state will dry up, or at least slow down.

Quality deer management, with its focus on habitat, is also much more justifiable to the public at large, he says, than traditional deer management, which tends to make sure few bucks ever live long enough to grow up. "If the human population had only twelve-year-old boys running around, with girls and women of all ages, you can imagine the social chaos we would have. Deer need adult males as much as we do."

Alt says he doesn't want to turn Pennsylvania into a trophy hunting state. Antler restrictions—in conjunction with increased doe harvests—are designed to do what's best for the deer themselves and their habitat.

The consequences of not using the tools at hand are a poor deer herd living in a poor habitat, Alt says. Pennsylvania has suffered under those conditions for too long, as evidenced by one of the bucks collared in Centre County. It died of malnutrition after having been born very late in the year, something that's probably attributable to some combination of poor habitat. "It was small enough to be able to fit through the holes in our drop net when we caught it, so we weren't surprised it didn't make it," said Eric Long. "It was very undersized."

"We have to manage deer so that they exist in the proper relationship with our forests," Alt says. "That's the right thing to do and we're going to attempt to do it."

"It's not about trophy hunting or big racks, though that's probably a side benefit," added game commissioner John Riley. "It's about stronger genetics and doing things the right way and having a buck-to-doe ratio that's right. And you have to fight for those things because not everybody understands it. They buy a license and they want to go into the woods and shoot a deer. Our role is to try and make it work for everybody and to try to remember what's best for the resource."

The promise of bigger-bodied bucks sporting bigger antlers is just the carrot to get hunters—who will admittedly have to sacrifice if they knock the size of the deer herd down—moving in that direction, Riley said.

Grund believes the state is on the right track. "Our goal all along has been to kill the right number of deer of the right sex and age in the right places," he says. "The shift in the age structure of bucks resulting from antler restrictions, together with the increased harvest of does over the last couple of years because of concurrent seasons, would suggest to me that we're beginning to do that much more. That's

Though the state's biggest bucks are often found in suburban areas, antler restrictions have moved more bucks into older age classes throughout the state.

not to say that we're done. We still have a lot more work to do with deer in Pennsylvania. But we are clearly making progress."

"I think some hunters may be pleasantly surprised by the effect of antler restrictions," Alt agrees. "Now hunters go out and if they don't see a buck by lunchtime of the first day, they figure they aren't going to see one because they've already been shot. With antler restrictions, hunters should start seeing bucks later in the day and later into the season. And at least some of those bucks that survive the first few hours and first few days are going to be ones that are legal to shoot."

If it takes a few of those big bucks to get people thinking about the right way to manage deer, there's nothing wrong with that, Frey said. "The big thing we need to do is to start to educate the general Pennsylvania hunter about the ins and outs, the whys and wherefores of scientific deer management," said Frey, holding a massive white-tail rack. "And there's no doubt these bones speak."

10

IN THE EYE OF THE STORM

Gary Alt doesn't look like your prototypical leading man. If Pennsylvania deer management was a James Bond movie, the folks in casting would probably take one look at him — short, bespectacled, with less hair than any action hero this side of Bruce Willis — and make him agent $003\frac{1}{2}$. Alt's appearance, though, belies a startlingly intense passion for Pennsylvania's natural resources.

I found this out early one midsummer morning. It was about 8:15 A.M. on a Monday when Greg and I pulled into the parking lot of the McDonald's in Lords Valley, Pike County. We made one trip around the building, but Alt's forest-green Ford Bronco was nowhere to be found. Our hearts sank.

"Great. Just greeeat!" Greg said, his voice rising to a yell as he leaned forward until his nose was just inches from the steering wheel. "Did I mention how much I hate my job right now? I hate it. Haaate it!"

I probably made things worse but, slaphappy from a lack of sleep, I couldn't help but laugh. Greg and I had been traveling all over the state to talk to people about deer. We were doing some research for a series of newspaper articles and were working primarily on our own time to do it. We'd already worked about fifty-odd days in a row without a break when we set up this particular weekend's interviews.

Our schedule called for us to leave my house at 5:00 A.M. Saturday, then travel three hours to Harrisburg to do a couple of interviews, starting at 8:00. We were to stay there Saturday night, backtrack ninety minutes south and west for a 9:00 A.M.

Dr. Gary Alt, former head of the Pennsylvania Game Commission's deer management section, shows the racks from two bucks in the same age class but with different antler growth owing to habitat.

interview Sunday morning, then head east for interviews in Valley Forge and Philadelphia Sunday afternoon and evening. Finally, we planned to drive from Philadelphia to Milford Sunday night, catch Alt in Lords Valley at 8:00 Monday morning, then drive five hours home.

The plan dissolved into misadventure pretty quickly. We had worked until 2:00 A.M. Saturday and so couldn't stay awake when it came time to drive across the state three hours later. We had to cancel our first interview to sleep in our compact rental car in a truck-stop parking lot.

After keeping our second appointment, we hustled north from Harrisburg to Millersburg in an attempt to squeeze in an unscheduled interview with Audubon Pennsylvania's Ron Freed. He was working Audubon's booth at the Ned Smith Center Nature and Art Festival. By the time we got there, though, all that remained of the festival were the bare skeletons of empty exhibit booths and the occasional napkin tumbleweeding its way across the park lawn.

Saturday wasn't any better. Having underestimated the distance between interviews, we were late for every appointment. We also ran into a storm that flooded the roads while trying to leave Philadelphia. I remember looking out my window as we were inching our way through the water. A glass bottle, like something tossed into the sea by a lonely man on a deserted island, floated past us in the slow lane.

It was all too much for Greg. When we finally made it to the hotel, he bought a case of beer and a bags of chips, vowing to ease his suffering—at least temporarily—with a good binge. Two Old Milwaukees and twenty minutes into Burt Reynolds's *Smokey and the Bandit,* he was snoring, and I had to turn the lights out and the TV off.

Now we were at McDonald's, but without the man we had come to see. We didn't know if we were at the wrong place, or if Alt had gotten tired of waiting and left, or if he had forgotten about us altogether. None of the possibilities were good. Of all the people we would interview about deer, Alt was the one we had to get, no matter what—not only because he was the newly appointed head of the Game Commission's deer management section, or because he was proposing the kind of changes that had ended Roger Latham's career fifty years earlier. We had to get him because everyone else we had talked to agreed that if anyone could turn Pennsylvania's deer management program around, it was Alt.

"He's very thorough. He's a hands-on biologist. And he's of course the best there is in terms of articulating good wildlife management to the people of Pennsylvania," John Oliver, secretary of Pennsylvania's Department of Conservation and Natural Resources during Governor Tom Ridge's administration, had told me a few weeks earlier. "He doesn't have a peer. He's that good. And he's so excited about this. It comes from the heart. It's just part of him to do this," Oliver added. "You've got to have that. You've got to have that if you want people to respect you. And he'll get the respect and support he needs. It's not going to be easy, but he'll get it. I don't know of anyone else who could do it. He's the man."

Things didn't quite work out that way in the long run. Alt would be the man—for a while, at least—but in the end he would burn out, just like Aldo Leopold and Richard Gerstell and Roger Latham before him.

That would come later, though. On this day, we wanted to talk with Alt and feared we might have missed him. We sat for a few quiet seconds, then Greg emerged from his funk and asked if I had Alt's phone number with me. I had to admit sheepishly that I did not.

"Maybe he's in the phone book," I said.

"Yeah, with our luck we'll find him listed right next to Miss Samsonite," Greg said, referring to the scene in *Dumb and Dumber* where Jim Carrey and Jeff Daniels arrive in Aspen after a cross-country drive, only to realize they don't know the name of the woman they're seeking. Looking down at her briefcase, the one they drove all that way to return to her, they see the name "Samsonite" and decide that must be her.

This was Greg's favorite movie—he'd been quoting from it for three days straight—and I couldn't help but laugh again. I certainly felt about as half-witted as Harry and Lloyd, the characters in the movie. I suggested we at least go inside to get some coffee and decide what to do.

We were just slumping into a booth when we saw Alt pull into the lot. We were saved! Our spirits renewed, we waited until he came in, then motioned him over to us. We shook hands, explained again who we were and what we were doing, and made a little small talk about where we'd stayed the night before.

Then Alt started talking about deer. He talked about the history of deer management in Pennsylvania. About the problems that existed. About where he wanted to see deer management go. About what role hunting could play in that. About what might happen to hunting if sportsmen didn't tackle the deer issue.

We ended up spending forty minutes or so in the restaurant, and if I was able to squeeze in more than one question, I can't remember it. I do remember wishing, desperately, that we could get to the car. Alt was laying out his vision of deer management in the twenty-first century and my notebook was a hundred feet away in the rental. I felt like a poor man at the base of a waterfall of cascading diamonds— riches were washing away downstream while my bucket was on the bank.

When we finally piled into Alt's Bronco, I climbed into the back seat and began scribbling as many notes from memory as I could. I needn't have worried. Some people are difficult to interview. They tense up and struggle to express themselves in full sentences. You have to roll up your sleeves and dig and sweat and strain to find a nugget of a quote.

That's not a problem with Alt. Get him talking, whether one on one or in front of an auditorium full of people, and he turns into a revival-tent preacher spreading the gospel of natural resource management. The shirt collar comes open, the voice alternately rises to a crescendo and falls to a whisper, jokes break up moments of solemn truth. His brow beads with sweat.

He gets results, too. When he's on, Alt could tell hunters he needed them to support missionaries helping whitetails in Africa, then pass a collection plate, and most would reach for their wallets while saying "Amen" all the while.

"He's an unusual guy. There aren't many wildlife biologists who have charisma," agrees David Samuel, the retired chairman of the wildlife biology department at West Virginia University and the man who advised Alt on his doctoral project. "Someone with his personality and brilliance, he's extremely convincing. It takes a unique personality to attempt what he's after, and he's got it."

That personality—and the drive and determination behind it—were forged under some unique circumstances. Growing up on a dairy farm in Lackawanna County, Alt was a tireless worker who appeared, at least to most, to be a slacker. Starting at age eight he got up at 4:00 A.M. every day to help with the cows. Four years later his older brother got married, leaving Alt and his father to run the farm.

By age thirteen Alt was hiring high school kids five years his senior to help his father bale hay, and firing them when necessary, too.

All that work did wonders for Alt physically—he was a regular winner in intramural wrestling, and he once did eight hundred sit-ups in an hour during a school competition, stopping only when his teachers told him class was over. It also turned him into a teenage field general of sorts.

"I suppose that's where I got my aggressive personality. I was always telling people where to go and what to do," Alt says.

"I raised six children and he was always the most ambitious of them," said Alt's father, Floyd "Buck" Alt. "I was always conservative in how much hay I would mow because I was afraid it might rain before I could get it in. Him, if I turned my back, he'd have half the farm mowed. He'd always get it in somehow, maybe by rounding up all of his friends to help, but that's the type of kid he was. He was always busy."

That frenetic pace didn't do much for Alt's academic career, though. He spent a lot of each school day catching up on his sleep, and ultimately graduated from North Pocono High School in the spring of 1969, ranked ninety-second out of a class of 132.

"I wasn't at the bottom, but I was sure headed that way," Alt said.

Looking up at the world, the schoolboy snoozer decided he wanted to go to college. Alt would have to pay for it on his own, though. His relationship with his much more conservative father had become strained, and Buck Alt refused to give him any money for school, worried that he'd go off to college and become "a long-haired hippie freak hooked on drugs," Alt remembers.

Undeterred, Alt worked on a construction crew, then became a skidder and chainsaw operator for the Newfoundland Lumber Company to earn some cash. The timbering job was especially rugged. In eighteen months, three of Newfoundland's eighteen employees were killed, and Alt was nearly smashed by an eighty-foot oak that twisted on its stump and fell, pancaking his hard hat after knocking it from his head.

This was just the first of several narrow escapes Alt would make over the next several years. Another came in January 1970. He had applied for a spot in the forestry program at Penn State University's Mount Alto campus at the same time that he signed up for the voluntary draft, which was taking men for service in the Vietnam War. Alt had passed his physical and was to report for military duty

January 15. Five days before that date, though, he received his acceptance letter from Mount Alto.

"I called up the army and said, 'Look, I know it's probably too late, but I just got accepted to college.' I didn't think they would care and was prepared to go off to Vietnam," Alt said. "But they said no, they'd give me a deferment, with a reminder that I would probably get drafted anyway as soon as I graduated."

At the same time, Buck Alt's best friend, Jack Grill, was working on Gary's behalf. Convinced that Gary was more interested in hunting—particularly deer hunting—than forestry, Grill wrote a letter and made a few calls to get him into Penn State's DuBois campus's new wildlife technology program, which was holding its first classes that fall. He also called a few people he knew there. It worked, and Alt was accepted for the September 1970 semester.

His stay at the school almost came to a premature end. Alt was sitting in class one day, just two weeks into the semester, when a guidance counselor interrupted the lecture to ask Alt to grab his books and follow him to his office. "I remember he was a young guy, maybe in his late twenties, and he smoked a pipe," Alt recalls. "We walked down to his office and he asked me if I knew how I got into school. I mumbled something about filling out an application and writing a letter.

"Well, he said that in the confusion of starting a new program and on Jack Grill's word, they had accepted me without looking at my grades and SAT scores. When they got around to doing that, they realized my grades were atrocious and my SAT score was more than three hundred points lower than anyone they had ever taken before.

"He offered me a complete refund right then and there if I would just leave. He said they figured I would come out ahead financially and they would come out ahead time-wise if I would just go," Alt said. "He said they didn't think I could compete with the other students.

"Part of me was devastated and part of me was mad as hell. If he had been an older man, or more confident, he would have just crushed me. But he was pretty small in stature and seemed as nervous as I was, so the part of me that was mad as hell won. I thought, let's try a little aggression and see what happens.

"I stood up and said, 'Are you telling me I have no choice? Because I don't know about your time, but I know about my money and I'm going back to class.' Then I stomped down the hall as far as the first men's room I came to and went in bawled my eyes out," Alt recalls with a laugh. "I showed him."

Actually, it took a little while, but Alt eventually proved his worth. That first semester was rough. He had to learn how to be a student, and catch up on all the learning he'd slept through in high school. But he poured himself into the task, determined to make his way through force of will and hard work.

"I remember I talked to one of his teachers from when he first started school there, someone I knew because I later taught there myself, and he said he remembered Gary sitting in the front row, just hanging on every word," said George Matula, supervisor of the wildlife resource assistance section of the Maine Department of Inland Fisheries and Wildlife. "He said he'd never seen a student so focused."

By the time he left the DuBois campus two years later with his associate's degree, Alt ranked third in his class. And he hadn't turned into a hippie—though he had enough hair and a big enough beard to pass for a Mormon.

The real turning point in Alt's life was yet to come. In summer of 1973, Matula, then a graduate student doing a master's degree project on black bears, met Buck Alt at a small airport. Matula kept his plane there, outfitted with radio transmitter antennas, to track bears. The two men struck up a conversation, and Buck Alt ultimately got involved in the work as a volunteer. Buck mentioned that Gary was studying to be a biologist and asked if he could lend a hand, too. The answer was yes, and a passion took root.

"When [Gary] started working on bears, he ate, drank, and slept bears. He was totally immersed in it," Matula remembered. "He never looked at it as a job. I can still see his eyes, just penetrating, you know? He was just so focused."

"It was almost a spiritual experience for me," Alt recalls. "Seeing bears, trapping bears, working with bears like we were, it was by far the most incredible experience of my life up to that point."

That bear work certainly shaped his immediate future. When Alt went to Utah State University that fall to finish his bachelor's degree, it was in the hope that he would return to Pennsylvania the following summer and again work for Matula, who planned to be doing his doctoral work on black bears. It wasn't to be, however.

Matula lost his funding, his project was canceled, and it looked as though Alt's bear days were over, too. When Matula called to offer the bad news, however, he mentioned, almost as an afterthought, that Penn State had an opening for a graduate student interested in working on bears.

Alt was one of more than a hundred students who applied for the post, and one of a much smaller number to get an interview. Home over Christmas break, he put on his one suit coat and only pair of dress pants, which were so short "it looked like I was wearing knickers," climbed into his 1963 Ford Falcon with 150,000 miles on the odometer, and drove to Penn State. It didn't go well, at least initially.

Unaccustomed to doing interviews, wet to the knees from the rain splashing up into the car around the Utah State food trays that were riveted in place where the floor boards were supposed to be, Alt struggled in that face-to-face meeting.

"I felt like a Miss America contestant trying to give the right answers, like 'I'd like to have peace for the world.' I was just terrible," Alt said. "Finally I pulled off my tie and said, 'Look, I don't know what I'm supposed to be saying here. All I can tell you is that I want this position so bad I would eat a bushel of rocks to get it. I'll give you every cell in my body if you hire me and you'll be glad you did before it's over.'"

His sincerity worked; he got the job. There was only one problem—Alt had not yet earned his bachelor's degree. He was nearly eighteen months away from gradu-ation, but only about six months away from starting what was a master's-level bear project. He hopped back into his Falcon, drove to Utah, and told his advisor that he needed to take fifty-three credits in twenty weeks so he could graduate.

"He just looked at me and said, 'Son, this is what we call academic suicide,'" Alt said. Alt pled his case, though, and the advisor ultimately agreed to sign off on a schedule that called for Alt to take twenty-eight credits one term and twenty-five the next, provided it was okay with the dean. He too had reservations, but he agreed to give Alt the chance, so long as he promised to abandon the madness if he got into trouble academically.

What neither man knew was that Alt was also planning to keep his two jobs—as "floor jock" in charge of sixty-four guys on the third floor of his dormitory, and as a stable hand of sorts at the Utah State deer pens—while taking all of those classes.

"I met with the sixty-four kids on my floor and said I had the opportunity of a lifetime. I said it meant a lot to me, but that I'd have to be pretty strict if I was going to pull it off," Alt said. "I even said I would put a bulletin board up on my door and told them I'd keep them apprised of my grades.

"What happened is that I never had to deal with anything on my floor from that point on. Stuff would happen. I'd hear it outside my door, but then somebody would say 'If you want to raise hell, go raise it somewhere else. You're not doing it here.' The kids ended up policing my own floor for me," Alt said.

With that help, and classmates sharing their notes—a necessity since he had three classes that met at the same time—Alt juggled work and school like a circus performer. He headed into finals week with eight tests in front of him. With an understanding of where his grades were strong and where they weren't, he studied more or less depending on where he needed the best marks. The result was that he finished the term by making the dean's list.

He didn't make it again the next term, but still finished with better than a B average. And seventy-two hours after his last test, he was back in Pennsylvania catching bears.

From June to November 1974 Alt caught seventy bears, more than anyone before had caught in an entire year's time. It was thrilling, daring, exhilarating work, much of it pioneering, too. Alt can tell story after story of climbing a tree to catch a bawling cub while the mother false-charged his father below, of having a bear that he thought was tranquilized awaken and stand on his chest inside a den, of having a bear literally rip off his pants in one quick swipe. It was his habit of climbing into bear dens with the bears still inside, though, that got everyone's attention.

Tim Carr, a forester in the Pennsylvania Bureau of Forestry, used to tag along as a ten-year-old when his brother Pat was working with Alt as a volunteer. He saw Alt climb into dozens of dens, at a time when no one knew whether you could do that without getting mauled.

"He'd crawl into these really small dens with nothing but a flashlight and a jab stick while we could hear the mother bear woofing and snapping her jaws. You'd be standing there and all of a sudden the bear would walk out first, with Gary still out of sight in the den," Carr said. "That would leave all of us on the outside standing around with our jaws on the ground, wondering what had happened to Gary. We'd stick our flashlights in to see and he'd always be in there, looking back out at us. The bear would have literally walked right over him to get out. That was pretty impressive. No one had ever done that before, but it was a daily thing for him."

It took more than that for Alt to get a job with the Pennsylvania Game Commission, though. He had gotten married in June 1976, but with the Vietnam War over and returning veterans getting all the jobs, Alt couldn't find work. It was only when the bear program reached a crisis stage that he found an in.

The Game Commission didn't have a bear biologist then, and its bear management program was not highly regarded. Harvests varied widely—from 605 in 1966 to the season being closed in 1970—and the stage was set in 1976 for more chaos.

Hunters wiped out nearly one-third of the total population during that one-day season, prompting outrage among antihunters and an investigation by the state House of Representatives' Game and Fisheries Committee. Lawmakers asked Alt to testify on the state of Pennsylvania's black bears the following April. He did, explaining his research and offering ideas on how it might be applied. Six weeks later, the whole committee went into the field with Alt and watched him work five bears he'd caught the night before.

Combined, those two appearances were so impressive that the chairman of the committee pushed the Game Commission to hire Alt. It did, for all of $6,900 a year.

"And it was a dream. It was a dream," Alt said. "I was independent, I was doing the research I wanted to do, and I felt I was helping the resource. It was almost perfect, really."

Not everyone was happy to see Alt get hired. One of his bosses tried to dissuade him from even taking the job by telling him that it was the lowest-paid position in the Commission and carried no health benefits—both lies. Others, including some who had overseen the bear program before his arrival, resented his hiring and tried to sabotage him with various commissioners. Alt persisted, succeeding by relying on the same skills that helped him overcome what may have been the greatest challenge the bear program faced.

In 1980 Alt suggested that the Game Commission get rid of its cub law, which prohibited hunters from shooting bear cubs. Such a law sounds nice in theory, but has no basis in biology. What's more, the only way to tell the age of a bear is to examine its milk tooth. Hunters, of course, couldn't do that before pulling the trigger. A bear's size didn't always tell the tale either. In areas of good habitat where yearling bears spent the summer bulking up, cubs often weighed nearly as much as their adult mothers by the time hunting season arrived.

"I knew there was no way to tell those big cubs from adults," Alt said. "I had shot hundreds of bears with a tranquilizer gun, and I couldn't always tell the difference. There were times when a bear would jump up on a rock or a log and I'd think for sure it was the mother, so I'd shoot. Then as soon as I pulled the trigger the mother would step out from behind some other tree."

Game commissioners weren't convinced. Going into a meeting with them, Alt was told that the eight-member board was aligned 6-2 against his recommendation. Those votes were set in stone, too, it was said. No amount of talking would change the commissioners' minds.

Alt went ahead anyway. He made an impassioned speech outlining why the cub law was bad for hunters and bears, several times almost taking the meeting out of order. He then started projecting photographs onto a screen. Each picture showcased several bears. Alt challenged commissioners—all of whom were lifelong hunters—to pick out the adult in each photo. Half a dozen slides flashed onto the screen, one after another, and commissioners picked out the wrong bear each time. When the meeting ended a short time later, the cub law was voted out of existence.

"I told them that protecting cubs was the wrong thing to do. It might make them feel good, but it was the wrong thing to do. Nobody could do it," Alt said "I think I won that decision 7-1.

"You can't go shooting your mouth off like that once a month. You have to save it up and when you need to shoot, make it a head shot. You will not win any war without winning the key battles, though. And when I see a key battle coming up, I will go to almost any length to win it."

Alt won the bear battle. Following his recommendations, the Game Commission closed bear season in 1977 and 1978 and began limiting the number of bear licenses available. In the early 1980s Alt began trapping pregnant female bears from areas with good populations and moving them to new areas of the state, like the mountainous regions of southwestern Pennsylvania. Those animals thrived and spread elsewhere, so that by the time Alt left the bear program to work on deer, the statewide population was as high as it had been in nearly a century, some fifteen thousand bears strong. The limit on the number of bear hunters had disappeared, too, and record numbers of hunters were shooting record numbers of bears, with the bear population still growing all the while.

Hunters noticed the change, and Alt reaped the credit. "I used to tease him because we'd go somewhere so that he could speak to a crowd and afterward little kids would come up and ask for his autograph," says Alt's first wife, Vanessa Caparo. "And I don't think it was always really the kids. I think there were some adults who wanted his autograph, but they sent their kids up to get it because the kids would do it. That always tickled me because that's the kind of thing we do to stars even though they're really just people. Not that he didn't deserve it for the work he did, but they really put him on a pedestal. And to me he was just my husband."

That adoration, mixed with Alt's resource-first attitude and the experience he gained on bears, are the things that made him the perfect man to take on Pennsylvania's deer management program when he did, says Bryon Shissler, the biologist at Natural Resource Consultants. "He took a bear program that was based on tradition and moved it toward science, and boosted the bear population in the process. I think that established a level of credibility that made him very much the right person to head the deer program. He was sort of prequalified to be the best guy to do this," Shissler says.

Still, it took a while for Alt to move to deer. Peter Duncan, executive director of the Game Commission from 1983 to 1994, tried to get Alt to take over the deer program in the late 1980s. The Commission was then in the midst of a "determined effort" to cut deer densities—which averaged forty or more per square mile—nearly in half. With doe license sales having reached the saturation point, the Game Commission was headed toward concurrent buck and doe seasons and expanded doe hunting, the same changes Alt would implement more than a decade later.

Duncan knew that this would not be easy. Every time the Commission had talked about going away from traditional seasons and shooting more does, hunters had complained and commissioners had backed off. "We heard the hue and cry from sportsmen, who were saying they didn't know where we hunted, but that they weren't seeing too many deer where they were," Duncan said. "We knew we had too many deer for the habitat, for forest regeneration to occur, for other wildlife species trying to share the woods with deer. But we weren't getting that message about the link between deer numbers and habitat across successfully."

Duncan was sure that Alt was the man who could make changes in that tense atmosphere. "I tried to get Alt over there to handle that a long time ago. Deer management is a very controversial issue. It's not warm and fuzzy like black bears. But I knew that given the opportunity, he'd provide the leadership," Duncan said.

Alt wasn't ready, professionally or personally, to make that leap, however, and turned Duncan down. He continued working with bears until 1999, when Vern Ross asked him to reconsider his decision of a decade earlier and take over the deer program. Alt still wasn't sure. He sought out his children, his second wife, Sharon, his father, and his friends for their advice.

"He asked me my opinion, and I remember how he said it," recalled Larry Schweiger, director of the National Wildlife Foundation and a contemporary of Alt's at Penn State University. "He said, 'I'm really in this safe and cushy place right now, and managing bears is so much easier than managing deer is ever going to be. If I do this, it could end my career, so I'm taking this very seriously.'

"I told him that I understood how dangerous this was for him, but that the over-abundance of deer was the most dramatic problem facing our forests, and that I could think of no one I would rather see at the helm leading the charge to fix it than him. I told him, 'I believe you can do it, I believe you can make it happen, and I believe you are the only one at that agency who can make it happen.'"

"I think he was more worried about how his taking the job might affect the kids and his family than anything," said Sharon. "He was afraid they might see him attacked in the media or by sportsmen, something they'd never witnessed, and worried how it might affect them at school or work. That's why he talked to the kids about the job and what it might mean for everyone.

"But they both encouraged him to do it," Sharon said. "It was kind of funny, too, because they used the same sort of words on him that he always used on them when they came for advice, like 'do the right thing.'"

They knew he would, too. "He and I have always talked about deer, even before all of this came up," said Alt's son, Garrick. "That's what the conversation always turned to. We always hunt together, and a lot of times we end up talking about deer. So I kind of knew he would do it."

Buck Alt did, too, though he was less than enthusiastic about the prospect. He worried that Gary would have a heart attack, either because of the full-bore pace he would undoubtedly set for himself or because of the stress inherent in the job. "When he said he was thinking about taking this job I told him he was crazy," Buck said. "Man oh man, he had that bear program going so good, he had his reputation intact, I said, why bother? I said, you've got no problems, and that deer job is loaded with problems, and I don't mean maybe.

"When he first started the bear program he wanted so bad to make out decent that he was working seven days and getting paid for five, but that's the way he was. And this is an even more longwinded thing. He can give a good talk. And he's always done what he said before, but boy, this is the biggest job he's ever tackled. It's a real nightmare. I can't help but wish sometimes that he'd just be a regular guy. But I knew he was going to do it anyway."

What ultimately convinced Alt were two things: assurances from his bosses that they would let him tackle the issue as he saw fit, no holds barred, and his concern for the resource. He had long known that Pennsylvania's forests had a regeneration problem brought about by trying to support too many deer. When Ross came to him, though, he looked, really looked, at the forest habitat for the first time. That did it.

"I always say, who knows how many bird's nests I ran over when I was chasing a bear," Alt said shortly after taking the job. "I was in a hurry. I knew what a browse line was, but I never paid much attention to it. I was obsessed with bears. Once I started paying attention, though, I didn't really feel like I had a choice, especially once my family said they supported it. I feel obligated to do this because it's the right thing to do. I loved the bear project. I miss them terribly. It was a hundred times more fun. But this is a hundred times more important. We have no alternative but to fix that forest ecosystem. It's not an optional thing.

"God, I want to fix this in the worst way," Alt said. "There are a thousand reasons to do it, and none not to do it, that I can see."

Alt began by studying the history of the state's deer problem with a vengeance. Two things struck him. First, the biologists who had gone before him had failed because they had never successfully communicated the nature of the problem to a mass audience. Second, they had failed because, without that base of support, they had tried to move too quickly. Every time they tried to close buck season, for example, a vocal minority of hunters had been able to defeat them politically within a year or two. Alt resolved early on not to make either of those mistakes.

"The first thing I have to pull out of my medical bag, so to speak, is education," Alt told us while sitting in that McDonald's in Lord's Valley. "Once people hear your message, they perpetuate it. They help you to counter the people who are keeping you from managing deer properly. Education is the key."

Alt put that tool to work right away. Starting in 2000, he spent three consecutive winters, from January through April, doing whistle-stop outreach tours. Like a politician running for office, he crisscrossed the state doing newspaper and TV interviews over breakfast, meeting with newspaper editorial boards in the afternoon, and giving lectures before crowds of sportsmen in the evenings. He traveled far and wide enough to appear at least once within twenty miles of every resident of the state.

At each lecture he would talk to hundreds of people about the need to balance the number of deer with the available habitat. More than once he reminded me of Teddy Roosevelt in one of those old black-and-white newsreels, with his animated style and bully pulpit mentality. He repeated lines like "we must kill the right number of deer of the right sex and age in the right places," and "we've got to stop looking at the deer and look at what's behind the deer" over and over again in high school auditoriums, gun clubs, and civic centers until they became campaign slogans.

The lectures were hot. Sportsmen opposed to Alt's ideas—which admittedly broke with decades of tradition—would show up ready to shout him down. Alt tried to head off some of that anger. He would remind hunters that the TV cameras were on, and that they represented their sport, in an attempt to keep them rational. Some, though, couldn't help but get out of hand. Alt absorbed their abuse like a sponge. Law enforcement officials within the Game Commission persuaded him to wear a bulletproof vest to his lectures. Armed officers accompanied him to each event and suggested that he always have an escape route from the stage to an exit should things turn violent. Alt, though, went out of his way to talk to hunters, always staying as long as it took for every single sportsman to get all of his questions answered.

"I never saw such expressions as I did on the faces of the hunters at those lectures. Initially I thought it was anger, but it was really concern," Alt said. "Sharon described it as a gut-shot look. These hunters were concerned about deer and deer hunting and they were hurting, confused, wanting help and answers.

"I can remember after each lecture we'd be off stage and in a corner, on their level. I was always told not to do that because if someone wanted to get you there you were dead. But I had to. If you try to maintain a distance from those people you'll never climb into their souls. And those hunters who stay three and four hours after a lecture to talk, they're the ones who go home and sway their friends and neighbors."

Marrett Grund, then Alt's right-hand man, remembers one meeting in January 2002. He traveled with Alt and some others from the Game Commission to Armstrong County to talk to hunters about that area's being a possible test site for antler restrictions. The hunters wanted no part of being guinea pigs. It was a charged atmosphere with the potential to get ugly, but Alt took charge. "The way he tempered the crowd, I was just amazed," says Grund. "If it would have been me, I would have probably walked off the stage. But he got control of the situation very quickly. By the time we left, I'll bet 95 percent of the people were happy or satisfied with things as he explained them."

"I think he's programmed in a way that maybe he could do that when others wouldn't be able to," says Alt's daughter, Lindsay. "When he's under pressure, he thrives. He doesn't get worked up, he just kind of sits back and relaxes, then comes charging out of the gate."

Doing one of his lecture tours required working about a hundred hours a week. Alt tried to make sure he ate decent meals along the way. He tried to get a good night's rest where he could. He listened to motivational and time management tapes while in his car. Still, it almost wasn't enough. After one particularly grueling lecture, in front of a crowd of more than eight hundred people that included a few very hostile opponents, Alt retreated to the men's room when it was over and broke down, overcome by the grind of battling those who opposed scientific deer management.

"The strain was incredible. I felt like I could never let my guard down," he recalled. "I felt like if I wasn't careful, if I became lax, if I didn't keep the train running, they'd hijack it again. It was an awful way to live. Even when we went out to eat or stopped for gas or went to get a loaf of bread, people would see me and come up to our table or stop me on the sidewalk and want to talk about deer. I couldn't escape it.

"It would have been nice to just get goofy once in a while. I like to have fun. It would have been nice to just hang out and do something ridiculous like pull my underwear up to my armpits and walk around like an ape or something, but I felt like I had to always be on, and that wears on you."

Amazingly, though, Alt started winning converts right away. Hunters who had never before thought about their sport as anything other than recreation started to see their role in protecting forests and farmlands and other wild places. They began to question the rationale for seasons that had existed for decades. They began to look at the possibilities of twenty-first-century deer hunting. Alt—who David Samuel always thought would make a wonderful professor—taught them to examine the possibilities, and most liked what they envisioned.

"He actually has sportsmen asking questions about what they can do to solve our forest problems, and asking how long it's going to take to turn around that habitat. Those are questions that weren't even on sportsmen's minds before," said Susan Stout, the Forest Service researcher. "I'll never forget the comment I got from one old grizzled hunter when we had a meeting in Warren County for farmers, foresters, sportsmen, and some others interested in deer. We were talking about how shooting more antlerless deer was the key to controlling the population. That was heresy to a lot of hunters, of course.

"But after this man heard Gary speak, he later came up to me and said, 'You know, you'll never get my generation to believe in shooting does, but we'll work hard to make sure the kids understand it.' What a breakthrough!" Stout said.

Ed Grasavage of QDMA knows how that old-timer felt. Just a few years ago he was the old hunter ready to bash Alt and his deer management strategies. He saw all the changes to Pennsylvania's deer hunting tradition swirling around him and decided he'd had enough. He set out to attend one of Alt's lectures with the intention of setting the biologist straight.

"I was almost on the verge of quitting, and I'm a lifelong hunter, a lifelong whitetail hunter. But I wanted to speak my mind before I quit. I couldn't wait to tell Gary Alt what I thought," Grasavage said. "I didn't know much about all of his changes, but I thought I knew all there was to know.

"Well, I got there and my mouth opened and I found out I knew little or nothing about white-tailed deer in Pennsylvania. I was just an average hunter out there in the woods sitting on a stump waiting for a deer to run through the woods so that I could shoot it. But everything he said made sense to me. Gary was probably the only guy who could sell the program to me and the general public because I and a lot of us were mad at the time. But he's just that credible. He's the most credible person I know. He's certainly changed my whole life," said Grasavage. "I was about to quit, and now I'm doing something deer-related every day. Now I'm as excited about deer hunting as I ever was when I was a kid."

Alt didn't convince everyone, however. The sportsmen who were among his earliest critics, largely members of the Unified Sportsmen of Pennsylvania, remain opposed to his policies and fear they are meant to appease everyone but hunters. Unified director Greg Levengood, for example, admits that Alt is a great public speaker. He thinks Alt's ability to reach out to others would make him the perfect man to lead a special program to recruit new hunters. He doesn't believe Alt is as well suited to manage deer, however.

Levengood and I were talking by phone in January 2004, just prior to the Game Commission's quarterly meeting. The 2003 firearms deer season had been a rough one in many ways. The weather on opening day and on the first Saturday—traditionally the days when hunters are most likely to kill a deer—had been marked by extremely high winds and near blizzard conditions in many places. Though time would show the overall harvest to be the fourth-highest ever, some hunters were complaining of not seeing as many deer as they were used to.

When Alt—speaking at a "deer overabundance" conference sponsored by the Audubon Society just after deer season, before final deer harvest numbers were available, and when pressure from hunters was heavy—said the job of lowering deer numbers was still not done, it was too much for some sportsmen, Levengood said.

"I think he has lost some credibility," Levengood said. "I think it infuriates people when he stands up there and says we have 1.6 million deer and need to knock the numbers down more, at a time when guys are hunting hard and just can't find any. I challenge Gary or anybody to take me out there and show me where all of those deer are and we'll be happy to shoot them. I mean, when you don't see the sign, you've got to ask yourself where the heck are these things? If those deer are out there somewhere, they should be leaving sign, and guys just aren't seeing it. I think sportsmen are pretty angry."

The Pennsylvania Federation of Sportsmen's Clubs, the state's largest sportsmen's organization with about one-hundred thousand members, had been one of Alt's bigger supporters initially. I remember sitting with Ray Martin one day in his home, surrounded by stuffed deer heads, a fanned turkey tail, a mounted bobcat, all tangible treasures of a life spent in the field, not long after Alt had taken the deer job. Martin told me then that the organization was glad Alt was in charge of

Dr. Gary Alt believes that harvesting more does will create better habitat for deer and hunters alike.

the deer program. With him at the helm, the Game Commission seemed interested in listening to hunters and considering their input.

"They're not perfect, and if they go the wrong way, or what we think is the wrong way, we're going to tell them about it," Martin had said. "But I'd say we're finally making some progress, which had to be."

By late winter 2004, the club's members were less enthusiastic about Alt, largely because they didn't think he was listening to them anymore. Like Levengood, the federation's Lowell Graybill worried that talk of wanting to shoot yet more deer in seemingly every region of the state was, literally, overkill. Hunters need to adapt, but biologists like Alt also need to listen to hunters—who pay for wildlife management in Pennsylvania by buying licenses—and take their point of view into consideration, Graybill said.

Referring to the job of managing deer as a "snake pit," as Alt did in one public setting, seems to cast hunters as the root of the deer problem, rather than as a part of the solution, Graybill added. "I've not heard anybody question his intent or his motivations," Graybill said of Alt. "If there were too many deer before, we're going to have to realize we might not be able to see thirty deer in the first three hours of hunting in the future. But I don't think, for example, that we should base the deer program just on what Gary says or on what the data says. I'm not suggesting we throw that out. But part of that has got to be taking into account what people are seeing in the woods, too.

"If Gary can present information in a way that doesn't end with 'there are too many deer' in every sentence, or 'you're just not hunting hard enough,' or 'look what's happening inside this exclosure,' I think that would go a long way in helping hunters look at the information and understand it. Hunters are not like one of the dart guns that biologists use to put down a deer," Graybill added. "You don't use him to drug a deer and then put him back in the gun cabinet until you need him again. You better include him in the process, especially when he's paying your bill."

Alt heard those complaints but refused to back away from what good science told him needed to be done for the state's deer and forests. The changes made to deer seasons and bag limits, the development of programs targeting deer on private, sometimes inaccessible lands, an urban/suburban deer management program, are all tools. The Game Commission is only beginning to use them, he would tell hunters. Sportsmen will almost assuredly see different deer seasons— with different opening and closing dates and perhaps different bag limits—in different wildlife management units in the future, with everything determined by the

In good habitat, a deer antler is the fastest growing tissue in the world, growing faster even than cancer.

differences in deer numbers and deer impacts, he said. Doe license allocations, which already vary by wildlife management unit, will become even more refined.

All of those decisions, though, have to be based on what's best for the state's forests, Alt says. If you don't allow the habitat to recover—no matter how long that takes or how much patience is required of hunters—there will be few deer. Hunters must keep their eyes on the prize: healthier forests that produce healthier deer for hunters who will be held in higher regard by society for making it all happen.

"I like deer, too. I like to hunt deer, especially in archery season. Some of my best memories are of hunting with my father and my son," Alt says. "Garrick and I wouldn't be as close as we are today if it wasn't for hunting. But I can't manage deer based on what I want or what other individuals want, hunters or otherwise.

"A lot of times as a deer manager I think of myself as a judge. Mentally, I step back and put on my robe and examine the situation. I try to separate myself from the feelings and emotions of the situation and ask myself not what do I want, but what is the right thing to do here? When I think I know what that is, that's what I do," Alt said. "That's not a pleasurable thing. Trying to manage wildlife properly is a lonely place to be. But I think that's the right thing to do, and how you make things happen. It's how you leave a mark."

Hunters—as well as the foresters, farmers, and other landowners who need hunters to control deer for them—need to realize, too, that some things are simply nonnegotiable, Alt says. A doctor doesn't ask his patient how to treat his cancer or put the choice of treatments to a vote of everyone in the waiting room. The doctor can let the patient choose between two treatments, if he knows either might achieve the same result, but he drives the discussion.

Likewise, biologists can't ask hunters—or foresters or farmers or suburbanites—if they want to fix the forest. They can, though, work with all of those groups on how best to tackle the problem. "You don't ask people if they want to take care of the environment. It's our job to fix it. Not fixing it is not an option," Alt said. "But we can talk about how to fix it. In the field, biologists have to set the goal. Then we can talk to hunters about choosing the path to get there."

Hopes were high early on that Alt would be the man to bring that kind of cooperation about. It was clear from the start that his credibility—earned over years of working with bears—would get him in the door with sportsmen, other Game Commission employees, and nonhunters.

"That's what surprised me the most when I came to Pennsylvania, the general public's admiration for him," Grund says. "Even within the Commission, you can go up to any wildlife conservation officer or office person or whoever, and they may not like him, but they respect him. From one end to the other in the Game Commission, everyone respects him very much. There are not a lot of people in the agency you can say that about. I think a lot of that has to do with his honest approach. Not too many biologists have ever walked up to a microphone and said, 'Yes, you're right, I made a mistake and I need to fix it.' It may make some people cringe to hear him say those things, but that goes a long way in gaining people's respect."

"People just trust him," agrees Bret Wallingford, one of Alt's contemporaries on the Game Commission's deer management team. "He had hard decisions to make in bear management, and he said that if he made them it wouldn't destroy the resource. Well, he made those decisions and they didn't destroy anything, so people are willing to listen to him. It's not so much that what he's saying now has never been heard before. Much of the message has not changed. The messenger has."

"I remember one time not long after he took the deer job, he was giving a lecture and telling people that despite all those years working in the woods, he never quite realized how bad the problem with our forests was," recalled John Dzemyan, the Game Commission land manager whose relationship with Alt goes back to the days they spent together at Penn State. "I thought, why's he saying that? It makes him look kind of dumb. But then I realized that if a guy like him had trouble picking up on it, how were the rest of us supposed to have known? We're not wildlife biologists out there in the woods every day.

"That's what makes him so good. He can put himself on the same level as so many people. There may be other biologists out there who know just as much, but put them in front of a crowd and they can't talk to people," Dzemyan said. "Gary can talk to senators and governors or the regular guy down at the suds and duds, so to speak."

Alt's courage, and his willingness to stand up for the resource, are unparalleled, too. In interview after interview, people told me about Alt's desire to do good. He simply wants to do what's best for deer—and for forests and hunters and other wildlife by extension—and will not waver from that.

"The interesting thing to me is how Gary can walk into a situation where many hunters think they are killing too many deer and tell them he wants them to kill more. That's tough, but he'll do it if that's what he believes," Samuel said. "What I love about Gary, what I admire about him as a biologist, is that he studied the situation, he studied the data, and he came out with proposals that were not going to be popular, but that were right. Not many biologists could do that, or would do that."

"I don't think you'll ever see him tuck tail and run from anything," agreed Garrick Alt.

Tim Carr believes that the mere fact that Alt took on the deer job is a testament to his strength. Leaving bears for deer was "like jumping into a pot of boiling oil," Carr said. No one knew for sure if Alt would survive, just as they didn't know if he would come out of all those bear dens in one piece. But he went in anyway because the job needed to be done. "He's not afraid to get in front of an audience and tackle an issue that's like gunpowder, where if you put a match to it, pow, it explodes. Because he studies an issue and determines what the right thing to do is, he has no problem telling an audience not necessarily what they want to hear, but what's right," said Carr.

Indeed, Alt is more than just a bear biologist with a salesman's gift for gab. A meticulous researcher with the ability to dig into the past and develop a vision for the future, he is a first-rate scientist, says Jim Grace, Pennsylvania's state forester. "I'm not exactly sure why he would agree to take on something like the deer program, to be honest with you, but I'm sure glad he did. If this is going to work, we needed someone to bring some integrity to the program and have it based on science," Grace says. "A lot of these different groups, they see someone different on stage and want to throw rocks at them and chase them away. They won't do that with Gary Alt. They won't be able to. It will be hard for anyone to disagree with him once he shows them all the facts."

The one skill that Alt has that pulls all of those other things—his honesty, integrity, courage, and science—together for audiences is his ability to speak to hunters. He can take science and deliver it in a way that's easy to understand. He can even make it fun, with a self-deprecating sense of humor.

"I think he's kind of funny. I know he tries to be. It doesn't always work, but he's always trying," says Lindsay Alt.

"I don't think Gary was ever very self-conscious at all," says George Matula, Alt's college professor. "Whenever it came time to do a talk or a lecture, I'd be a nervous wreck, you know? But not him. He's great at telling stories, and he was just so focused on the message that he always found a way to get that message across. I never saw him struggle with communications at all."

"He's probably the best biologist communicator I ever met," says Bob McDowell, retired director of the New Jersey Division of Fish and Wildlife and a close friend of Alt's for about thirty years. "He's very passionate about what he does, whether it's bears or bow hunting. And he communicates that to whomever he's talking to. That's why he's the guy. He's the man. The state's very lucky to have someone like him, quite frankly."

Game commissioner Roxane Palone, who would later be disappointed with the way Alt left the Game Commission, agreed. She said Alt brought "the total package" to the agency, with his blend of intellect, education, skill, enthusiasm, and experience. Like anyone, Alt made mistakes made along the way, Palone said. But he was always willing to admit to them and move on to something else. "It takes a large amount of courage to stand up for the conservation of our natural resources like he has. As he travels around Pennsylvania, he encounters detractors and people who disagree with him," Palone said. "But Gary can handle that because he believes wholeheartedly in what needs to be done to manage deer for the future of hunting. He's a very special person."

The level of professional dedication and devotion required to earn such accolades does not come cheap, though, and Alt has paid a price for his years at the top of his profession. He's met thousands of people over the years but is really close friends with few. He purposely holds some people at arm's length so that his decisions aren't compromised by personal feelings. "If I have to choose between someone being my friend or respecting me, I'll have them respect me," Alt said. "It's not that I don't care what people think about me. But I can't operate that way."

In his early career, all of those hours spent chasing bears through the woods, from sunrise to dark and even later in the summer, left little time for anything else. The weekend work, the lectures, the requests to appear at banquets and hearings and on TV shows—it all became too much. His marriage to Caparo crumbled after seven years and two children.

"That was the major flaw with our marriage, his work. He was always a good husband and dad, but his work was number one," Caparo said. "If he had stopped, he would have imploded, I think. Years later I can still see how it works."

"I'd go somewhere to do a lecture and spend three or four hours with all of these people who were telling you how wonderful you are. Then I'd get in the car to go home and the whole way there I'd be asking myself why I felt so miserable," Alt remembered. "I would wonder what was wrong with me, what was wrong with my life, what I was doing wrong and what I could do to fix it. It was no way to live, that's for sure."

Two decades later, Alt's life was torn apart a second time, again at least partly because of work. He and Sharon—his constant companion, who traveled with him from lecture to lecture and meeting to meeting—divorced. I got the news one day while trying to catch up with Alt on the phone. I called his work number and got his answering machine, so I called his house. Sharon answered and broke the news.

It was an eerie conversation. I immediately recalled a phone conversation we'd had a few years earlier. I had been sitting at my kitchen table and Sharon was at hers. She had chased Gary out of the room so that she could talk freely about his decision to take the deer job and how it was affecting their life. They had seemed so optimistic then, so committed. "We're putting Gary's career on the line, our life on the line, and, if we hadn't talked about it, our marriage on the line," she had said. "It encompasses our whole life, but the cause is so great, we'll never walk away from it."

In the end, Gary, at least, could not. In April 2003, during a break at the Game Commission's quarterly meeting, Alt, Sharon, Grund, and I went to lunch at one of Alt's favorite haunts. He always eats at the same handful of restaurants and always orders vanilla ice cream for dessert, Grund told me.

"Sharon and I like to go out for ice cream, and if we go a hundred times, she'll try a hundred flavors. But seventy-seven of those times she'll go, 'Ewww, I don't like this' and want to finish mine," Alt said with a laugh, screwing his face up like a child who has bitten into a lemon. "I know what I like and I'm satisfied with my choices."

I think that was the only time Alt smiled for the next two hours. He seemed beaten down, worn out, exhausted. He talked openly of retiring or resigning or just leaving somehow. Sharon was pushing him to go, he told me later, fed up with the constant work and strain of managing deer. I remember coming home and telling Greg that I feared for Alt and the Commission and the direction of the deer management program all at once because he seemed so depressed.

Alt did in fact submit a letter of resignation shortly thereafter. He rescinded it, though, and soon filed for divorce instead. He had made his choice.

What drives Alt is a desire to, in his own words, "leave a mark" by making a difference for this and following generations. He's read a lot about great leaders in history, people who rose up at times of crisis and strife to do the right thing, to see what they did and how they did it. He looked around and decided that white-tailed deer and forest regeneration and the fate of hunting at the dawn of the twenty-first century represented his opportunity to leave that mark. He wouldn't—he couldn't—not take it.

"I've always said that if I was going to lose in this effort, I wanted to lose because I did all I could and it just didn't work. I don't want to lose because I didn't work hard enough," Alt said. "I have to stand up for what I believe in. So long as I know I did that, I'll have no regrets, not matter how this all turns out."

Going through the crucible of trying to change decades of deer hunting tradition while also suffering through a divorce tested, even scarred, Alt. Lindsay noticed that he became a little more streetwise, maybe a little less trusting, a little less inclined to believe that everyone is as sincere as he might once have thought. She's equally sure he had to do the job he did, though.

"When he talks about those years touring the state to talk about deer, I think it burned him. I don't think he would ever want to do it again," she said. "But I think he's glad that he did it, too. It's not his entire life, so if you ask did it take a toll, I think it did, but it's not the only thing he has going. I think what's important is that he knows he's doing the best job he can and that he's doing what he thinks is right."

Once he'd made his decision to stay, Alt brightened considerably over the next few months. Whenever I talked to him on the phone or in person, he seemed like the Gary Alt of old, the one Greg and I had met that day in Lords Valley. He was full of enthusiasm. His team was still together—the Game Commission and Alt at one point persuaded Grund to stay rather than move to another agency in state government—and he was ready to move the deer program forward again. His team was excited, too.

Grund likes to say, not really jokingly, that when he was in Wisconsin and decided to apply for a deer job with the Game Commission, some of his peers viewed it as suicidal, given Pennsylvania's poor reputation for managing whitetails and the way sportsmen and politicians chewed up and spit out all those who tried. Under Alt's direction, though, working with deer in Pennsylvania became, if not always fun, at least challenging professionally in a positive way.

"He doesn't try to intentionally motivate you, but you can't help but want to work for him," Grund said. "Everyone who's involved in our deer team meetings looks forward to going to them, just to be in that environment and work with him. We don't always agree. It's not always consensus. Sometimes it's amazing that we work together at all, but we do, and Gary facilitates that. I think a lot of the things that business schools try to teach their students when they're trying to make them into leaders just comes naturally to him."

Ultimately, though, Alt's renewed commitment could not last. By December 2004, after weeks of rumors about his departure, Alt left the Game Commission. The Commission issued an official statement that he had retired, and insiders tried to spin things to suggest that he had left because it was best for his pension or because he needed and deserved a break from the constant pressure of trying to balance deer management with a crumbling personal life.

Alt, though, tells a different tale. He left, he says, because he was not convinced the leaders of the Commission were committed to doing what was right by deer and their habitat. In fact, he says, they had actively tried to keep him from doing his job. Vern Ross, Alt charged, had asked him to back off his request for antler restrictions after Alt had spent the previous three months touring the state telling hunters how necessary they were. Later, Ross and Alt's immediate supervisors began sending representatives of the agency's upper management to his deer team meetings in an attempt to "rein him in" and quash any ideas that were deemed too radical before they ever came to public light.

It was all too much. Alt said as much in a conversation we had just a few days before he submitted his resignation. He had given his bosses an ultimatum—provide some kind of assurance that they would let him do what needed to be done or he was gone. "If I have a chance to solve this, I'm willing to do it. But if I have no chance, I'm not going to stay with it," he told me. "I always said that when the time came that I could no longer be effective, I would leave. I would rather starve than perform malpractice. I'm not going to do it," he said.

That time had come. No one, Alt said, so much as called him to see what it might take to get him to stay. There were too many hard feelings by then, too much animosity. The Commission let him walk, and then—at least privately—reacted angrily when Alt went public with some of his reasons for leaving.

For his part, Alt expressed no regrets about his decision. He's proud of the changes his team was able to enact and proud of the research they did to support them. If there's any disappointment—and there clearly is, despite his relief at being away from the grind of piloting a ship through a hurricane—it's not so much with failing to accomplish everything he dreamed of in regard to deer, habitat, and hunting. His biggest disappointment, he says, is knowing that it was largely people within the Game Commission who doomed his program.

In trying to save the Game Commission and its deer hunting traditions, those people may—and probably will—destroy all that they hold so close, Alt says. "Proper resource management is a lot like proper parenting. Sometimes you have to make your kids do something even though they absolutely do not want to do it. But you do it because you know it's in their best interests.

"You can't let those kids drive ninety miles an hour, you can't let them do drugs, and you can't let hunters drive this management program into the ground. That's not optional. If you can't fix the forest, people in the future are going to see a whole lot less everything, deer, turkeys, squirrels, chipmunks, everything. If you can't grow a new forest, nothing else matters."

Alt admits he could be hard to work with. He was always pushing, always challenging, always demanding to know the why of things. But he wouldn't do anything differently. "I'm a real bastard to manage, there's no question about it. I am only interested in doing the right thing. That's cost me, I'm sure," Alt said. "But you can't effect change without upsetting some people.

"I think in any profession, anything you look at where someone tried to make a difference in the world, it's not pretty. It's not pretty. You look behind the scenes and it can be horrible. You cannot fix problems without making changes and you cannot make changes without controversy. You become seen as a problem. You become seen as dangerous. But you can't fix problems without upsetting people.

"Managing deer or any other wildlife resource properly requires taking risks, just like cutting hay," Alt said, recalling those long-ago days on the farm. "It's not that I like taking risks, but you're not going to make significant positive change without taking risks. It's just a matter of knowing when to take them and whether it's worth it. It's like a big chess game. You've got to figure out the moves you need to make to be able to do what you want to do. It's not textbook stuff. You'll never learn it in a classroom. And you're going to catch hell no matter what you do. You might as well catch hell for trying to do what you think is right."

Alt always tried to do that. Like Ralph Abele, the legendary conservationist who carried his resignation letter in his pocket every day of his career as executive director of what was then called the Pennsylvania Fish Commission, as a signal that he would quit before he would compromise his principles, Alt remained steadfast in his beliefs.

He knew that this might cost him. I remember the last thing he had said to Greg and me that day in Lords Valley. We had talked for close to eight hours, driving all around Hemlock Farms looking for deer to photograph. After dinner at one of Alt's favorite sandwich shops, we were saying our goodbyes when Alt tried one last time to explain why he had taken the deer job.

"I believe so deeply in this cause. Sometimes I literally lay awake at night, asking myself, am I doing the right thing? Have I overlooked something so obvious that I'm going to screw this up? I probably have one chance to turn this around," Alt said. "I might get killed yet. But I won't come this way again. And I wouldn't feel right if I didn't try."

If Alt did not succeed completely, he didn't get killed, either. And he expects to remain a player in the deer management debate. He's already been approached by several organizations that want him to carry his message about deer management to the public on a broader, even national, scale.

"I think if Roger Latham could come back to life, he and I could have an interesting conversation," Alt said. "I think I understand more clearly now what he went through than I did in the beginning. I read what happened to him. And I thought I knew what he went through. Now I know for sure.

"I guess my ego was big enough to think that I could change things when no one else did. I guess I'm going to have to swallow that now. I'm choking on it. But I'm not giving up and I'm not going away. I'm just giving up on solving this problem from within the Game Commission."

How history will treat Alt remains to be seen. Schweiger, though, believes Alt will take his place in the lofty heights beside the likes of Leopold and Latham. "Gary Alt figures out what is right and stays on it no matter how much people beat him up," says Schweiger. "And he's been beat up tremendously, and he's never wavered. He so inspires me. He's one of the great wildlife scientists in America today.

"We take him for granted because he's a homegrown boy from up there in Lackawanna County, but he's internationally known and respected as a scientist and as a communicator. We're really privileged to be around him. When the final chapters of this whole story are written, we will see we have had a conservation hero in our midst in Gary Alt."

11

A WILD CARD IN THE DEER MANAGEMENT DECK

Dressed in his camouflage jacket and overalls and his knee-high rubber boots, Jim Loree looked as if he had just walked out of a John Deere catalog when Greg and I met him. That was appropriate, I guess, considering that Loree is both a white-tailed deer hunter and a deer farmer.

The remnants of some past "crops" were visible when we walked into the little office he had recently built on his Warren County farm. Hanging on the wall were a number of whitetail mounts. One, a buck taken in 1925 by his grandfather, stood out not only because the taxidermy was beginning to show signs of age but because the deer—while no slouch—was like a white-tailed version of Mini-Me next to the bruisers around it. Ten or so absolutely monster bucks were hanging on the wall, all wide-racked and heavy-beamed.

Those deer were just the best of the best. In the corner of the office, stacked in a big pile, were antlers from a number of other animals. Each antler contained at least four points, if not five or six, of varying thicknesses. It was an impressive collection. Loree's best-ever typical buck—Sterling, son of Silver—boasted a rack that scored 245 points at three years old. That's almost sixty points higher than Pennsylvania's state-record typical white-tailed buck.

It's the genes behind those big deer that allow Loree, vice president of the Pennsylvania Deer Farmers Association, to get $3,000 for every buck fawn and $2,500 for every doe fawn he sells. An adult buck, scoring in the 230s by age five, might

Jim Loree, owner of Loree's Whitetails, shows off some of the racks produced by deer on his commercial deer farm.

bring $40,000. If these prices seem steep, they're not so high that Loree can't sell every deer he wants to.

"It's just like with a championship horse," Loree said. "If you just want to buy the old nag down the road you can get it for half of nothing. If you want a championship horse you've got to pay for quality. Even the people who are trying to get a bargain don't want to get junk. It costs so much to raise deer or take care of deer anyway that people don't want to chintz on a deer."

Things weren't always like that. Loree, closing in on thirty years of working for a steel fabrication plant when we talked, started raising deer as a hobby in 1985. A hunter himself, he wanted to see if he could raise a world-record whitetail. He had some 200-class bucks—"everybody's goal," he said—by his second generation. Still, farm-raised deer were a bit of a novelty then. That's true no more. The Pennsylvania Game Commission estimates that there were 726 permitted deer farms in the state in 2004, along with an untold number of nonpermitted ones.

"The whole industry is becoming more widespread. We've got everything from the guy who has two or three deer in his back yard to full-blown ranching-type operations," said Tim Grenoble, chief of technical services for the Pennsylvania Game Commission.

Deer owners need a permit from the Commission only if they plan to sell or give away some of their deer. If they just want to keep them as pets, there are no regulations involved. "You can have a hundred-deer herd without needing a permit so long as you don't get into what is known as transfer of possession," Grenoble added. "That's when the permit kicks in, when you're giving them away, selling them, selling the venison, whatever."

To get and keep a permit, a farmer has to provide evidence that he got his deer from a legal source and maintain a ten-foot-high fence around his farm to keep wild and domesticated deer from intermingling. Breeders have to file an annual report, too, that details how many deer they started the year with and how many they ended with. They must also report the number of deer bought, sold, and butchered, as well as how many died from illness.

Farms also are subject to annual Game Commission inspections designed to make sure the deer are being treated humanely. "A farm's got to have shelter, it's got to have shade, it's got to have room to move around," Grenoble said.

Most deer being raised by permitted farmers are destined to be shot on hunting preserves. As of 2005 there were about a hundred high-fence shooting preserves in Pennsylvania—good enough to rank the state in the top five nationally—where hunters could pay for the chance to kill a farm-raised deer. They come looking for not just any deer but bigger deer than they might expect to find in the wild, and with less effort.

"In today's society, everything is so fast paced anymore, there's more acceptance for the whitetail market, for the hunting preserve market," Loree said. "People want to shoot a nice deer, but they don't have time to go out of state and spend several weeks looking for one. It's not so much that people go to hunting preserves knowing they're going to get a deer, it's that they know they're going to see quality bucks in there."

"That's the benefit of selective breeding, the genetics," added David Creegan, owner of Creegan Quality Whitetails in Bedford County and a member of the Pennsylvania Deer Farmers Association board. "We can provide bucks that score 180 points as two-year-olds."

Just what all these deer farms and preserves mean to the state is unclear. Agriculture is big business in Pennsylvania. The state ranks fourth nationally in milk production, with more than 9,200 dairy farms and 560,000 dairy cows. That's enough to support 40,000 jobs and create $4.2 billion in local economic impact. With more than 28,000 beef producers and 1.6 million beef cattle, the beef industry generates another $1.5 billion for the economy, according to statistics from the state's Department of Agriculture. Pennsylvania's poultry and swine industries are big, too, with the state home to more than one million hogs, for instance.

Deer farming doesn't compare on that level. Nationwide, there were just about 11,000 or so deer farms raising about 550,000 deer and employing about 23,000 people in 2005, according to Phyllis Menden, executive director of the North American Deer Farmers Association in Appleton, Wisconsin. Those farms generate billions of dollars in spending each year, and Pennsylvania is one of the top states in terms of its number of deer farms, she said. But neither Menden nor Loree could put a dollar figure on the industry's impact on Pennsylvania.

The Pennsylvania Deer Farmers Association has talked of doing some kind of survey to measure that impact, but had not yet done so when Loree and I spoke. He expects that the numbers would be significant, though, especially when the feed, equipment, and materials farmers buy to raise deer, the gas spent to get them from sellers to buyers, and the money offered up by hunters who come in from out of state to shoot a big farm-raised deer are all factored in. "It's a big industry for this state. It's amazing the revenue it's generated. It's tens of millions of dollars every year, if not more," Loree said. "It's a shot in the arm for the state, really."

"It is a significant and growing industry," agrees Dr. Paul Knepley, animal health division chief for the Pennsylvania Department of Agriculture.

If there's a problem with all of that, it's something else deer farms are often linked to. That's chronic wasting disease, or CWD. Chronic wasting disease is a neurological disease found in deer and elk. It belongs to a family of diseases known as transmissible spongiform encephalopathies (TSES), or prion diseases. Related to but not exactly the same as scrappie in sheep, bovine spongiform encephalopathy or mad cow disease in cattle, and even Creutzfeldt-Jakob disease in humans, it attacks the brains of infected animals and produces small lesions that destroy tissue.

Symptoms of the disease—which strikes male and female deer with equal vengeance—include weight loss, excessive salivation, difficulty swallowing, head tremors, lethargy, and loss of wariness. It is always fatal, with most of the deer and elk killed by it actually perishing from pneumonia. The animal dies after weeks or months of sickness during which it gradually deteriorates, hence the term wasting.

Sick deer don't always look sick, though, at least not right away. Studies have shown that the disease can persist in a deer's body for up to twenty-five months and in an elk's body for thirty-four months before killing it. This has raised questions about how long the disease incubates in an animal before becoming noticeable. At one point, scientists thought the disease didn't show up until a deer reached sixteen months of age, at a minimum. In New York, however, one of the first deer there to test positive for CWD was just eleven months old, so there are few answers.

Indeed, it's how little scientists understand about the disease overall that's most troubling. CWD was first diagnosed in captive mule deer in Colorado in the 1960s and in a wild, free-ranging herd of elk in 1981 in Rocky Mountain National Park. It's possible, though, that the disease has been around much longer, said Colorado Division of Wildlife veterinarian Michael Miller. Testifying before a U.S. House of Representatives panel on CWD, Miller said the disease may have existed for decades without anyone realizing it. "Based on what we now know about its distribution and occurrence, it is quite plausible that CWD actually arose in captive and/-or free-ranging cervids forty or more years ago," Miller said.

Wasting disease is not the only ailment that afflicts deer, of course. Whitetails also get anthrax, tuberculosis, and epizootic hemorrhagic disease, or blue-tongue. But these are viral and bacterial infections that are short-lived and not always fatal. Chronic wasting disease, by comparison, always kills and can persist in the environment for years, according to Bryan Richards, CWD project leader for the U.S. Geological Survey's National Wildlife Health Center in Madison, Wisconsin. This makes it potentially much more dangerous.

"CWD has no immunization, no treatment, no live test, a long incubation period, and can be transmitted before the onset of clinical signs," Richards said. "You put those facts together and it becomes perhaps the worst-case scenario for a deer manager. He's most likely going to find it in an animal that was infectious for some period of time before turning up. And you have to deal with it because it shows no signs of burning itself out. It's tough, but there's no cookbook for managing this disease."

If there's one thing experts agree on, it's that monitoring of deer herds—captive and wild—is key to preventing the spread of wasting disease. Such monitoring has being going on for a relatively short period of time, though, at least in the eastern United States. CWD was seen for a long time as a western ailment since it was confined to a small area in Colorado and Wyoming for the first few decades after its discovery. It has since spread to Nebraska, Kansas, Montana, Oklahoma, South Dakota, New Mexico, Utah, Minnesota, Wisconsin, Illinois, Alberta, and Saskatchewan, however. In March 2005 it turned up in wild and captive deer in Oneida County, New

York, just about eighty-five miles from Pennsylvania's border. It was found even closer to Pennsylvania in September 2005, when a two-and-a-half-year-old buck killed by a vehicle in Hampshire County, West Virginia, was confirmed to have the disease. Hampshire County is just thirty miles south of the Pennsylvania state line. Subsequent testing revealed that five deer in that county had CWD. There's speculation that it exists in other places already, too, but has yet to be found.

"It used to be a case of 'if CWD showed up here.' Now it's not if, but when, we find it," said Vern Ross, then executive director of the Pennsylvania Game Commission. "That's why we have to be on the lookout for this disease. It's bad news."

CWD can move from area to area and state to state in one of three ways: on the back of a trailer, as deer farmers ship live animals around; in the back of a truck, when a hunter takes an infected carcass home from his hunting grounds; and on four legs, with sick deer walking from place to place. Of those possibilities, wildlife managers consider the movement of live animals to pose the greatest risk.

There's speculation, for example, that the interstate movement of CWD-positive captive elk and deer is the reason CWD jumped the Mississippi River and made its way hundreds of miles east of any previously known location to Wisconsin in 2002, said Bob Manwell, public affairs manager for the Wisconsin Department of Natural Resources. Elk from CWD-infected herds were imported into Wisconsin during the 1990s. Captive whitetails on two Wisconsin deer farms turned up positive for CWD in 2002. And deer—including one that was later shot and tested positive for CWD—escaped from one of those farms.

Not long afterward, CWD showed up in the state's wild herd, albeit in animals some distance away from those farms. Officials looked for a link between the sick captive and wild deer but were never able to find a "smoking gun." The truth is, they may never know how the disease showed up in the state, Manwell said.

That's not surprising, said Beth Williams, who was a professor of veterinary sciences at the University of Wyoming and the person credited with discovering CWD (Williams died in 2004). "It is clear the disease has been present in the deer-farm industry and moved from state to state because of the deer-farm industry. That's very clear," Williams said. "What is less clear is the relationship between deer farms with CWD and CWD in free-ranging wild deer populations."

This hasn't stopped wildlife agencies from focusing on deer and elk farms as likely culprits—perhaps the most likely culprits—for spreading the disease, though. In September 2001, for example, Pennsylvania was one of nineteen states to receive elk from four different farms that tested positive for CWD. "That's when

The Game Commission has been sampling hunter-killed deer for evidence of chronic wasting disease, a fatal illness that affects both deer and elk. Biologists fear that if this disease shows up in Pennsylvania, deer herds will have to be drastically reduced.

we first realized our animals were wide open to CWD," said Bob Boyd, the Game Commission's point man on the CWD issue.

The Commission responded a few months later. In August 2002 it enacted a ban on the importation of live deer and elk into the state that lasted until January 2003. Deer and elk farmers immediately assailed the ban, but Vern Ross said it was necessary in light of CWD's potential impact on Pennsylvania's wild herds and the huge hunting economy they support. A 1998 study by the Center for Rural PA concluded that hunting annually pumps $4.8 billion into Pennsylvania, supporting more than forty-five thousand jobs. "Moving live, infected animals is the most high-risk opportunity for spreading the disease," Boyd said. "Our interest is in protecting wildlife. We had no choice."

The ban was eventually replaced by regulations requiring that those who would bring deer and elk into Pennsylvania submit an application to the Game Commission at least ten days prior to shipment and wait for the application to be returned. Each shipment must be accompanied by a certificate of veterinary inspection. Most important, only certain animals are allowed to cross the state's borders. Live cervids from a state without documented evidence of CWD must have been in a monitored herd for at least three years before they can be imported. Deer and elk coming from states that do have CWD must come from a disease-free herd that's been monitored for at least five years.

Many other states have enacted similar rules. For Pennsylvania's deer farmers, this means that while they can move deer freely from farm to farm within the state, they have to have proof that their herds are CWD-free if they want to do business elsewhere. This has led Pennsylvania to develop its own monitoring program. Run by the state's Department of Agriculture, it is designed to dovetail with a national CWD certification plan released in the summer of 2004 by the U.S. Departments of Agriculture and Interior. It calls for regular inspection of captive deer herds and testing of all deer sixteen months and older that die.

Pennsylvania's monitoring program has the support of most of the state's bigger operators, says Deer Farmers Association president Dave Griffith. In June 2005 more than half of the state's captive deer—more than ten thousand animals— were in the program, "and the number is growing daily," Griffith says.

"If a deer farmer wants to be able to sell deer out of state, market pressures dictate that he should be a part of the program," Knepley said. Loree adds, "The program is good to have. It kind of forced everyone to become aware of what the potential problems are."

The weakness of the monitoring program initially, according to people like Boyd, is that it was completely voluntary. No farmer had to participate if he didn't want to. That was bad, Boyd said. "Monitoring is a means of early detection. We need to know right now whether CWD is here," he said. "If it's here, it didn't get here through natural dispersal. It moves too slowly. We have to look at ways that are more likely. Inside the fence, it can be controlled. You just kill everything. It's hard, it's devastating. But you can manage it. Once it gets outside the fence, you're screwed. You're toast. Once it's out in the wild, it's like letting the genie out of the bottle."

A mandatory monitoring program finally went into effect on October 1, 2005, about one month after Governor Ed Rendell officially signed off on the state's CWD response plan, which was more than two years in the making. There were still questions even then, though, about who might be responsible for paying for that testing. That wasn't surprising: money had been the sticking point all along when it came to implementing a mandatory surveillance program. Game Commission officials had balked at paying the $500,000 annual tab, saying it was a misuse of sportsmen's dollars to test captive deer. Agriculture officials said they didn't have the money either, or the staff to carry out the testing.

In the fall of 2005, state officials were hoping that the U.S. Department of Agriculture would agree to reimburse the state for the cost of monitoring captive deer and elk. The only potential holdup was that state USDA officials had suggested that deer farmers themselves be the ones doing the testing. The USDA—along with those at the Game Commission and sportsmen—were not too keen on that idea, for an obvious reason.

Pennsylvania's CWD response plan—drafted by representatives of the state's Game Commission, Emergency Management Agency, Departments of Agriculture, Health, and Environmental Protection, and the U.S. Department of

Agriculture—takes an aggressive stand on trying to contain any outbreak of cwd. If the disease is found in wild deer herds, officials will identify a containment zone and try to lower deer numbers to as close to zero as possible. If the disease shows up in a captive herd, the plan calls for immediately "depopulating" that farm. That means killing all of the deer on it and shutting down the farm indefinitely, essentially putting that farmer out of business.

While there is some indemnity money—something on the order of $3,000 per animal—available for farmers who lose their herds, that's not a lot, according to Melody Zullinger, executive director of the Pennsylvania Federation of Sportsmen's Clubs. It's conceivable that a farmer with a cwd-infected deer might be tempted not to report it rather than risk losing his business. That's why testing needs to be mandatory. "We don't care who regulates them, we just want someone to do it," Zullinger says. "I don't think it's a matter of if we're going to find cwd anymore. I think it's a matter of when we find it. The question is, do we want to spend $500,000 now to keep it at bay or do we want to spend $23 million later to deal with it. It's just so frustrating, it drives me crazy. This should be a nonpartisan issue. It's a public health issue."

Some would like to just rid themselves of deer farms altogether and be done with it. When the members of the Northeast Association of Fish and Wildlife Agency Directors, representing thirteen state and Canadian wildlife management agencies, met in April 2005, they approved a resolution endorsing the elimination of captive cervid populations in the Northeast.

The Game Commission was the only state agency not to agree to it, simply because it's not practical to suggest such a thing in a state where deer farming is so entrenched—some operations are fifty or more years old—and so "well connected politically," Ross said in a letter to his fellow directors. "While elimination of captive cervid populations may be an attainable goal in jurisdictions with a small and politically insignificant captive cervid industry, and I would applaud such action in those areas, here in Pennsylvania this is not the case," Ross wrote. "It would be unrealistic for the Game Commission to eliminate captive cervid populations in Pennsylvania, and divisive and counter productive to be on record as supporting such action."

"The problem with that [resolution] is that it's twenty years too late," Boyd added. "In states with little or no cervid industry, that's great. In Pennsylvania, with almost eight hundred operators, some of them people who have invested their whole lives and all of their earnings in something, you can't do that. You can't get away with that."

Indeed, Pennsylvania's deer farmers already feel as though they're being unfairly targeted. Farmers are sensitive to the threat of cwd, Loree said, but they shouldn't have to bear the brunt of fears about the disease. "I'm not saying it's not something to be worried about, but it's been hyped so much," Loree said. "We're really scrutinized, I tell you. We all need to make sure the animals we're moving are healthy, but you get to the point where you feel like you're being picked on."

David Creegan agreed, saying he suspects wasting disease has existed, undetected, for a long time in a lot of states, the by-product of hunters and wildlife managers allowing deer herds to grow unnaturally large over the last fifty years. No one will believe that when it's eventually discovered, though.

"The deer herd is in the millions nationwide. It's higher than it's ever been. When you start running numbers that high, Mother Nature is going to take care of itself," Creegan said. "But, yeah, we'll get blamed for it. We're going to find it in Pennsylvania. I'm not sure when and I'm not sure where, but we're going to find it. And who's going to find it? Us, the deer farmers, because we're looking for it. If they would test a hundred thousand roadkills, they'd find it there, too."

That's not happening—the routine testing of roadkills, that is—but the Game Commission is looking for cwd in wild deer. Beginning in 1998 the agency began doing cwd testing on deer that were collected because they appeared sick. If running those tests didn't seem particularly important then—given that cwd was still considered a western disease—it quickly became a priority when wasting disease showed up in Wisconsin, Boyd said. Teams made up of Game Commission personnel, state Department of Agriculture veterinarians, and usda employees have been sampling hunter-killed wild deer in ever greater numbers each fall ever since. Team members go to butcher shops around the state, pulling brain stems and lymph nodes from deer, then sending the samples to be tested. Five hundred deer were tested for wasting disease in 2002–3. Two thousands were tested in 2003–4 and four thousand were tested in 2004–5. The Commission also does tests annually on tissues from hunter-killed elk. All of those tests—deer and elk alike—have come back negative.

Still, no one can say cwd doesn't already exist in the state's wild deer herd. The problem again is money. Testing deer and elk samples in amounts like those seen over the past few seasons costs more than $120,000 annually. Testing obviously sick deer that die by other means—like the fifty collected in 2003—probably costs another $500 per deer, factoring in the wages and benefits of a conservation officer who spends eight hours picking up the animal and driving it to State College or Harrisburg for testing and the expense of having the lab examine it. The state gets some help from the U.S. Department of Agriculture to cover these costs, but the Commission picks up most of the tab.

From a statistical perspective, for the Game Commission to be 99 percent sure CWD was not present in even 1 percent of the deer herd, it would need to test ten thousand animals a year, Boyd said. That's not likely to happen, given what it would cost. Instead, the agency has to settle for doing the best it can. "I don't see that we're going to get to that [ten thousand] figure," Boyd said. "It's just too much burden and it's too expensive."

A step the Commission did take in fall of 2005—much to the delight of deer farmers—involves deer and elk killed outside the state. For a number of years prior to 2005, the Commission had issued an annual news release advising hunters to consider leaving high-risk animal parts—lymph nodes, brains, and spinal cords—behind if they killed a deer or an elk in a state with a CWD problem. Hunters would be wise to return only with clean skull caps and antlers, clean hides and boned meat, the advisory said.

The advisory had no law or regulation behind it, though, and hunters were free to ignore it even if they did know about it. The result was that hunters, albeit unknowingly, brought CWD-infected carcasses back to Pennsylvania with them. At least fifteen contaminated animals made their way into Pennsylvania in 2003, along with another four in 2004. Whenever possible, Commission personnel collected those parts and incinerated them. In one case, though, a group of sportsmen returned home with an entire elk carcass, then butchered it and disposed of the backbone in a landfill before the Commission could get there.

"They boned out the meat like they should. But where did the backbone go? It ended up in a landfill. That is bad. That's what we don't want to see," said Boyd. "We don't know enough about how the disease is transmitted, so we don't want any infected carcasses dumped in a landfill or the back forty," agreed Cal DuBrock, director of the Game Commission's Bureau of Wildlife Management.

These days, that suggestion that hunters leave high-risk carcass parts behind when they return to Pennsylvania after a hunt elsewhere has the force of law behind it. In July 2005 game commissioners gave preliminary approval to a regulation that allows their executive director to ban the importation of those parts. Final approval came in October. And in the interval—in September, at the same time it created the mandatory CWD testing program for captive deer—the Department of Agriculture instituted an importation ban on its own.

The ban essentially makes it illegal to bring brains, spinal cords, and the like back from states with documented evidence of CWD in its free-ranging deer and elk herds. The only exception to the rule involves the states of New York and West Virginia: Pennsylvania's ban in regard to those states applies only to New York's designated CWD containment zone and West Virginia's Hampshire County.

Enforcement of the ban is of necessity a hit-or-miss kind of thing, said Mike Dubaich, director of the Commission's Bureau of Law Enforcement. The agency won't be "setting up road blocks" looking for carcass parts to come into the state, he admitted. Having the ban in place does give the Commission the authority to act if it gets word of illegal parts coming in, however.

The Commission could yet act to institute another ban, too. The same change that gave the executive director the authority to stop certain animal parts from coming into the state also gives him the authority to ban the feeding of deer "if the spread of CWD poses a threat to human safety, farm animals, pets or wildlife in the Commonwealth."

The Game Commission already prohibits the feeding of elk and black bears. Feeding deer is hugely popular with a lot of people, though, a fact Ross admitted when he said he would not stop the practice "unless and until" CWD posed a threat to the state's deer and elk.

There is evidence that allowing people to feed deer is dangerous for the animals themselves, however. A study released in February 2003 by the Canadian Cooperative Wildlife Health Centre concluded that while artificial feeding of deer does not cause disease, it makes the spread of disease much more likely because it concentrates animals in unnaturally high numbers. "If one or more animals are harboring an infectious organism or prion, its transmission to unaffected animals is facilitated by the increased frequency of contact among animals congregating at the feeding site," the report said.

Pennsylvania wildlife officials have known since at least 1997 that artificial feeding does more harm than good. That year the agency's Bureau of Wildlife Management received a report on the winter feeding of deer and turkeys. It determined that winter feeding programs are "a wasteful use of resources under any circumstances" and "should be actively discouraged as a waste of money and effort as well as being potentially harmful to wildlife and habitat."

Other states have banned feeding. The Wisconsin Department of Natural Resources prohibited the practice after wasting disease appeared there in 2002. The New York State Department of Environmental Conservation acted at the same time. It was not a popular move. A New York lawmaker, in fact, was scheduled to introduce legislation that would have lifted the ban the very day that wasting disease was discovered there.

That proposal quickly died, as well it should have, said DEC spokesman Michael Fraser. "Certainly the ban met with some opposition. But I think recent news, as unfortunate as it is, shows we're moving in the right direction," Fraser said.

The Vermont Agency of Natural Resources was moving in 2005 toward banning the feeding of deer, too. The agency had long discouraged people from feeding deer, but talk of a ban began in earnest when CWD moved to Wisconsin. Even then, though, there was a lot of opposition to the idea, and things might have gone no further had the disease not moved next to Vermont's doorstep in New York, said John Hall, a spokesman with Vermont's wildlife agency. "Now that CWD has suddenly appeared 150 miles to our west in New York, people without exception seem willing to accept anything that seems sensible. If this didn't seem sensible before, it does now," Hall said. "It may show up anyway, but the feeling seems to be that we should at least try this."

In Pennsylvania, it's a decades-long tradition for some sportsmen's clubs to buy corn by the ton to feed deer through the winter. Feed, hardware, and sporting goods shops across the state sell deer feeds, too. The Game Commission's Roxane Palone would like to see all of that come to an end, as she's convinced that artificial feeding really has no place in managing wildlife. She's less sure that this is a fight she can win, though. That's why she's been trying to get the Commission to at least do more public outreach explaining why feeding deer and other wildlife is not necessarily a good thing. "I think we'll discuss a ban, but I think socially and politically it's going to be very controversial," she said.

"It's one thing with bears to ban feeding because you can say this is a dangerous animal and someone's going to get hurt, so if you don't stop feeding it we're going to cite you," agreed commissioner John Riley. "But what do you do with the eighty-three-year-old woman who feeds deer because she thinks they're beautiful and so do her grandchildren?"

There may not be room for much of that kind of sentiment, though, given how expensive and drastic are the measures for dealing with an outbreak of chronic wasting disease. Consider the situation in Wisconsin. When CWD showed up there, researchers did some computer modeling to see just how big a problem it might be. The model suggests that, left unchecked, chronic wasting disease could wipe out deer herds on a statewide level in the eastern United States—where whitetail populations are much denser than are mule deer and elk populations in the West—within twenty to fifty years. In those "core" areas of Wisconsin where CWD was first discovered, deer herds could be significantly reduced within as little as eight to twelve years, the model predicted.

Now, this model, like all others, is based on assumptions, meaning that if one thing is wrong, much of the model's conclusion can be wrong. But there's no denying that CWD spread across several counties in Wisconsin in a period of less than four years, solely as a result of natural, wild deer movements, said Paul Knepley. "A dense population of deer does not lead to CWD. However, if CWD is introduced into an area with dense deer populations, it could spread very quickly," Knepley said.

Even in the West, where deer are less numerous and much more spread out, CWD has shown an ability to expand across the landscape. Colorado, for example, has been living with CWD for decades. It tests more than twenty-five thousand deer and elk for the disease each year. While it hasn't seen its deer herds decimated by CWD, it has experienced a slow but steady increase in CWD—particularly in buck deer—over the past decade. The infection rate in northeastern Colorado now stands at about 7 percent.

"Someone once described it as an epidemic in slow motion," said Todd Malmsbury, chief of information for the Colorado Division of Wildlife. "We believe that left unchecked, not over years but over decades, the disease will continue to spread and infect more of the deer population. That would mean, over decades, declines on the size of our herds. Whether it could ever wipe out populations is less clear, but the need to manage the disease is obvious. Based on what we know, if we don't try to control this disease, it will spread not only in Colorado but across the continent."

CWD can persist in the environment for a long time, too. Scientists know that CWD is not transmitted from deer to deer by a germ, like the common cold. What's more likely is that something coming out of the sick deer—whether it be saliva, urine, feces, eye secretions, or something else—comes in contact with an otherwise healthy deer, making it sick, too.

That contact doesn't have to be immediate. Research conducted by the Colorado Division of Wildlife and others indicates that the disease can live on in an area long after the deer that initially carried it there dies or wanders off. Researchers confined healthy deer in three sets of separate paddocks. In the first set, healthy deer were exposed to another live deer already infected with CWD. In the second set, deer were exposed to carcasses of deer that had died of CWD. In the third set, deer were confined in paddocks where infected deer had previously been kept. Healthy deer in each paddock contracted CWD within one year.

"Although live deer and elk still seem the most likely way for CWD to spread geographically, our data show that environmental sources could contribute to maintaining and prolonging local epidemics, even when all infected animals are eliminated," said Colorado Division of Wildlife veterinarian Michael Miller, the principal author of the report resulting from that study. "You can remove all of the animals, plow up all of the ground, disinfect everything, let it lie fallow for a year, and if you put animals back in there, they'll get CWD," Boyd said. "That's how bad it is, this issue of habitat contamination."

Knowing all this, when CWD was discovered in the southern third of their state, biologists in Wisconsin—where deer and deer-related activities like wildlife viewing generate about $1 billion a year in economic activity—decided not to take any chances. They established a 411-square-mile deer eradication zone encompassing those places known to have CWD, then loosened deer hunting regulations within that perimeter. They offered unlimited deer tags, extended seasons, developed a sharp-shooting program using conservation officers and biologists, and even let farmers shoot deer from tractors.

The goal was to lower deer densities from an average of about sixty per square mile to five or fewer deer per square mile inside the zone, and to ten to fifteen deer per square mile in a buffer around the zone. The hope was that, by managing herds at those low levels for an indefinite period of time, the disease might be conquered. "The message we're trying to get out is that what we're trying to do here is eradicate the disease, not the deer herd. But the only way to attack the disease is to lower deer densities," said Bob Manwell, senior public affairs manager for the Wisconsin DNR.

If eradication sounds like an extreme policy, it's really an accepted means of trying to snuff out or at least curtail the spread of disease. More important, it may be the only hope for beating the disease. "If you don't try something, it's pretty much going to be all across the state," Beth Williams said. "They're kind of conducting a grand experiment, if you will. I actually support what they're doing. And if it works, it may be something you could try in Pennsylvania if you suddenly get a case or two of a deer with CWD. It may be a way to stop it early. If it doesn't work, there aren't a whole lot of options. It makes sense to try to keep it out," Williams said.

"It's extremely important that states do everything they can to keep the disease from occurring in their areas and, if it does show up, to knock it down as quickly as they can to keep it from becoming established," Malmsbury added. "I always use the example of my daughter. If you pack twenty-three or twenty-four first graders in a class, and one comes in with pink eye, guess what happens? My daughter gets it and then she takes it home and Mom gets it and then things get real interesting for a while. Whenever you have high densities of animals, be they human or otherwise, transmission of disease is always more likely."

Eradication, when tied to a largely mysterious disease like CWD, poses three problems, however, as officials in Wisconsin found out. First, no one knows for sure if even such a lethal policy will be enough to get the job done. "In trying to lower deer densities, states are going by the best available science," Bryan Richards said. "But will it work? We have no idea. No idea."

Second, saying you're going to kill lots of deer and being able to do it are not necessarily the same thing. And third, it's tough to fund such a policy when you start losing customers.

In the first year or so after CWD was discovered, hunters, perhaps fearful of a disease about which so little is known, were slow to respond to the increased opportunities to hunt in the eradication zone. Landowners in the largely privately owned zone didn't exactly throw open their doors to unknown hunters, either.

Things have since improved on both counts. Biologists and conservation officers acting as sharpshooters are killing eight hundred or so deer a year in the eradication zone, and hunters are taking their share, so progress is being made, Manwell said. But deer numbers in the eradication zone are still much higher than they should be. "Three years ago, we had fifty to sixty deer per square mile in the eradication zone," Manwell said in mid-2005. "We're not sure how close we are to that five-deer-per-square-mile goal now. They've knocked that head per square mile down by 10 and 20 and even 30 percent in some units, but it's going to be a multiyear effort, for sure."

That begs the question, can hunters, landowners, and biologists ever hope to eradicate CWD if given the chance? The Wisconsin episode would seem to indicate that the answer is perhaps not, said Duane Diefenbach of the Cooperative Fish and Wildlife Research Unit at Penn State. "That's troubling, because even if you want to eradicate deer, you can't. Then what?" Diefenbach asked.

That's a question that has real implications for Pennsylvania, said David Wolfgang, a veterinarian at Penn State University's College of Agricultural Sciences. If wasting disease shows up in the state's big woods counties, where deer hunting is a tradition anyway, lowering deer densities will be difficult. If it shows up in urban areas like Philadelphia and Pittsburgh, where hunters already have difficulty getting access to deer, it could well be impossible. "If that happens, all bets are off," Wolfgang said. "In those suburbs where we are having great difficulty bringing deer numbers down, and where deer congregate, eating shrubbery and landscaping plants, dealing with CWD would be a political nightmare. Many of the people living in the suburbs like having lots of deer around."

What made things worse for Wisconsin was that the discovery of CWD was accompanied by a panic-induced drop in hunting license sales. That meant that revenues were dropping at the same time that expenses—namely, the cost of monitoring the disease—were skyrocketing.

The Wisconsin DNR collected more than five hundred deer from every county in the state—more than forty thousand deer total—in 2002–3 to test them for CWD. The cost of that effort, the largest of its kind in world history, was $14 million, in a year when the agency's total operating budget was less than $80 million.

At the same time, hunting license sales were dropping by 10 percent. This was not solely attributable to discovery of CWD—a survey of people who bought a license the year before the outbreak but not after showed most dropped out because of a lack of time—but fears of CWD ranked second, Manwell said.

With federal and state money slow to come that first year, Wisconsin wildlife officials had no choice but to pull money from existing programs to pay for their CWD monitoring effort. "Wildlife programs in particular took a pretty big hit. It has caused a lot of hardship, certainly," Manwell said.

Things have gotten somewhat better. By 2005 the Wisconsin DNR had recovered most of the lost license sales attributable to CWD, Manwell said. The state saw its second-best deer harvest ever in the fall of 2004, too.

Still, the agency has continued to spend between $4.5 and $5.5 million every year studying the disease, with no end in sight. Wisconsin—having now identified two separate CWD infection sources—has uncovered positive cases of wasting disease every year since 2002, and its CWD management zone has since expanded into neighboring Illinois.

The Pennsylvania Game Commission would, like Wisconsin, have to spend tens of millions of dollars if chronic wasting disease showed up there. Its CWD response plan calls for reducing deer numbers drastically in the area where the disease pops up—"ground zero"—just as Wisconsin's plan did, with the size of the eradication zone to be determined by the landscape.

The buck study Eric Long carried out in Pennsylvania showed a clear relationship between the percentage of forest cover and how far young bucks move. Deer disperse farthest when the habitat is most broken up. In solid woods, they move less. "So, for example, in an area with 60 percent forest cover—Pennsylvania's average—the average dispersal distance will be less than six miles," Long said. "However, in an area with less than 30 percent forest cover, the dispersal distance would be twelve to twenty-five miles." Knowing what type of forest cover surrounds "ground zero" for CWD, scientists could predict how far the disease might travel via natural deer dispersal in a year's time and could set up their eradication zone accordingly.

Still, the thought that the Game Commission might have to manage CWD in such a way, with all its attendant monitoring, at the same time that hunting license revenues were falling is a terrifying thought for an agency that gets no general tax dollars. "It will throw a monkey wrench into the state's deer management plan, that's for sure," Diefenbach said. "The Game Commission couldn't afford to deal with it without some sort of state or federal assistance."

"To deal with CWD, you're looking at a tremendous expense, money that would have to come from somewhere else, like habitat improvement," Boyd agreed. "And it's money you're spending while your license sales, your principal source of income, are going down. It's a double whammy. Your expenses go up while your income goes down."

Of course, it's the fear that chronic wasting disease could hurt people that causes some hunters to back away from pursuing deer. Because of its similarity to mad cow disease and Creutzfeldt-Jakob disease, many have wondered if CWD is transmissible to humans. The answer so far is probably not. Scientists have tried injecting CWD—which had never been found in any wild animal other than a deer or elk prior to September 2005—directly into the brains of cattle, to see if the disease could jump the species barrier. Even under those conditions, only five of the thirteen animals injected became sick.

The disease itself—at least to some degree—did what scientists could not, however. In September 2005 Colorado Division of Wildlife officials confirmed that a bull moose taken by an archer tested positive for CWD. This marked the first time ever that a wild animal other than a deer or elk was confirmed to have the disease. Moose are members of the deer family, so it's not unbelievable that one could contract CWD, said Miller, the division of wildlife veterinarian. But Colorado had been testing moose for the disease since 2002, and had gone through 288 hunter-killed animals without a single positive occurrence before this case, so finding an infected animal was a bit of a surprise.

Even at that, though, there's no evidence to date that CWD has ever made or could make the jump from deer to people, according to research conducted by the World Health Organization and the National Centers for Disease Control. Scientists with the Centers for Disease Control have studied the incidence of Creutzfeldt-Jakob disease (CJD) in areas with long-standing evidence of CWD, for example. If the disease could move to humans, scientists reasoned, they might expect to see higher rates of Creutzfeldt-Jakob disease in humans populations in those areas. So far, there's been no evidence of that occurring.

A paper resulting from a study written by Beth Williams and several others concluded that "the lack of evidence of a link between CWD transmission and unusual cases of CJD, despite several epidemiological investigations, and the absence of an increase in CJD incidence in Colorado and Wyoming suggest that the risk, if any, of transmission of CWD to humans is low."

In the same paper, though, researchers admitted that there is still a chance the disease could spread to humans, just as mad cow disease did. "The transmission of BSE to humans and the resulting variant CJD indicate that, provided sufficient exposure, the species barrier may not completely protect humans from animal prion diseases," the report said. "Because CWD has occurred in a limited geographic area for decades, an adequate number of people may not have been exposed to the CWD agent to result in a clinically recognizable human disease. The level and frequency of human exposure to the CWD agent may increase with the spread of CWD in the United States."

Given that possibility, the World Health Organization and most wildlife agencies recommend that hunters limit their potential exposure to the disease by avoiding eating meat from animals that test positive for CWD or that even look sick. Hunters should also use gloves when dressing carcasses in the field, bone out the meat, and minimize handling of brain and spinal cord tissues. Hunters should avoid eating the deer and elk tissues—namely, the brain, spinal cord, eyes, spleen, tonsils, and lymph nodes—of otherwise healthy-looking animals from areas with CWD, as well.

At the same time, though, Williams said hunters need to keep the threat of CWD in perspective. People live around animal populations with rabies, she noted. People can't ignore that disease, but they shouldn't worry about it excessively, either. The same is true with CWD. "You look at rabies, that's a real disease with a real human link," Williams said. "By comparison, the situation with CWD is that it will in all likelihood have an impact on deer herds, but not necessarily be a human pathogen. It falls into the realm of something that we need to be concerned about, but not anything to panic about."

Gary Wolfe, project leader for the CWD Alliance, an information clearinghouse formed by thirteen sportsmen's organizations, including the Rocky Mountain Elk Foundation, Boone and Crockett Club, and Mule Deer Foundation, agrees. He hunts an area of Colorado where CWD is endemic and has to have any animal he kills boned out on site before he can take it home to Wyoming for butchering.

It's true that's a bit of an inconvenience, Wolfe says. But the mere presence of CWD is no reason to stop hunting or to stop hunting any particular area, he says. That's one of the main ideas the alliance tries to get across in the instructional CD it makes available to sportsmen. "There is no such thing as 'mad deer disease,' even though I saw that in a lot of headlines," Wolfe says. "The important thing for hunters to remember is that this is no reason not to hunt out of state. My message to hunters is that fear of CWD should not keep a person from enjoying the sport of hunting. You just have to take a few extra steps up front. I know, myself, I'm more concerned about the drive to my hunting spot or getting knocked off my horse or kicked by my horse or getting shot by another hunter than I am about chronic wasting disease. It doesn't even make my top-fifteen list of risk factors."

Sportsmen may be getting the message. In New York, the initial reaction to the discovery of the disease's existence there was surprise, said Tom King, president of the New York State Rifle and Pistol Association, the state's largest sportsmen's group. The fact that the disease hadn't moved east from Wisconsin in three years probably lulled some into thinking it would never get to New York. But when it showed up it didn't necessarily spawn a panic either. "I don't think it's a fearful thing yet," said King, who hunts with his son in an area of Colorado where CWD is endemic. "I think sportsmen are aware of it and are waiting to see what happens next. But I don't think it's going to end deer hunting in New York."

That's good, because if hunters stop hunting over concern about chronic wasting disease, the impact could be enormous. Andrew Seidl, an associate professor of agricultural and resource economics at Colorado State University, did one of the first studies of the potential economic impacts of chronic wasting disease. Released in 2003, the study estimated that CWD could cost the nation $100 billion a year, and that rural areas that depend on hunting, wildlife watching, and game farms would suffer the most.

The study factored in expenses—like the cost of giving federal aid to farmers who lose their herds and state game agencies that have to do testing and monitoring—as well as lost revenues absorbed by sporting goods stores, gas stations, restaurants, and the like if fewer hunters headed to the woods.

"The economic implications of this disease are manifested in a number of ways," Seidl wrote in the report resulting from his study. "Government agencies incur costs in research, surveillance and disease management activities. Countries may have trade restrictions imposed against entire industries due to an outbreak. Consumer demand may suffer temporary or permanent damage due to perceived risks of meat products.

"Producers of farmed cervidae may have their herds quarantined, restricting sales and movements, or depopulated," the report continued. "Business and communities may lose revenues from decreases in cervid hunting and wildlife viewing, and participants in these activities lose recreational benefits."

The study assumed a worst-case scenario, Seidl said, but showed just how significant the risks really are. "The bottom line is that while we really don't know what the total economic impact is going to be, we can see that wildlife is a large and important industry," Seidl was quoted as saying in an interview with a Denver newspaper.

Bruce Morrison, wildlife disease specialist for the Nebraska Game and Parks Commission and chairman of the National CWD Plan Implementation Team, is not sure $100 billion is an accurate reflection of what CWD might cost. There's no doubt, though, that some communities rely on hunters and the money they spend to get through the winter. He's seen that in western Nebraska and suspects it's true in rural communities all over the country, including Pennsylvania.

The best long-term hope for keeping that money flowing is to invest in learning more about CWD now, he said. That's going to be an expensive proposition in and of itself, he admitted, even given the close cooperation among federal and state agencies and universities. The national CWD team, organized by state wildlife officers, figured it would take $100 million to study the disease over three years.

That research would, though, result in a plan outlining what needs to be done to combat CWD, and by whom and at what cost. "To me, if you can spend $100 million to save $100 billion, that's not too bad a bargain. It could be a pretty big deal," Morrison said.

Wolfe agreed, but said he hopes that hunters—through their already cash-strapped game agencies—are not asked to pay for all of the needed research alone. "The best we can say right now, unfortunately, is that we really and truly don't know what the long-term impacts of CWD are going to be on our deer and elk herds. We just don't know, so we'll be justified to err on the side of caution," Wolfe said.

Allowing bucks to live longer not only produces the kind of big racks cherished by hunters but is good for the deer themselves, as it allows more mature bucks to do most of the breeding.

"But what we're dealing with right now is more than just a wildlife management issue," Wolfe continued. "With all of those unknowns, this is a public safety issue and a lot of research needs to be done. I don't want to see sportsmen be the only ones picking up the tab on chronic wasting disease. If sportsmen pick up the whole bill, a lot of other very important wildlife programs are going to go down the tubes."

Help may be forthcoming. The USDA has granted money to state wildlife agencies to study and monitor the disease. Federal legislation to provide additional funding for CWD research and control efforts, upgrade diagnostic laboratories, and create a National Chronic Wasting Disease Clearinghouse has been discussed, too.

Malmsbury, for one, hopes that all of this research gets done, not just for the sake of hunters but for everyone's sake. "Disease left unchecked can have a negative impact on wildlife," Malmsbury said. "That's important not only to people who like to take home and consume these critters, but to people who just like to see wildlife and have these animals around. I think the vast majority of us want to have our native species. And disease like this clearly threatens that wildlife."

Loree doesn't disagree. He's just hoping that deer farmers don't have to bear too much of the blame or pay too much of the bill for monitoring CWD or dealing with it if and when it shows up in Pennsylvania. He treats his deer very well, giving them special high-grade feed mixes and trying to provide conditions that minimize stress, which in turns affects antler growth. He worries over them, frets over them, pampers them in many ways. But they remain products. He has names for many of his deer, but only one or two—like Penny, an old doe he's had since his early days of raising deer and who meets us at one of the gates to his deer pens—are like pets.

"People think of Bambi and all that crap. Deer are vicious. They'll kill you," Loree said. "White-tailed deer, bucks, well, all deer really, but bucks especially, are vicious. Those sons of guns are nasty."

Maybe that—and the money the deer bring—is why Loree doesn't mind selling deer knowing they're going to be shot, any more than a cattle farmer worries about selling a steer that's destined to become beef in a grocery store meat case. "I can load one into a box and ship it off, knowing it's going to be shot in three to four months. That doesn't bother me," Loree said. "But if one runs into a fence here and breaks its leg, that just tears my heart out. I can't take it. I have a lot of respect for these animals, I really do."

He certainly doesn't want to see any of his animals infected with CWD. But he's not as worried as some others. "I think CWD is a big scare," Loree said. "I don't truly believe it's that big a deal. Out west they have it and they're dealing with it. Rabies is a serious disease, too, and you never hear anything about it. Is it that big a problem or it is more hype? I guess the jury is still out on that, but I have my opinions."

Others disagree. More CWD tests were done in 2002 alone than in all the previous years combined nationwide. These kinds of precautions need to continue, Williams said. If not, it's likely that wildlife populations infected by CWD will lose favor with the public, thereby lowering the value of all wildlife and the level of care afforded it. "This is an important issue that not enough hunters are paying attention to," Boyd added. "If they think they've got a problem not seeing enough deer now, wait until CWD shows up. When we get CWD, those problems are going to seem small. I hope we don't get it, but we need to be alert in case we do."

"I don't believe we've found it in the last place by any means," Bryan Richards added. "I think that's why states have to continue to be vigilant with their surveillance. You're not going to find it if you're not looking for it. This is one of those things where prevention is very important. It's unlike other diseases. Once you get it in your free-ranging deer herd it's very hard to control. The consensus among states is that if you don't have CWD, you don't want it."

12

A LOOK TO THE FUTURE

It was midsummer and Mandy, Derek, Tyler, and I were in Harrisburg. I was so glad to be there. We'd spent the past three days camping at Assateague Island National Seashore with Greg, his wife, Jill, and their son, Jared. It had had its moments of fun—camping on the sand, waking up to see sika deer wandering past just outside the tent, getting out of the ocean to see wild ponies napping near the beach towels.

The mosquitoes, though, had been relentless. Our last night in camp had been spent huddled around a picnic table under a screened canopy, counting down the hours until we could leave and dreading the thought of having to run the bug gauntlet from the tents to the vehicles the next morning.

Staying in a hotel in Harrisburg had never felt so good. I was working through the day, covering a meeting of the Pennsylvania Fish and Boat Commission, while Mandy and the kids hung out at the hotel pool. The evenings were ours to spend together.

One night, before going to dinner, we stopped in a Gander Mountain store. We went back to the gun department so that Derek and Tyler could look at the youth-sized rifles and shotguns, like the pint-sized .22 rifles with brand names like the Cricket and the Chipmunk.

Derek, who was less than six months away from turning twelve and looking forward to being able to hunt for the first time that fall, tried shouldering a long-barreled, adult-sized bolt-action .30-06 rifle. He had to nearly bend over backward to be able to hold it level, but he didn't seem to mind. He was too excited.

"What kind of animals will I be able to hunt this year?" he asked, taking aim at one of the fluorescent lights on the ceiling.

"Well, you'll be able to hunt all kinds of small game, like squirrels, rabbits, pheasants, and grouse. You'll be able to hunt turkey. And you'll turn twelve just in time to hunt does in October," I said.

"Does? You mean I get to hunt deer? Ahh, cool!" he said.

Derek didn't realize it then, and still doesn't now, but chances are that the hunters of his generation will grow up with more opportunities to hunt deer than their parents could have ever imagined. But those increased opportunities will be accompanied by equally dramatic changes in the backdrop against which hunting is enjoyed.

One thing the hunters of tomorrow may have, for example, is the chance to hunt on Sundays. As of the fall of 2004, Pennsylvania was one of only six states— all in the Northeast—that still prohibit Sunday hunting. The ban, similar to one that forbade Sunday fishing in the state until 1937, is a remnant of the state's "blue laws," which also previously prohibited stores, movie theaters, and the like from being open on Sundays. The ban dates back to 1873.

"When I was a kid, you couldn't buy gasoline on a Sunday," said the fifty-something Steve Mohr, a former game commissioner. "They weren't allowed to be open. The department stores weren't allowed to be open. When I was twelve and we were travel- ing to Clinton County to do some hunting or fishing, we carried two five-gallon cans of gasoline because we knew we wouldn't be able to buy it. But times change."

Pennsylvania's Sunday hunting prohibition is not a complete ban. Hunters can pursue crows, foxes, and coyotes on Sundays. Whether to allow Sunday hunting for more species has always been the question. Those who favor Sunday hunting believe it would have many benefits. Ray Smith is a professional hunting guide. He takes dozens of Pennsylvania hunters to Kansas and Texas each year to pursue turkeys and white-tailed deer. Getting sportsmen from elsewhere to hunt those same species in the woods around his Lycoming County home, where they are as plentiful as anywhere, is a lot tougher.

There are a couple of reasons for this, Smith said, but the biggest is that it's ille- gal to hunt on Sundays in Pennsylvania. Hunters who work through the week and might not be able to get off until Friday just don't want to travel to Pennsylvania for one day's hunting. "It would be much easier for me to sell a hunt, be it for deer or turkeys or small game or whatever, if a person could have a long weekend," said Smith, owner of River Valley Outfitters. "A working man could have a good hunt without having to miss a lot of work. But right now, there's no real advantage for people to come to Pennsylvania to hunt."

Barry Wickes, president of the Pennsylvania Tourism and Lodging Association, which represents seven hundred hotels, motels, resorts, and bed and breakfasts across the state, believes Sunday hunting would be a boon to the state's economy, too. "If a guy wants to hunt Saturday and then he can also hunt Sunday, he's going to have to stay overnight somewhere and spend some money on lodging, gas, and food. So it's going to have an impact, a positive economic impact," Wickes said.

More than just a money issue, though, Sunday hunting would be a great management tool, too, particularly for deer and nuisance waterfowl, said state representative Marc Gergely, an Allegheny County Democrat. "Times are changing. We need, in Pennsylvania, to step forward and discuss these things," Gergely said. "It's not 1950 any more. I know that since I took this job as state representative, I hunt far less than I used to and that's because of my work schedule. It's tough to get a day off through the week especially and sometimes Saturdays are even tied up. I'm often free on Sundays, but I can't hunt. How is that doing me, or the biologists who would like people like me to shoot a few deer, any good?

"You can give me all the Mondays in the world to hunt deer, but it's not going to do me any good, because I can't hunt. I'm convinced there are lots of people in the same situation. That's the way the world is today," Gergely said. "We need to match opportunity with reality."

"I have a son-in-law who has to work a lot of Saturdays," Dave Laden, the Philadelphia deer hunter, added. "He can't get around it. He has a family and working Saturdays is a condition of his employment. It's not an option. He has to do it. If he had Sundays, though, he could hunt. Sundays would open hunting to a whole new crowd."

Commissioner Roxane Palone is also a proponent of Sunday hunting. In an age when so much of the Game Commission's focus is on giving hunters more opportunities to shoot deer, opening Sundays to hunting would be a dramatic step forward, she says. "Sunday hunting is probably one of the most important changes we need for the future of managing deer. Certainly there would be more opportunities for small-business owners and other people who work six days a week to get out and get out with their children," Palone says. "We do everything else on Sundays. I'm not saying that's right or wrong. But if we have lottery tickets on Sundays, we have all of our stores open on Sunday, liquor stores are now open on Sundays, why not have hunting, too?"

Ralph Saggiomo of the Unified Sportsmen said Sunday hunting is critical to recruiting new hunters from among the youths who can play soccer, see a movie, or play on a computer every day of the week. "I'm sixty-eight years old. Do I need Sunday hunting? No," Saggiomo said. "But do my children need it? Yes. Will my grandchildren need it probably even more? Yes."

Pennsylvania has debated the merits of Sunday hunting before. In the late 1990s the House Game and Fisheries Committee held six hearings around the state to gauge support for legislation that would have allowed hunting on the two Sundays that fall during the rifle deer season. Representative Bruce Smith said that most of those who testified at the events opposed the idea. Even Dan Surra, who sponsored that legislation, admitted that "we got our heads handed to us politically."

Still, interest in the issue has remained high, and in the summer of 2005 the state legislature was again examining the idea of Sunday hunting. A resolution sponsored by the House of Representatives directed the Legislative Budget and Finance Committee to study the economic impact of Sunday hunting, its effect on commercial hunting grounds, and what measures might be undertaken to protect landowners who don't want Sunday hunting on their property.

The resulting report was written by Rob Southwick of Southwick Associates, a fish and wildlife economics and statistics consulting firm based in Florida. He said that his research determined that allowing hunting on just the two Sundays that fall within the two-week firearms deer season would create 1,630 new jobs and generate $184 million in economic activity and $5.4 million in additional state sales and income taxes. If Sunday hunting opportunities were expanded across the entire fall, those numbers would be even bigger: 5,300 new full- and part-time jobs would be created, and $629 million in economic activity and $18 million in additional sales and income taxes would be generated.

More important, perhaps, 53 percent of hunters surveyed said they support the idea of Sunday hunting and would get afield more often—an average of 4.7 days per year, on average—if Sundays were available to them. In addition, people who were at one time hunters but have since given up the sport might return to the hunting ranks if they knew they would have more opportunities, Southwick said. "If they know they can hunt more than one or two days a year, they might be more likely to get back into it," he said.

Not everyone likes the idea of Sunday hunting, however. As part of his research, Southwick interviewed landowners—most of them members of the Pennsylvania Farm Bureau—and asked what they thought of Sunday hunting. Quite simply, they don't like it. Eighty-two percent said they oppose or strongly oppose hunting on all Sundays in the fall. Eighty-one percent said they oppose hunting on the two Sundays in deer season. This was not surprising, given that the Farm Bureau has been the biggest opponent of Sunday hunting in Pennsylvania for more than a decade.

This is not to say that every farmer opposes Sunday hunting. Phil Long, a bureau member from Westmoreland County, said he would be open to Sunday hunting if it meant that hunters could shoot more of the deer that eat up to $15,000 worth of his crops every year. Fellow Westmoreland County farmer Ron Ambrose would trade Sunday hunting for fewer deer, too.

But this is the minority view among farmers, Crawford County farmer Doug Gilbert said. The Farm Bureau polls its members on the Sunday hunting issue each year at its annual convention. So far, the majority of delegates have always opposed it. In the fall of 2004, for example, the Farm Bureau approved two resolutions of its own. One opposed Sunday hunting. The other urged the Game Commission to add a third week to the rifle deer season as an alternative to Sunday hunting if more time is needed to control deer.

The farmers who put up with trespassers, littering, and other intrusions like having one day—Sunday—when they don't have to worry about people knocking on their door or shooting too close to the house, Gilbert said. What's more, they're willing to act to keep things that way. "If farmers have to go to the extreme of posting their land to have one day to themselves, they will. That's the simplest way to put it," he said.

Even so, there might be more support for Sunday hunting now than there used to be. The Pennsylvania Federation of Sportsmen's Clubs, which had never supported any Sunday hunting measure out of respect for the landowners who provide places to hunt, recommended at its fall 2004 convention that the Game Commission allow Sunday hunting for groundhogs. The federation noted that Sunday hunting for crows, foxes, and coyotes "has not caused any specific issues concerning public discontent, over-harvest or safety issues."

The club also noted that farmers and landowners have significant property damage due to groundhogs digging dens, and that there is a need to establish more liberal seasons for harvesting them. Groundhog hunting on Sunday "would increase hunting opportunities for the sportsmen."

A second resolution—meant to support the idea of Sunday hunting in general—did not pass the federation's board, but there was more support for the measure than there had ever been before. Some were willing to at least try Sunday hunting on public land, said executive director Melody Zullinger, so "the tide is changing."

The Pennsylvania Game Commission—which has never taken a formal stand on Sunday hunting—has surveyed sportsmen about the idea several times, and these surveys also seem to indicate that attitudes are changing. In a 1991 survey, 62 percent opposed Sunday hunting for deer. In 2001 only 50 percent opposed Sunday hunting of turkeys, and in a 2002 survey, 61 percent supported Sunday hunting of groundhogs.

Given such evidence, Governor Ed Rendell has asked his Advisory Council on Hunting, Fishing and Conservation to explore the pros and cons of Sunday hunting as well, said his press secretary, Kate Philips. Robb Miller, Rendell's sportsmen's adviser and leader of the council, thinks Sunday hunting is an idea whose time has come. "I like the idea of Sunday hunting," Miller said. "Until the governor tells me to back off—and I don't think he will—this is one of those issues we need to educate ourselves about. I mean, why not have it? It would be great for retaining the hunters we have and recruiting new ones. That's very important."

Others must feel the same way, judging by the flurry of Sunday hunting legislation proposed in recent years. State lawmakers introduced three different bills in 2004 and several others in 2005 that would allow Sunday hunting in one form or another. One of these, sponsored by Representative Ed Staback, a Lackawanna County Democrat, would remove all of the prohibitions on Sunday hunting from state law and give the Game Commission the authority to include Sundays when setting seasons, if it so chose. He too cited retaining and recruiting new hunters as a key reason for sponsoring the bill.

"Personally, I would like to see the Game Commission use their data and input from hunters to decide whether a particular season should utilize a Sunday hunt and if such a change is best used statewide or only in some areas," Staback said. "I want to start that dialogue." It's critical to start talking about the issue now, he said, because it may take a while to resolve the issue in Pennsylvania, if the experience of other states is typical.

Ohio dabbled in Sunday hunting for a few species, then went to full-blown Sunday hunting in 2002. Members of Ohio's farm bureau initially opposed the idea, fearing they would be overrun with hunters, said Randy Miller, assistant chief of the Ohio Division of Wildlife. Those attitudes changed, though, when the state agreed to strengthen its trespass laws. "Enforcing trespassing is one of our top priorities now," Miller said. "If we get a call and we have an officer to send, we go. Our farmers seem pretty happy with that arrangement."

Maryland allowed hunting on private property on two Sundays—November 2, the first day of the archery deer season, and November 30, the first day of the rifle deer season—for the first time in the fall of 2004. Just getting those two days took four years of work, though, said Bill Miles, a registered lobbyist who worked on the issue. "When I'm on my deathbed, it will be the greatest legislative achievement of my career," Miles said. "It was a major, major, brutal undertaking. But we won."

Gergely believes it's only a matter of time before the public demand for Sunday hunting brings it to Pennsylvania, too. "We're in Sunday hunting's childhood stages. Not its infancy, but its childhood stages," Gergely said. "We've just got to keep chipping away at it."

Another potential deer management subject that's been debated recently is whether it should be legal for hunters to hunt deer over bait. Some believe regulated baiting could be a useful tool, especially in urban settings where deer are a problem but where access to hunting them is very limited.

Representatives from the Game Commission's southwest and southeast region offices and Bureaus of Wildlife Management, Law Enforcement, and Information and Education spent part of 2003 researching the pros and cons of baiting. There are studies, the committee found, that indicate that hunters hunting over bait take more deer than those not using bait. This is especially true with shelled corn in winter, when wild foods are scarcer. It's true, too, that while few deer will travel outside their normal home range to get to a bait pile, those that do may use predictable routes to get there, making them more susceptible to being taken by a hunter.

The committee ultimately recommended against allowing hunting over bait, though, for several reasons. First, on the practical side, deer learn quickly to avoid bait piles until after dark, when hunting is not allowed, thereby limiting their harvest. Second, it is bucks and fawns—and not the adult does the Game Commission would most like to see harvested—that take bait most often. Third, baiting could lead to unnaturally high concentrations of deer and promote disease.

There are also social reasons for not allowing baiting. The committee decided that those negatives—which include the possibility that it might turn off some landowners and encourage illegal activity—outweighed the positives. "Based on information available, it is not clear to what extent baiting would be useful in attaining the lower deer densities that we are trying to achieve in those areas," reads the committee's report.

"Baiting is not the panacea some people think it is," said John Smith, the Game Commission's law enforcement supervisor. "We don't think it will work to the extent that it's going to control deer populations in those metropolitan areas." As alternatives to baiting, Cal DuBrock has suggested increasing the number of

In an effort to make it easier for hunters to kill deer, especially in suburban areas, the Game Commission has made some changes to its regulations. One change is to allow hunters to use crossbows in some areas.

antlerless permits available, rewriting the urban deer control program to allow nonpolitical subdivisions—like homeowner's groups—to get permits for deer removal, or giving hunters an additional tag for every one they fill in urban and suburban areas.

Laden says that such tools don't address the core problem of dealing with deer in urban areas: getting hunters and deer in the same places. If hunters aren't going to be able to get where the deer are, wildlife managers need to consider ways of bringing the deer to the hunters. He suggested that hunters might draw deer from nonhuntable areas to huntable ones by placing bait out only at certain times of day, for example. "None of the tools presently employed to address the problem of too many deer do anything to draw deer out of unhuntable areas for the purpose of removal," he says.

The Game Commission has been reexamining the idea of allowing baiting for deer. That's not a bad thing, said Greg Isabella, a game commissioner from Philadelphia. He isn't sure yet whether baiting is an answer to some deer problems or not. Sportsmen, biologists, commissioners, and others need to keep an open mind, though. "Maybe this is something that needs to be looked at," Isabella said. "Deer aren't stupid. They are going to run to areas where hunters can't chase them. It's a problem."

The future of Pennsylvania deer management might also include citizen task forces. The New York State Department of Environmental Conservation uses them—they are bodies made up of farmers, landowners, hunters, municipal officials, and others. Task force members don't get to say how many deer an area should or will have entirely on their own. Instead, biologists give them a range of acceptable deer numbers and task force members decide where on that scale to let the population fall. Critics pan the task forces as superficial, powerless bodies whose real purpose is to pacify people with a stake in deer, while also deflecting criticism from the Department of Environmental Conservation.

Some people in the Game Commission like the idea of using citizen task forces to help manage deer, however. Jeannine Tardiff, a biologist in the agency's deer management section, was finalizing plans to create a citizen task force for one of the wildlife management units in southeastern Pennsylvania in late 2005. It was expected to be up and running in 2006. If it works, it could serve as a model for similar task forces in other parts of the state, she said.

But can a task force like that really help settle some of the deer debate? If anyone wants to know how such a group might work, all they need to do is look to the

Bedford County Deer Damage Control Committee. This group—which includes a county commissioner, conservation district board member, Federation of Sportsmen's Clubs representative, wildlife conservation officers, farmers, woodlands owners, and biologists—has met regularly since the early 1990s to talk about deer issues in Bedford County.

Greg and I traveled to Bedford to sit in on one of their meetings one summer afternoon. It was in many ways a trip similar to those we had taken to the state's northern tier, as the county, cut by the rugged Allegheny Mountains as they pass through the south-central portion of the state, has long had lots of deer. Committee members believe it has been suffering of late because of that.

"There's nothing any of us like more than to go into the woods and see some deer," said Don Morris, a member of the Woodland Owners of the Southern Alleghenies and a member of the committee. "I hunt, and I like to see a rack in the crosshairs. But there's a limit to how many deer you can have, and we've just got too many."

Morris explained this as we walked some of the hundred-plus acres he owns. Already there's evidence the area is suffering the same kind of ecological damage—browse lines, acre upon acre of forest with no understory—found in places like the north-central part of the state. He led Greg and me to a power line–like swath that was cut through his woods more than ten years ago. It had never been mowed or cut since. It should have been full of young trees reaching pole timber stage, but it wasn't. Little was growing above knee height. That's because the deer have been keeping it trimmed back, he said

"There are no hardwoods in there. There's nothing in there but black locust, and that's because deer don't like to eat it much. The only thing that's coming back is junk," Morris said.

The Bedford County Deer Damage Control Committee was formed to help address that issue. Farmers, for example, can outline just what kind of deer damage problems they're facing. "The agricultural community will sustain a certain amount of damage. They will feed a certain amount of deer. But when they get overburdened, as is the case now, you have to do something," said committee member and Bedford County commissioner Dick Rice.

Thanks to the communication generated by the committee, sportsmen, who might not otherwise have known about or understood the seriousness of the problem, can help find solutions, said committee member Luke Williams, a representative of the Bedford County Federation of Sportsmen's Clubs. "We try to work with

Don Morris is a member of the Bedford County Deer Damage Control Committee. The committee might be an example of how task forces could assist in deer management.

the landowners whenever possible. We write letters, we work with the state federation on seasons and bag limits, we try to get hunters in places with too many deer, whatever we can," Williams said.

Committee members don't think they've solved all of Bedford County's deer damage problems by any means. They do think they have made progress, however. "I think this committee has helped to educate the Game Commission about the deer problem in this area," said committee member and state representative Dick Hess.

"More and more average hunters are becoming more and more aware of our forest deforestation problem," added Terry Miller, district manager for the Bedford County Conservation District and a committee member. "That's not going to have an immediate impact, but it's going to have a real good long-term impact. We're also seeing more and more people open their land to hunting. And this is a lot of land that might have tended to be posted."

Ron Johnson, president of the Woodland Owners of the Southern Alleghenies and a board member of the county conservation district, said deer management is the most political issue he's ever been involved with in Pennsylvania. He believes the committee can help defuse that, though. "I've heard rumblings about people wanting to sue the Game Commission or get help from the legislature or whatever," Johnson said. "Hopefully, if people and agencies can work together through groups like ours, none of that will really be necessary."

Don Garner, the Game Commission's information and education supervisor in the south-central office, praised the work of the group and its dedication to finding solutions. "Bedford County has too many deer, to be sure. But the committee is looking for ways to fix that instead of going off into their separate camps, and they've been doing it since before it became a trendy thing," he said.

Longer deer seasons are something else tomorrow's deer hunters will enjoy. Game Commission biologists know they can sell only a limited numbers of doe licenses each year, Gary Alt told me. At some point, you run out of hunters to buy them.

It's true, too, that hunters are less likely to fill their second and third doe tags when they're limited to shooting deer in a narrow timeframe. It might be too much to butcher several deer at a time, or freezer space might become an issue, or something else. Whatever the reason, hunters are less efficient when it comes to filling second and third doe tags.

If hunters are able to harvest several deer, but spread it out over a longer period of time, they might be more interested and more successful, Alt believes. Biologists are already talking about what they can do to help hunters in this way. "I envision, in the long term, you're going to see us have longer antlerless seasons and offer much more recreation. I think that's going to be good for hunting, and good for controlling the deer population," Alt says. "And it's not only going to be good, it's going to be necessary."

Within the past few years Alt and his staff have suggested a few new seasons. While none has gotten as far as making it onto a Game Commission agenda, that day may yet come, and soon. One idea Alt had tossed around was holding a September doe season. It could offer several distinct advantages. First, it could remove does that are destined to be harvested anyway earlier in the fall. This would lessen the competition among deer for food and send the remaining deer into the winter in better health. Second, an early season could improve breeding efficiency, as bucks would waste less time and energy breeding does that aren't going to survive hunting season.

An early season would also give hunters more time to hunt, an important consideration if there are going to be fewer hunters to control deer numbers in the future, as Marrett Grund pointed out. It would also spread the overall deer harvest out and make it less dependent on things like weather.

The timing of a pre-rut season has been a hotly debated subject. "We're not too sure we want to have an early rifle season overlap with archery season," Grund said. "That might be too much. That's why we're thinking about perhaps the last week of September."

Department of Conservation and Natural Resources officials like the idea of a September season, Merlin Benner said. One of the criticisms leveled at the DCNR by hunters is that it makes the areas where it wants deer removed too hard for hunters to reach. The agency has tried to address this concern and make things easier for hunters by opening more gated roads. There were about three thousand miles of state forest roads open to public travel in 2004, and the agency opened another 450 miles of gated roads for deer season.

The problem, Benner said, is that there are only so many roads that can be opened. Some areas have no roads, and new road construction is unlikely given the competing missions and demands of the department. And the roads that do exist are largely dirt. They can't handle a lot of traffic in late fall and winter, when the ground might be wet or snowy. They get no winter maintenance, either, which means they might be snowed in for deer season, just when hunters most need access to them. These roads would be in better shape and could handle more traffic in September, when the weather is better. "We made it clear to commissioners that we could open a lot more roads if we had an earlier season during the drier time of year, before snow and ice," Benner said. "For us to be able to open more roads and not have a huge environmental problem, we need an earlier timeframe."

Biologists never did formally recommend a September season, but they may yet do so. They may also try for another variation on a season they did propose but saw rejected before it made it to a vote. The idea was to hold a doe season the week before buck season opened. It might have run from the Saturday before Thanksgiving through the following Saturday, or—to avoid putting deer and bear hunters in the woods at the same time—opened on a Saturday, closed Monday through Wednesday while bear season was in, then reopened and run through Saturday.

The thinking, Alt explains, was threefold. By allowing hunters to chase does before bucks were legal, it might ease the pressure on antlered deer and educate them about hunter pressure a week before they became legal game. By including two Saturdays and the Thanksgiving break, when youngsters are off school and some adults are off work, it might have encouraged lots of participation. Third, a November season would make the doe harvest less dependent on the weather than it is now. With more time to hunt, a few bad days mixed in aren't so critical.

Commissioners ultimately didn't vote on the November season. At a meeting held at the Commission's Harrisburg headquarters, executive director Vern Ross, regional directors, and bureau directors squashed the proposal. In a statement explaining the decision, Ross said that "given the concerns about such a season's impact on the end of the turkey season and the statewide bear season—as well as other social issues about impacting family plans for the Thanksgiving holiday—the agency staff has decided against moving this idea forward as a formal proposal for the board to consider."

That's okay, but the need to get hunters in the woods with more opportunities to kill deer is not going to change, Grund said. If those particular ideas won't fly, others with the same goal will have to be found.

Different deer seasons for different areas of the state are a possibility, too, for the same reason. The day is likely to come, Alt says, when deer seasons in wildlife management units north of Interstate 80—where deer experience an earlier rut—might open sooner than deer seasons in southern units. Seasons in some units might last for months, too, especially on DMAP lands, while seasons in other places might be measured in weeks. "Pennsylvania's never going to have a two-week buck season followed by a three-day doe season again," Grund said. "It's probably going to become much more like the southern states, where you measure deer seasons in months."

Biologists have also considered the idea of making some doe licenses time sensitive by giving them an expiration date. Bryon Shissler says the Commission may reach a point when just lengthening deer seasons won't be sufficient to get enough does harvested. At that point, the idea would not be to make it tougher for hunters to take a doe but to inspire them to be more diligent about getting out and filling their tag. "It would be a situation where you would use it or lose it," says Shissler.

Some believe that landowners—specifically the DCNR and even the Game Commission itself—might have to think about helping hunters reach the places where deer need to be removed, too. Sam Dunkle said there was a time when the Game Commission took hunters deep into the woods on flatbeds trucks. The hunters could hunt all day, meeting back at the drop point at designated times to have their deer hauled back out. Those who hunted all day with no success could meet at the drop point at dark for a ride back out of the woods. With Pennsylvania's hunter populations aging, now might be the time to consider a similar program again, he said.

Ben Moyer, a respected outdoors writer from Fayette County, has suggested something similar. In an article in *Pennsylvania Outdoor News*, Moyer said it's the prospect of dragging a deer out of the woods—rather than the mere hike back in—that keeps a lot of hunters close to roads. If the DCNR and other landowners want to get around this problem, they need to start thinking of ways to make it easier for hunters to get where they need to be.

"What about patrols of DCNR personnel that could transport hunters and their deer back out to parking areas? It pains me to suggest this, but what about ATVs?" Moyer wrote. "What if we allowed hunters with DMAP permits, who we can assume are most likely to focus on a particular area, to use ATVs to bring out their deer? Why couldn't we arrange for successful hunters to call a special cell phone number to arrange for pick-up?"

There may even be a role for the legislature to play in deer hunting's future, apart from the question of Sunday hunting. The Game Commission sought a license fee increase from the legislature in 2005. The agency isn't likely to see that money until at least the 2007–8 license year, but already some are thinking that the agency should ask for a change in what each license is good for.

Right now, a hunter who buys a general license is allowed to shoot one buck a year. In order to harvest a doe—the type of deer biologists really want him to shoot—he has to apply for a license through a lottery. No one thinks legislators will make a general license good for a doe and require hunters to apply for a buck tag—that would be political suicide—but what about making that general license deer tag a tag good for either sex? Or including one doe tag with each general license? That would certainly make it easier for hunters to bag a doe and, done in conjunction with a license fee increase, ease the financial hit on the Commission of selling fewer doe licenses.

The day may also soon be coming when the state, through some act of the legislature, will have to find ways to encourage landowners to keep their properties open for public recreation and deer removal, says Dunkle. This may take the form of tax breaks, outright payments of some sort, or giving landowners who leave their property open to hunting technical expertise in managing their land for wildlife. There are all sorts of possibilities.

"New York is leasing much of its recreational land. That's an idea Pennsylvania rejected years ago, but it's something that might be worth revisiting in the future," Dunkle says. "It's a win-win situation if we can encourage individuals to leave their land open to public recreation. We're in our infancy here in Pennsylvania as far as that's concerned, and as far as dealing with what's public versus private land."

Some think finding a new way to support the Game Commission is critical to the future of managing deer as well. Currently the agency is funded almost solely

Because as much as 90 percent of the hunting population is made up of deer hunters, what happens to deer hunting will go a long way toward determining the fate of hunting in general in the future. Here, members of the Buffalo Valley Sportsmen's Club protest the January Pennsylvania Game Commission meeting, hoping to gain support for their effort to cut doe license allocations for the coming year.

by license revenues, making hunters its core constituency. More than a few people have wondered in recent years—especially in light of the deer debate—whether that model can work in the future. Can a commission that has traditionally catered to hunters do the right thing for forests and deer, and survive in the long term, if this means angering hunters who want more deer in the short term?

Some scientists believe the answer is no. The authors of the Deer Forum Report—a final version of which came out in January 2005—concluded that the Pennsylvania Game Commission will remain incapable of dealing with the issue of overabundant deer until it reduces its dependence on one constituency, namely, hunters.

It's going to take a long time—a period measured in years—for the state's forest habitats to recover from years of deer overabundance, says Jan Beyea, a consultant for and former vice president of the National Audubon Society and one of the report's authors. An agency that is tied to just one group of supporters that has traditionally lobbied for more deer may not be able to survive their demands long enough to get the job done. "It's going to take a lot of commitment to overcome that lag time between when you start to lower deer densities and when the forests start to recover," says Beyea. "The challenge of ecosystem management is that delay."

It's not a challenge the Game Commission is up to meeting in its present form, according to the report. In its major findings regarding policy and administration, the report said the Game Commission needs funding other than just license dollars and timber revenues if it is to meet its "broader conservation goals."

The report noted, for example, that managing deer according to ecosystem considerations "would lead to the conclusion that deer densities in some parts of the state should be reduced below levels that would be set solely by considerations of deer health and condition." Getting to that point will be all but impossible until the agency has a wider constituent and funding base, the authors noted.

The study recommended that the Game Commission employ more wildlife biologists, ecologists, and other scientifically trained staff. It should also lead by example by putting sections of some game lands into the deer management assistance program. The report also concluded, however, that it will require the oversight of the state legislature to make sure these things happen. The "commissioner system should be reviewed by the Governor and General Assembly," it says. "If the system is retained, it should be changed to ensure that the commissioners represent all of the citizens of Pennsylvania, not just those who hunt."

The Game Commission should also be monitored until it's clear that it is bringing deer densities down and implementing ecosystem management. "An annual review of PGC's mission, organization, skill mix, policies, funding adequacy, funding sources, and priorities, along with the sociopolitical obstacles it faces, should be conducted by an independent entity appointed by the Governor and General Assembly," the report concludes.

Opponents of the report, including many within the Game Commission, took its recommendations to mean that the agency should be merged with the state Department of Conservation and Natural Resources and that the opinions of hunters should be minimized. "My concern is that the authors of this report are merely trying to create a structure for managing deer that marginalizes hunters' views and opinions," Russ Schleiden said. "The Game Commission, as a state government agency, historically has directed deer management, with input from the state's varied stakeholders—hunters, biologists, farmers, foresters, landowners, and local officials—and we believe that the current process is working."

The state legislature examined the idea of a Game Commission/DCNR merger in 2004. Its study determined that a combined agency might save $5 million annually. Sportsmen made it clear in a series of public hearings that they don't want to go that route, however, and the idea ultimately faded away.

The Deer Forum's authors do not necessarily believe that idea should be revisited, says Ron Freed. They recognize, however, that the Game Commission, despite its best intentions, will always struggle to do what's right by deer, wildlife, and habitat, so long as it hears only from one group interested largely in one species—in this case, hunters interested in deer.

The report, by suggesting that the Commission broaden its funding base and meet mandates for all wildlife, offers ways for the agency to do the right thing while remaining independent, he said. "I don't think you're going to do real ecosystem management with an agency that answers to just one constituency. It just isn't going to happen," Freed said. "Given that, what we're offering is not a proposal for merger, but an alternative to merger."

Peter Pinchot, a forest landowner from Pike County, director of the Milford Experimental Forest, and grandson of former Pennsylvania governor Gifford Pinchot, says that no matter what form the state's wildlife agency takes, it has to do one thing: make sure its wildlife management policies serve all of its species and people. When it fails to do that, it risks losing its "moral authority" to manage wildlife. "It's reform we're talking about," Pinchot said. "The merger may be one way to bring about that reform, though whether it's the best way or the only way has yet to be determined. It's really the end result I'm promoting, rather than the means."

Hunters themselves are going to have to change in the future, too, Jan Dizard, the sociology professor at Amherst College, says. Some people will never accept hunting, no matter what. Davis and Irons are evidence of that, at least when it comes to Fairmount Park. They want no part of hunting in their back yard. "We know more about white-tailed deer now than we ever hoped to know. We wish it would be over. We have other things to do," Davis said. "But we will continue to do anything and everything we need to do to stop this. That's a commitment that will last into infinity."

If hunters want to be accepted by the vast majority of people who are neither hunters nor antihunters, though, they have to work at it, Dizard says. The nation has undergone a cultural shift, he believes. Whereas many people once hunted as children, or at least knew someone who did, this is no longer true in an age of rampant suburbanization. Hunters, and deer hunters in particular, need to make a conscious effort to reach out to their neighbors and explain what it is they do and why.

"Hunters have always been a minority, but they embodied certain common values, like self-reliance and a connection to nature. That's not as true any more," Dizard says. "Hunters are becoming a social minority, too. I don't think that's sunk in yet.

"Perceptions of hunters have changed for the worse in a rather steady way. Fewer people hunt or know hunters, so hunters and nonhunters confront each other as almost total strangers, with no social bonds. It's ready-made for a cultural clash. There are some real soul-searching moments in front of us."

John Organ, a wildlife program chief for the U.S. Fish and Wildlife Service, likewise thinks hunters must be proactive in selling themselves as contributors to the good of society. To do that, they need first to understand how the public perceives deer hunters and how deer hunters think of themselves. Hunters have played a historic and proud role in conservation, he says. Some hunters may have forgotten this, though, and some nonhunters may not realize that role ever existed. To change this, hunters, wildlife agencies, and the outdoor media all have to give voice to the good brought about by hunting. This means talking about everything from why killing is integral to hunting—the "paradox of taking life to sustain life"—to making sure proper hunter behavior is enforced.

"We've got to change the image of deer hunters and deer hunting. I think it's tarnished and I think it's tarnished in some of the areas we need to be hunting," Organ says. "We've got to make hunting a fiber of the community again."

Hunters need to get to the point where people look at them as making a "civic contribution" to society, he said. Hunters need to distance themselves from the "beer, brag, and blood" stereotype and position themselves as people who can be respected for what they do and the role they play in promoting conservation for everyone. He suggested that agencies like the Game Commission may be able to help in this respect by offering classes that train hunters in everything from woods skills to dealing with the public. Such people, who have made a commitment to being knowledgeable and been recognized by the state in some way, could serve as a "cultural core" of hunters.

"That's where we need to be," Organ says. "I think we're at a crossroads, really. I think the next couple of years are going to tell us a lot about where we're going. I feel optimistic in that we're seeing more and more leadership coming out of different circles. But there are still a lot of challenges before us. A lot is going to depend on how hunters, and the whole hunting community, really responds. We do have to start to change. In Pennsylvania you've made some great strides. What Gary Alt has done has been nothing short of miraculous. There's a foothold there," he says. "Now we've just got to keep moving forward."

Steve Horsley, the research forester, agrees. Pennsylvania needs deer hunters, he says, but it needs deer hunters who are willing to serve as conservationists and who are respected by the rest of society. "Hunters do a tremendous service for the rest of us in Pennsylvania," Horsley says. "They help us to regulate deer, a species that is able to accommodate itself to a variety of conditions. The woods have changed a lot over the last hundred years, and deer have adapted to those changing conditions. So hunters are doing a good thing for us. We certainly need more of them. But this is a tough problem. It's certainly something Pennsylvania is going to have to face up to."

Shissler, too, says that deer hunters can be as important to the future of wildlife management as they want to be. They have to show themselves ready and willing to take on that role, though. That means sacrificing by bringing deer numbers down in some areas in the short term for the long-term good of the state's forests. "They can't have it like it used to be because they've already spent the principal. Whether it's your retirement or your habitat, you can't spend the principal and then turn around and spend it again," Shissler says. "But I don't think deer hunting's ever going to be any better than it's going to be in the future. I know people like to talk about the good old days, but I think the best days are yet to come if we do this right. By the same token, if we don't, we as hunters are going to pay a tremendous price."

Some hunters are ready to accept the challenge of managing deer and increasing public acceptance of their sport. Mike Foust of Johnstown, president of the United Bowhunters of Pennsylvania, says that many hunters are willing to sacrifice—and bear the mantle of the conservationist—to do what's right for the health of the state's forests. "If we take care of all those other issues, we'll have plenty of deer to hunt," Foust says. "Let the numbers fall out where they will, and we'll make do with whatever deer are available."

If not everyone is so adaptable, that's not hard to understand, according to Schleiden. Change never comes easy, especially when the potential rewards are so far away that some will never see them. But come it must. "When you're sixty-five or seventy, like some of our hunters are, there is no long term. What do you say to that? I know what to say, that we've got to keep moving forward, but I don't think they want to hear that," he says.

Alt has said many times that he envisions a day when public school teachers rely on biology books that outline the role of hunters in promoting forest health. He dreams of a day when landowners turn to sportsmen to help keep their property's ecosystem in balance.

These things have begun to happen already. At Lutherlyn, a Butler County camp affiliated with the Evangelical Lutheran Church that also does environmental programs for elementary school groups and others, children are taught a game in which a certain number are predators and others are deer, some healthy, some not. The deer try to run from one line to another in a sort of Red Rover–like game without getting caught by the predators standing in the middle. The game is designed to show that healthy deer are harder to catch and better at survival. Instructors talk about how, through hunting, deer numbers can be controlled for the sake of the deer themselves.

At Shaler High School in Allegheny County students have studied forest regeneration and deer impacts right on campus, doing things like fencing off some stump sprouts and leaving others unfenced to see how they respond in the presence of deer. They've treated some areas with fertilizer and let others go, and even sprayed vegetation with various so-called deer repellents to see what happens. It's all been an eye-opener for many of the students there, says Dave DiPasquale, a teacher who coordinates the project.

"I think what was neat was that there were a few students who didn't even think we had deer on campus, but we've got a whole herd. So number one, we've raised awareness," DiPasquale says. "Number two, we had two groups, the tree huggers who were against hunting and the hunters. Some of the students were really appalled by hunting and they went looking for other solutions. What a lot found, though, was that short of killing some deer, there's nothing you're going to do to keep their numbers down. Not everyone who was against hunting turned to support hunting, but a lot did."

"I think this issue of deer management might be the thing that gets more youngsters involved in hunting," Gary Alt says. "In a kid's world hunting is not cool, or not as cool as it was twenty years ago. If we can't change that, if we can't get teachers to start talking from the other side, showing hunters as someone who can help keep our forests healthy, it's over. And that's going to happen in a generation. It's going to happen in twenty years.

"But that doesn't have to be. We have such an opportunity to do what's right here. I still think we can. I'm more optimistic than I ever was just a few years ago," Alt says. "If you look at how far we've come already, I mean, jeez. If you'd have told me hunters would accept antler restrictions and concurrent seasons and early doe seasons and all the other things we've dumped on them, I'd have said you were

If all the deer management changes undertaken in Pennsylvania do what biologists hope, the state's buck-to-doe ratio should be closer to one to one in the future.

crazy. But they have accepted those things and we're better off for it. We just need to keep this thing moving."

"If you talk to any of the professionals in this field, they all agree that deer management in Pennsylvania is only going to become more challenging in the future. We need to aggressively harvest does now, then maintain that in the future," adds Grund. "But that probably won't be easy. In fact, if I had to guess, I would say that deer management in Pennsylvania is going to be challenging right up until the day we retire."

I think of that when I look at an old, brittle newspaper clipping we found in my grandfather's attic when his health forced him to move into a smaller, easier-to-negotiate home. The clipping is from the April 27, 1943, issue of the now-defunct *Pittsburgh Press*. On one of the sports pages is a small box of text called "Sparks from the Campfire by Johnny Mock." It includes several short items on fishing subjects, such as how some papers in the Lock Haven, Williamsport, and Emporium areas were running headlines about fishermen unhappy with having to do all of their angling close to home because of the shortage of gasoline resulting from the war.

What caught my eye, though, was a three-sentence blurb: "The deer hunters can look for a doe season in 1943, at least, in some of the counties where the surplus population is extremely heavy. The buck season will probably open on the Monday nearest to the first of December. That means Nov. 29." I can't help but wonder how the hunters who read the paper reacted to that one line. The 1943 doe season was the first in the state in three years. It surely must have caused a firestorm of controversy.

It's now more than sixty years later and not a whole lot has changed. Williamson, who as a very young man knew Richard Gerstell, knows as much. Williamson's father worked for Gerstell in his post–Game Commission career at the Civil Defense Agency in Pennsylvania, and the old biologist and the future biologist often talked. One thing Gerstell always said was that he never saw much change in Pennsylvania's deer management debate, despite his hard work and the work of those who came after him. "I remember he remarked then that things hadn't changed a bit. There was the same lack of trust at the Game Commission, the same lack of trust of science that existed even then," Williamson said.

As for Roger Latham, if he never expressed any bitterness about being forced out at the Game Commission, he never quit talking about the need to control deer, either. Whether through his writing for the *Pittsburgh Press* years later or through the slide shows he put on for sportsmen's groups and others, he always worked to "raise awareness of what he believed was the central conservation issue in the state," says his son, Roger Latham. "He never wasted a minute talking about how he wished things had been different," Latham says of his father. "That wasn't his character. But he never quit talking about the issue either."

Gary Alt has been burned by the deer management debate, for sure. He entered the deer arena "full of piss and vinegar," he says. Half a decade later, he's been beaten up so many times it was hard not to take some things personally. "I won't say it has destroyed my life, but it has left scars that will never heal. We never should subject anyone to that kind of anger," Alt says. "It's very, very caustic."

I hope there's a way to get beyond that and position deer hunters as an important part of Pennsylvania's future. I think of the 2003 firearms deer season, when I was hunting a favorite spot near the border of Linn Run State Park and Forbes State Forest in eastern Westmoreland County. It was the second day of the firearms deer season and there weren't many hunters in the woods. I saw just two or three all day.

I had passed on shooting several antlerless deer on the opening day, partly so as not to bring my season to too quick an end and partly because I wasn't sure the smallish-looking deer weren't button bucks. On this morning, though, shortly after 9:30, a bigger doe wandered out in front of me about sixty yards distant, walking along a bench marked by big oak trees. She turned to look at me as I raised my .30-06 to my shoulder. It was the last decision she ever made. I gave her one last look, settled the crosshairs behind her shoulder, and squeezed the trigger. The rifle roared and she fell in her tracks.

I walked and slid down the steep, rocky mountainside separating the bench I was on from the one with the doe, thankful that she hadn't run off into the greenbriars. When I reached the deer, I laid my rifle on the ground, took off my gloves, and knelt to spend a moment admiring her. She really was a beautiful animal. I ran my hands over her brown-gray coat and down her slender, strong legs to her hooves. I stroked her ears and looked into her eyes, those deep, dark pools of wilderness, and offered a silent prayer of thanks.

Looking around at the mountainside we were on, I felt a real connection to that deer and the place we shared. The year was 2003, but we were both threads in the fabric of life and death that had blanketed that mountain for thousands of years.

I slipped off my vest, took my license out of its holder, and tagged the deer before field-dressing her and heading down the mountain, across the stream and to the Jeep for the ride home. I knew what awaited me there. Derek and Tyler love to fish, hike, to catch crayfish and salamanders and frogs, to shoot their BB guns and bows. Both have gone hunting with me, too. On the days when I went without them—like this one—I could always look forward to them greeting me at the door when I got home.

"Whadya get, whadya get?" Tyler would ask excitedly from the other side of the screen door.

If I had brought some game home, they'd shout the good news to Mandy, then follow me to the kitchen or the garage to help clean it. If I came home empty handed, Tyler would let everyone know, with the kind of innocent but brutal honesty only a child can muster.

"Ahh, dad didn't get anything again," he'd say, then walk away to play with his action figures.

On this day, though, we would share the excitement of the hunt—the paradox of taking life to sustain life, as Organ said—and the feeling of bringing home a part of the wilderness we love and treasure. It's a feeling I hope never goes away, for me, for Derek, for Tyler, and for everyone else who loves white-tailed deer.

INDEX